BUSINESS COMMUNICATIONS

BUSINESS COMMUNICATIONS

R.T. CHAPPELL
MA, BSc(Econ), DPA, FCIS, FBIM, Dip Ed
*Formerly Dean of the Faculty of Business & Management
Harrow College of Higher Education*

and

W.L. READ
BSc(Econ), ACIS
*Formerly Head of the Business Studies Department
West Ham College*

FIFTH EDITION

Pitman

Pitman Publishing
128 Long Acre, London WC2E 9AN

A Division of Longman Group UK Limited

Fifth edition first published 1984
Reprinted 1985, 1988, 1989, 1991

© Macdonald & Evans Ltd 1984

British Library Cataloguing in Publication Data
Chappell, R.T.
Business communications. — 5th ed.
1. Communication in management
    I. Title II. Read, W.L.
HF5718 651.7

ISBN 0 273 02963 0

All rights reserved; no part of this publication may be reproduced, stored in a retrieval system, or transmitted in any form or by any other means, electronic, mechanical, photocopying, recording, or otherwise without either the prior written permission of the Publishers or a licence permitting restricted copying in the United Kingdom issued by the Copyright Licensing Agency Ltd, 90 Tottenham Court Road, London W1P 0BR. This book may not be lent, resold, hired out or otherwise disposed of by way of trade in any form of binding or cover other than that in which it is published, without the prior consent of the publishers.

Produced by Longman Group (FE) Ltd
Printed in Hong Kong

PREFACE TO THE FIFTH EDITION

Our object in writing this book has been to provide an introductory textbook to the study of communications in business. We have deliberately restricted the fullness of our treatment of the subject so that the main points can receive consideration in a book of moderate length.

As the economic system throughout the world becomes increasingly complex, more and more opportunities occur for both men and women to reach managerial status. We have, therefore, borne in mind particularly the needs of those who have, or hope to have, responsibility for supervision.

In his task of directing the activities of others, the manager uses words as his tools, and this book covers the problems involved in using English, whether written or spoken, for this purpose. Correspondence and the telephone, reports and committee meetings, and external publicity are among the aspects dealt with. Study questions will be found at the end of each chapter.

We have also included a chapter on the teaching of communications since there is a very great need for a discussion of the principles of teaching applied to this field. A select bibliography is provided to assist readers who wish to pursue the subject of business communications further.

Though the book is necessarily brief, we have been very conscious of the fact that this is a field of management where there are few absolute answers to the problems which can be applied irrespective of the changing circumstances. We have been content at various stages in this work to pose questions for discussion rather than to attempt to give a rigid pattern of machinery for communication, and hard and fast rules for the use of what is, after all, both a living and a changing language.

In the preface to the fourth edition we drew attention to the organisational trend towards decentralisation of large units. This trend has continued into the eighties with the development of new computers and word processors. In the United States the proportion of professionals with hands-on experience of terminal operation is about 30 per cent compared with 10 per cent in the United Kingdom, but we can expect the British percentage to increase quickly to match the American situation. The development of networks with responsibility for decision making placed lower down the management line will enrich the work of junior executives but at the same time demand a high level of expertise in the processes of communication.

Whether the communication is in the form of a telephone call, a written memorandum or a screen presentation on a visual display unit, the initiator of the message must think clearly about the ideas he wants to convey to the recipient. The need for a sound training in the purposes and processes of communication remains paramount and this need is acknowledged not only by commerce and administrative organisations but by the professional examining bodies and the Business and Technician Education Council (BTEC).

The authors hope that the fifth edition will provide a further opportunity for managers and organisations to be helped in the essential task of improving their communications.

Readers may also find it useful to have the following list of names and addresses of organisations from which further information may be obtained.

British Association for Commercial and Industrial Education,
16 Park Crescent,
London, W1N 4AP

British Productivity Council,
Carlisle House,
Southampton Row,
London, WC1

Industrial Society,
48 Bryanston Square,
London, W1H 1BQ

ACKNOWLEDGMENTS

In writing this book the authors have received invaluable help from a variety of sources. Our professional colleagues have given us the benefit of their advice and where we have received help from organisations we have acknowledged their assistance in the text. Thanks are due to the following bodies for permission to reprint questions taken from past examinations set by them:

Institute of Chartered Secretaries and Administrators
Royal Society of Arts
Institute of Transport
London Chamber of Commerce and Industry
National Examinations Board in Supervisory Studies
Civil Service Commission

R.T. Chappell
W.L. Read

1983

CONTENTS

PREFACE TO THE FIFTH EDITION   v

I. INTRODUCTION   1
Meaning of communication; Need for communication; Objectives of communication; Management/staff communications; Methods of communication.

II. LINES OF COMMUNICATION   17
Line management; Job descriptions; Job evaluation; Joint consultation; Suggestion schemes; Horizontal communication.

III. THE SPOKEN WORD   51
Clarity and brevity; Be precise; A note on vocabulary; Communication by silence; Public speaking; Lecturettes; Oral instructions and orders; Interviewing; Advantages and disadvantages of the spoken word; Listening; Oral examinations.

IV. THE WRITTEN WORD   63
Correct English; Unnecessary words and phrases; Use words that will be understood; Examination technique; Essay writing; Article writing.

V. MIND YOUR Ps, Qs, and COMMAS!   86
A look at grammar; Punctuation.

VI. BUSINESS CORRESPONDENCE   101
The importance of sound business letters; The purposes of business letters; Letter construction; The form of the letter; Business jargon; Internal communication; Finding and making an application for a job.

VII. SUMMARISING INFORMATION 118
The method of summary; Tense; A specimen précis; Summaries of correspondence.

VIII. REPORT WRITING 142
The informal report; The formal report; Style; A note on quicker reading.

IX. COMMITTEES—THEIR VALUE AND GENERAL STRUCTURE 158
Development of the use of committees; Modern committee uses; The advantages and disadvantages of committees; Size of committees and sub-committees; Officers of committees.

X. COMMITTEES—THEIR ORGANISATION AND PROCEDURE 169
Essentials of a valid meeting; Notices; The chairman; Procedure; Minutes; Conclusion.

XI. ASPECTS OF EXTERNAL COMMUNICATIONS 183
Introduction; Use of telephones; Public relations; Advertisements for company meetings; Consumer and consultative councils.

XII. THE TEACHING OF COMMUNICATIONS 197
The place of the formal lecture; Informal teaching techniques; Criticism of reports; Teaching aids.

APPENDIX I. EXAMINATION PAPERS 205

APPENDIX II. SELECT BIBLIOGRAPHY 213

INDEX 215

CHAPTER I

INTRODUCTION

MEANING OF COMMUNICATION

Communication is any means by which a thought is transferred from one person to another. There have been many other definitions, but this seems to be the best.

This book will discuss the lines of communications through which information is transmitted. One example of this is joint consultation, which has been described as a means of getting to know the other person's point of view.

As well as considering this collection of procedures—the machinery of communications, as it is sometimes called—we shall deal with the effectiveness of different kinds of communication. We must ask ourselves whether our purpose has been achieved: whether our communication has had maximum effect.

NEED FOR COMMUNICATION

As production and distribution have become increasingly complex and the size of organisations has increased we have all tended to become specialists. Some of us specialise in production, others in buying, others in selling, and so on. When specialists communicate with others who have a similar background they talk a language all their own. This technical jargon has its advantages, because it saves a great deal of time, yet the more specialised the nature of our work, the more we find ourselves unable to communicate with those who do not possess our specialised knowledge.

We should all try to remember that it is always important to speak and write as clearly and concisely as possible. In this way we shall be able to get our ideas across more effectively and avoid misunderstanding. In addition, time will be saved in answering queries which arise from those who cannot understand the exact point we are trying to make. This, of course, means that we should take care and pay attention to what we are doing. We should not try to emulate the dear old lady who always knitted while she was talking, so that she should have something to think about.

Later chapters of the book will deal with the written and spoken word and visual aids in detail. Here we emphasise that there will often be a conflict between the need for speed and the necessity for clarity. For example, we all like to revise the written words for which we are responsible. If, however, we spend too much time on the grammar and construction of our letters and memoranda our output may well be negligible. Fortunately, there are techniques which enable us to reconcile speed with clarity of expression.

OBJECTIVES OF COMMUNICATION

One of the objects of good communication is that everyone should be aware of what the organisation wants to achieve. This end may be attained by what is called a common doctrine. The organisation must have an objective, purpose, aim, or goal. The ways of ensuring that employees are aware of the common doctrine are dealt with in this book.

The policies of the organisation should offer guidance to all: wise policy-making is dependent upon a good two-way communication system.

Training ensures that there is a similarity of outlook and a uniform method of attacking problems. Of particular importance is the training provided by an induction programme which should have the purpose of introducing a new employee to the background of the company, its objectives, general organisation, regulations, communications system, leading personalities, and amenities. Further, it should seek to describe the highlights of its achievements in providing goods or services and thus its economic and social value to the community.

Large companies will provide a specific course but smaller companies will often offer an informal programme of induction. Both approaches should enable the newcomer to understand his job, his relationship with both his colleagues and his immediate boss, and how his tasks relate to the work of the organisation as a whole.

MANAGEMENT/STAFF COMMUNICATIONS

Introduction

SCOPE OF COMMUNICATION

As we have defined it, communication is clearly a vast subject. It is, nevertheless, possible to resolve it into two main aspects—the internal and external relationships of the organisation. Most of the books written on this subject deal almost exclusively with the internal, that is the "control" aspect. We have, however, devoted a chapter to certain aspects of external communication (*see* Chapter XI). The matters affecting the organisation's reputation in the outside world are to us fundamental and warrant a reasonably detailed consideration even in a short book.

However, *within* a company, communications may be said to deal with the way in which information may be presented to management, staff, and workers. There is also the upward movement of information, so that the feelings of staff and workers are made known to the management.

Since communications are of joint interest to management and employees, in some companies the communications policy is wholly or partly written into the organisation's rules, i.e. the rules governing conduct within the business. In other companies this policy statement appears in writing in some other document. The advantage of having the communications policy in writing is that all employees should understand that there is a formal procedure for dealing with grievances. Most of these documents emphasise the need for employees to approach their supervisor *before* they see their shop steward.

COMMUNICATION AND PRODUCTIVITY

As a nation, we have experienced a doubling of our living standard over the period of the past twenty-five years. Striking as this appears at first sight, the improvement has been achieved with an increase of the order of 3 per cent per annum in the gross domestic product per head. Although this rate of growth is rather more than that obtained in the last few years of the period, it should surely be possible for a better performance to be attained throughout the whole of the economy to ensure an increase in real national income.

It is vital for us to ventilate this issue and to find out, if we possibly can, the answer to a fundamental problem. Is it possible for us to discover the main factor, or factors, which prevent our obtaining greater output? It is imperative for us to do this, because as a nation engaged in importing most of our food and raw materials we must produce more if we are to survive at all. After all, there has been a notable growth in the standard of living of most people in the country since the early days of industrialisation.

Water power brought forth factories located near the sources of the water. Later productivity increased when steam was used as a motive force. Controversy, however, still rages about the extent to which the improved productivity was offset by the appalling conditions which existed in the early factories built in the towns situated on the coalfields. Other forms of power—gas, electricity, oil and now nuclear power—have enabled output to be vastly increased at lower cost per unit. Moreover, it has become technically possible for factories to be set up in parts of the country away from the grim surroundings of the coalmining areas.

Many of the problems of production have been solved by the application of engineering skills and knowledge during this century. Taxation, too, has been used to reduce the inequalities of wealth and income which were characteristic of growth of the capitalist system. In addition, trade unions have been able, by collective bargaining, to abolish many inequalities and to institute recognised rates of pay. In all of these ways, aided by the emergence of a welfare state, the condition of the people has been enhanced.

For example, at the time of writing two out of three adults in the country now invest in stocks and shares either directly or indirectly, e.g. through their trade unions' funds. Another way in which money is invested indirectly on the Stock Exchange is by taking out insurance policies, the premiums of which are invested by the insurance companies. Most of us, therefore, have an additional interest in ensuring that the country's output increases substantially.

Yet from the early days of industrialism there has been constant and often bitter strife between employer and employee. Improvements in the general standard of living over the past two centuries have oddly enough done little to ease the situation.

The evolution of the principles of scientific management has, however, indicated methods by which relations between employer and employee can be improved out of all recognition. It is in this way, principally, that the economic welfare of us all can be improved.

A study of communications will, we feel confident, lead to the conclusion that the paramount need in present circumstances is for constructive co-operation between management and employees.

The management

EVOLUTION OF MANAGEMENT

It is now an established fact that it is essential for a great deal of attention to be paid to the human factor in management. The pace of technological advance has undoubtedly been very rapid during the last seventy years, and much technical ability of all kinds is clearly required to master the complexities of present-day production and distribution. However, it becomes more and more apparent that to be really successful the manager requires qualities over and above those which set him on the first rungs of the managerial ladder.

Before considering in detail the place in management of good communications we shall dwell briefly on the evolution of management. We are also going to say a few words about the meaning of the term as we intend to use it in this book.

It is generally agreed that the main factors which gave rise to management as we know it today were the growth of company legis-

I. INTRODUCTION

lation and the realisation of the advantages of large-scale production. The Industrial Revolution, which occurred in this country in the period 1760-1830, resulted in the need to build up very great amounts of capital. The Companies Act of 1862 confirmed the principle of limited liability, which inaugurated the divorce between management and capital.

So much capital was needed to take full advantage of the benefits which the introduction of steam power had brought about that the net had to be cast wide. The number of investors increased considerably.

A parallel, although generally somewhat latter, development was that of large-scale organisation. This took place not only in the private sector of the economy but also in the public sector. Furthermore, this movement was not confined to Britain but was worldwide.

MEANING OF MANAGEMENT

What then is meant by "management"? Perhaps the best definition is that it is the art of directing human activities so as to secure the greatest possible conformity with the policy of the organisation. It must be clearly understood that we are not dealing here exclusively with problems which confront the manufacturing industry. Many management writings deal only with the subject in these terms.

We live today in a mixed economy where several different forms of business organisation of both the public and private sectors exist side by side. Management cannot now be considered to relate to manufacturing concerns only. A much wider field of activity than this should be meant by the term.

In all types of large organisations the problems and difficulties which arise seem to possess common characteristics. This largely explains the movement of managerial staff from one form of organisation to another.

Professional bodies, too, have not been slow to realise this fundamental transformation of the activities of their members and students. The Institute of Chartered Secretaries and Administrators (formerly the Chartered Institute of Secretaries) gives increasing emphasis to providing facilities for training in management and administration.

The staff

COMMUNICATION AND EMPLOYMENT

The government has accepted responsibility since 1944 for the maintenance of a high and stable level of employment. In recent times the percentage of the working population unemployed has, of course, varied with the conditions prevailing both at home and overseas.

There have frequently been more vacancies than there have been registered unemployed.

Even a policy of full employment did not assume that every person would be in employment all the time. The architect of Britain's post-war social security system, Lord Beveridge, assumed that the full employment threshold was 200,000 unemployed! Since the end of the Second World War there have been periods of less than full employment resulting from changes in demand and technical developments. The high levels of unemployment in the nineteen-seventies and eighties seem destined to continue for some years, if not indefinitely.

There are many economic and social implications resulting from the shift from low to high levels of unemployment. For example, how can we finance large numbers of people, who are not working, without producing inflation with its adverse effects on those with fixed incomes? This will become a growing problem for a community faced with the prospect of an ageing population.

Should we not consciously pursue a policy of total personal development rather than continue to plan for the seemingly unattainable object of full employment? Some observers, including Clive Jenkins, secretary of the technician's and supervisor's trade union, ASTMS, have suggested that it would be desirable to provide full-time education up to the age of twenty-five. Some EEC countries have introduced national early retirement schemes; work-sharing, too, has its advocates. But our concern here must be with the effect on communications of the adoption of more worker-oriented policies by both employers and central government.

Today, prospective employees of all grades require more information than ever before. Despite the difficulties of securing a job, potential recruits still need this material before deciding to join an organisation.

Potential employees wish to know the facts about the income which they may expect to earn, and the conditions of service, where these are not standard throughout the industry. In addition, such matters as the education, training, health, safety, and welfare provisions are all of growing concern to the employee in present-day conditions. Employers are required by the Contracts of Employment and Industrial Relations Acts to give new employees details of their conditions of service.

So that a considered opinion can be given it is also necessary for the employee to be aware of the policy of the firm and of its achievements, not only in financial but also in real terms. Employees will also want to know the future plans of the organisation. These may not always be generally available, in case detailed information is given to competitors, thus having a detrimental effect upon the success of the proposals.

Much interest is also shown in the ways in which it is intended to increase the productivity of the organisation. In the ultimate, the continued success, not to say survival, of the country depends upon our increasing national productivity. This must therefore, not only nationally but also regionally and locally, be a matter of great importance to us all.

PROMOTION PROSPECTS

Not every employee of the organisation will wish to progress to a more responsible post, but the opportunity of promotion must be clearly available for those who display potential.

People in the organisation should know their promotion prospects. If they are not clear about this it is a failure of the communication system. It is common to hear that we are told when we are doing badly, but never praised when we are working well. This is all too true.

Some organisations have a yearly review of establishment or pay. It is a sound idea to have, in addition, an annual interview of all new entrants by the departmental head. The entrants can then be told frankly what their promotion prospects are.

METHODS OF COMMUNICATION

Selecting the right method

It is sometimes a problem deciding which method of communication to adopt.

This book attempts to deal with the problems of management likely to confront those who are or who hope to be responsible for the supervision of the work of others. In such a book it is necessary to consider separately what we have called the means or media of communications, i.e. the methods by which we shall get our message across.

In practice, however, managements always find that more than one method has to be used to achieve any desired object. The methods used will, of course, depend upon a number of factors, for example, the amount of time available and the geographical location of the people who are to receive the message.

Some managements, for example, insist that important policy statements should be made personally wherever possible. In these circumstances other methods of communication can be used to reinforce the earlier spoken announcement.

We must always, in communication, consider the person we want to reach. Some people prefer to deal with their business matters by word of mouth. It is important to be able to judge how the other person will react. Communication is a two-way process. A face-to-face oral contact or a telephone call will often produce immediate results whereas a letter will remain unanswered.

Dictators know well the importance of effective communication. Even democratic governments now understand the need to explain to the public the value of supporting certain policies. For example, Her Majesty's Treasury produces a monthly bulletin on financial problems and the manner in which economic, financial and industrial problems may be approached. Semi-official bodies such as the British Standards Institute produce periodicals for general industrial circulation.

The means of communication used will depend upon a number of factors. As we discuss the methods in turn we shall see that our personal knowledge of the person we wish to contact, the time available, and the cost of the communication are among the points we shall have to bear in mind when deciding how to communicate.

Most of the ways by which we communicate require some action. Thus we communicate by writing, by speaking, and by making gestures. But we also communicate by passive means, although often not so effectively. We may communicate our thoughts, our intentions, or our views by doing nothing, by remaining silent, or by doing or saying a certain amount and no more.

Governments are often told what their supporters think by abstentions from voting at divisions in the House of Commons. Significantly, too, at by-elections the electorate may communicate dissatisfaction by refraining from voting rather than by voting for an opposition candidate.

Managements may communicate their indifference to the problems of their staff by not arranging for the training of their supervisors and operatives or by not making any consultation arrangements. A manager may communicate his impatience by meaningful glances at his watch during an interview with an employee. The same manager may communicate cynicism be reprimanding, while smoking, an employee who has disobeyed the company's rule forbidding smoking on the factory floor.

Readers will find it an interesting exercise to observe in their office or factory the ways in which people communicate other than by writing, by speaking, or by making gestures.

Communication by *writing* is discussed in Chapters IV-VIII, and by *speaking* in Chapters III and XI. For convenience we shall deal here with the third *visual* method. The use of visual aids for teaching purposes is covered in Chapter XII.

I. INTRODUCTION

Visual methods

If information and figures are presented visually the meaning and implications are always more readily understood by everybody concerned. It is also important for management purposes to grasp the trends or rates of change at the earliest possible moment. Visual methods enable the trends to be presented to the manager much more easily than in any other way. A number of methods of showing information visually are now in general use.

For the sake of completeness a few notes are given in this chapter on several of these methods, and examples are given where considered necessary.

A more detailed explanation is provided in most good books on statistical methods.

CHARTS AND GRAPHS

Pie charts are widely used to indicate how a total is made up. Usually pie charts (*see* Fig. 1) should not be employed for the purpose of

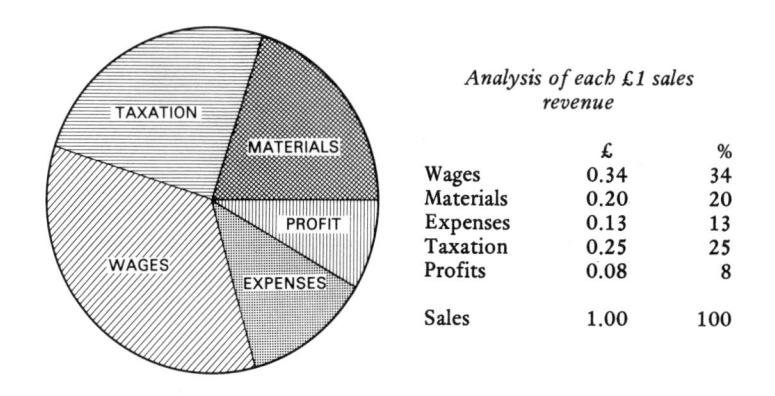

Analysis of each £1 sales revenue

	£	%
Wages	0.34	34
Materials	0.20	20
Expenses	0.13	13
Taxation	0.25	25
Profits	0.08	8
Sales	1.00	100

Fig. 1. *Pie chart.*

making comparisons. Other methods, to be detailed later, are much better in these circumstances.

Bar charts, on the other hand, present information in a form so that comparisons can be made easily (*see* Fig. 2).

A *compound bar chart* shows, in addition to how the totals are made up, comparisons between totals (*see* Fig. 3).

Pictograms (*see* Fig. 4.) may also be used to make visual comparisons in a way that may be easily grasped. In effect, the pictogram shown is a type of horizontal bar chart.

Graphs usually show time along the horizontal axis and quantity along the vertical axis (*see* Fig. 5).

Z charts are so termed by reason of the shape taken by three graphs superimposed (*see* Fig. 6).

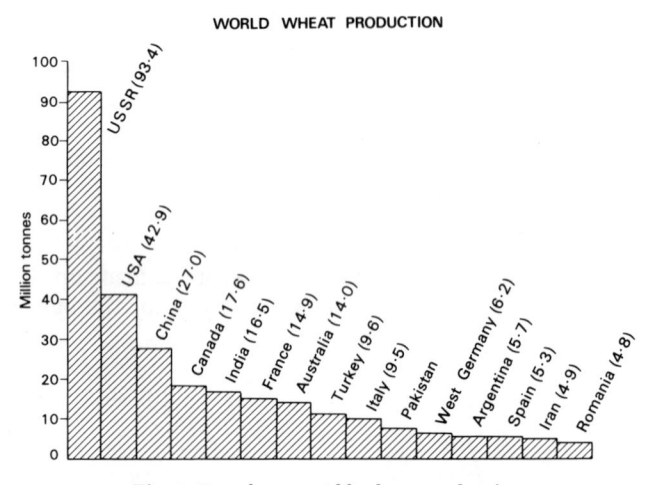

Fig. 2. Bar chart: world wheat production.

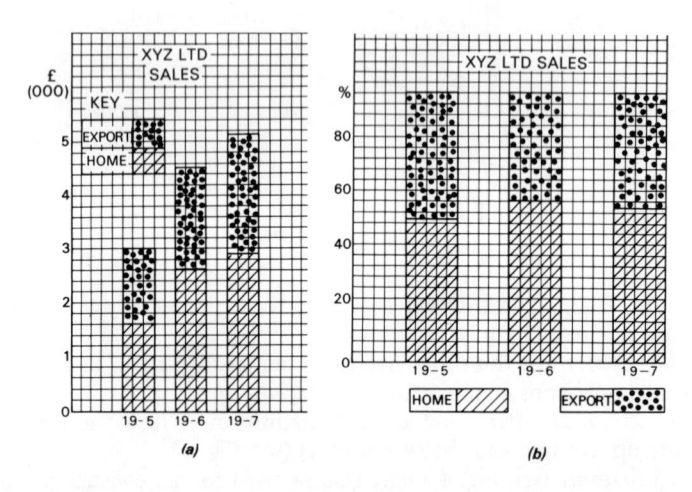

Fig. 3. Compound bar charts: (a) component bar chart; (b) percentage component bar chart.

I. INTRODUCTION

PEGASUS VAN MANUFACTURING CO. LTD
OUTPUT OF VANS

OUTPUT	
19-4	2004
19-5	2996
19-6	4219
19-7	5324

Fig. 4. *Pictogram.*

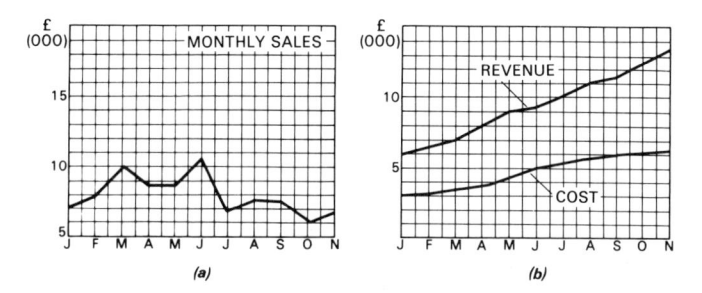

Fig. 5. *Graphs:* (a) *simple sales graph;* (b) *revenue and costs graph.*

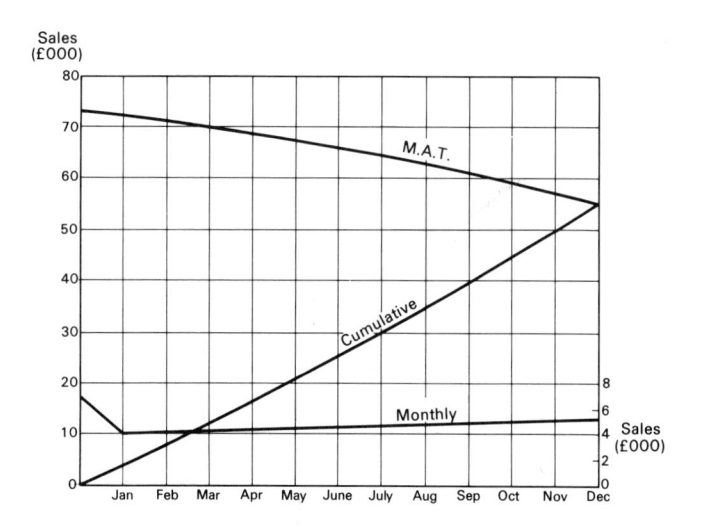

Fig. 6. *Z chart: MAT = moving annual total.*

On a single sheet, usually for a term of one year, are shown: (1) on the lowest line the monthly totals: (2) on the sloping line the cumulative monthly totals since the beginning of the year: and also (3) on the top line of the graph the moving annual total for the previous twelve months. The moving annual total is obtained by adding to the total of the preceding twelve months the next monthly total and subtracting from this sum the monthly total for the corresponding month of the preceding year. For example, for the month of January 19—8 the total for January 19—7 to December 19—7 is written down. The monthly total of January 19—8 is then added and the monthly total for January 19—7 subtracted. It is possible to plot two or more years' results in different colours on the same chart. In this way month-to-month and year-to-year trends are clearly visible.

Gantt charts. Managements are deeply concerned with variations from the normal. Progress charts of various types, such as the Z chart mentioned above, are helpful with this end in view. Of particular value in progress recording is the Gantt chart, which is a horizontal bar chart used to compare actual with scheduled performance.

MAPS

Maps may be used to give geographical information in a succinct and logical fashion. Figure 7 illustrates various ways in which such maps or cartograms may be used. Figure 7(a) shows how shading may be used to break down an area into manageable portions, selecting boundaries according to the data available. Figures 7(b) and (c) use dots to indicate the distribution of branches, etc., and Fig. 7(d) shows a combination of map and graph.

FILM, FILM STRIPS, CLOSED-CIRCUIT TELEVISION AND VIDEO

The psychologists tell us that words are the least effective way of communicating. Managements have been slow to realise this fact. So have educationalists, whose slogan has for too long been "chalk and talk"—often with greater emphasis on the talk. But faced with the need to solve the problems of communications, managements are now making increasing use of visual aids. Film strips are available both with and without sound. Slides can also be purchased or made.

Films and videos can be very effective, although they are less adaptable than either film strips or slides. Some large firms maintain their own film and video production units. Smaller organisations can also use these media and buy or hire films, video cassettes or film strips. Many companies have come to appreciate the value of closed-circuit television as providing support for their security and other control systems. CCTV, as it is usually called, also provides the training manager with a useful visual aid, and this aspect, together with the use of video, will be considered in Chapter XII.

I. INTRODUCTION

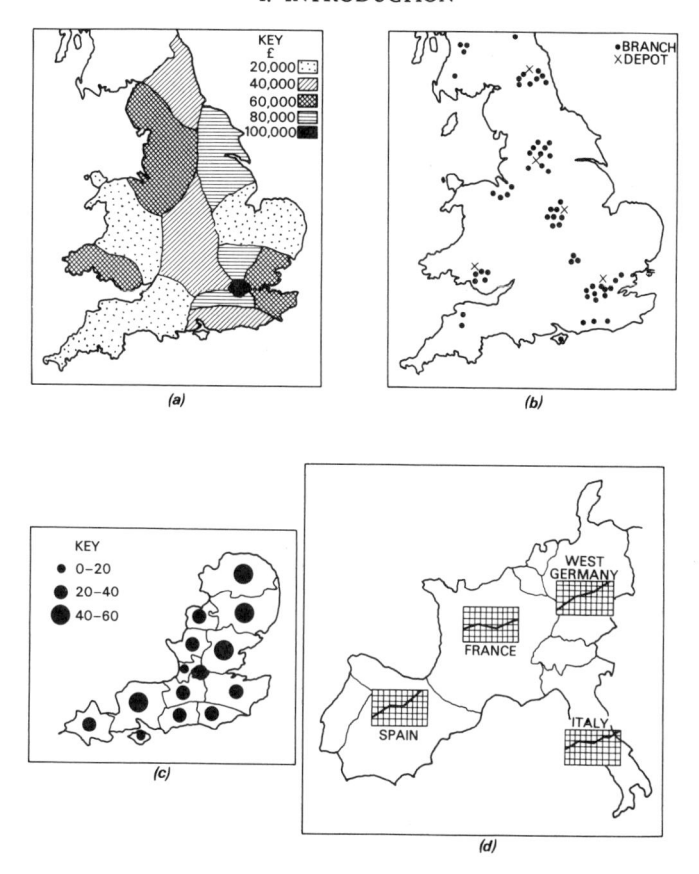

Fig. 7. *Maps for cartograms.*

Over the past few years there have been striking improvements in the efficiency of the equipment. This is not the place to discuss in detail the types available, and even if it were, the speed of technical change is very rapid. The latest information at the time of going to press would soon be out of date. However, many people who are not technically minded will find that after a very short period of instruction they are able to master the handling of modern visual aids equipment.

POSTERS

To consider posters last among the visual methods of producing material for communications purposes does not mean that we in any way underestimate their importance. For example, a real contribution can be made to the success of the communications policy by the way in which essential information is presented to all those employed by the organisation.

Most facts and figures can be displayed by such methods, which are both effective and simple. We have been able to obtain one or two first-rate examples of these techniques of communication which are illustrated in Figs. 8 and 9.

(Courtesy of RoSPA)
Fig. 8. *A poster issued by the Royal Society for the Prevention of Accidents.*

I. INTRODUCTION

(Courtesy of RoSPA)

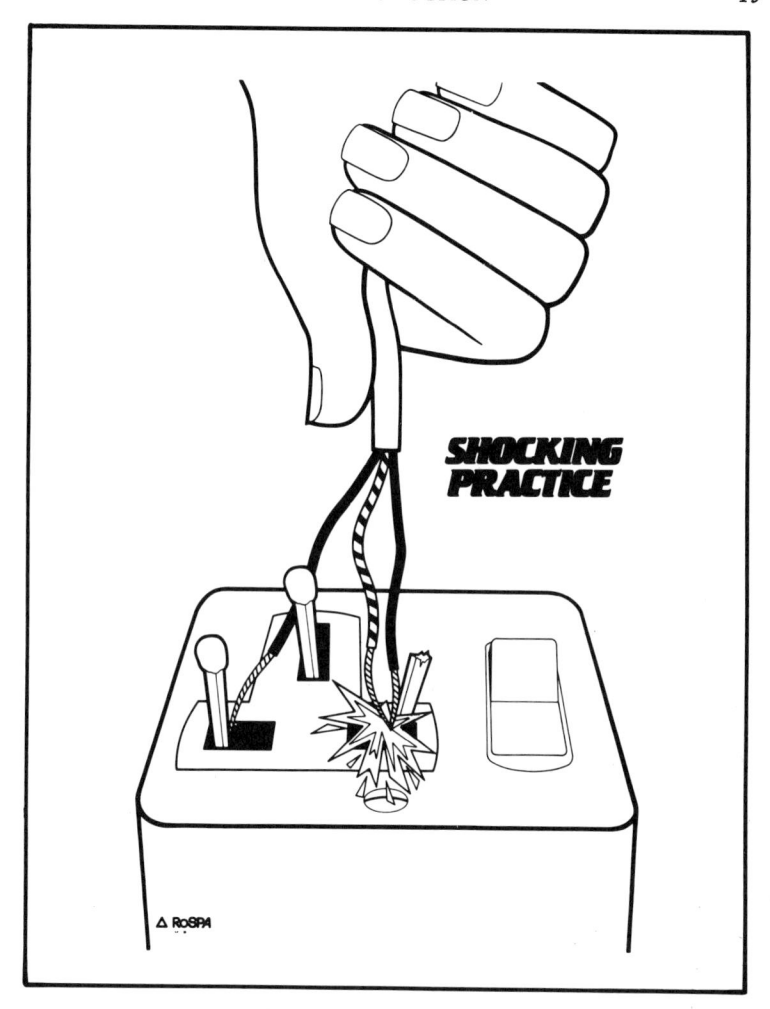

Fig. 9. *A poster issued by the Royal Society for the Prevention of Accidents. Such posters can contribute to the success of a company's safety and communications policies.*

There are, however, several less-obvious applications of the use of posters for communications purposes. For example, very little is written about the activities of the consumer and consultative councils which have been set up in many of the nationalised industries. We have, however, dealt fairly fully with their functions in Chapter XI. Many of these councils use posters for publicity purposes. The

North Thames Gas Consumers' Council, which provides a two-way channel of communication between North Thames Gas and the consumers, is a case in point.

A large-size poster setting out the aims of this consultative council is exhibited in every showroom in the region. The posters are renewed annually to keep them up to date. Similar posters are sent to every local authority in the area for display in council premises. Distribution is also made to other organisations representing consumer interests. Moreover, copies are sent to each member of Parliament whose constituency falls within that area of North Thames Gas and to the editors of all local newspapers.

QUESTIONS

1. What is meant by "communication"?

2. Discuss, with reference to any factory or other place of work with which you are familiar, the argument that more industrial disputes are caused by lack of information or a communications breakdown than for any other reason.

3. Do you consider that all organisations should appoint special officers to deal with the whole of their communication system?

4. Discuss the advantages and disadvantages of the various methods of visual communication.

5. How far is the management of a firm which produces motor vehicles for an international mass market justified in communicating to its employees its proposals for future development?

6. The board of directors of a manufacturing company decides to have a written statement of its sales policy, production policy, finance policy, and personnel policy. If you were preparing two of these what matters would you include in them, and why?

7. The CD Company has never issued internal statements of its sales policy, its production policy, or its personnel policy. A newly appointed chairman wishes the board to consider the desirability of formulating and publishing statements of policy.

(a) Consider the advantages and disadvantages of such a course.

(b) Prepare for submission to the chairman a list of the headings, that is, the names of the subjects, that might be included in such statements.

CHAPTER II

LINES OF COMMUNICATION

By lines of communication are meant the channels through which information is transferred from one person to another. Communication is essentially a two-way process; information has not only to be sent but has also to be received and understood. It has, in addition, to be acted upon. Machinery must be available through which there can be downward communication (from superior to subordinate), upward communication (from subordinate to superior), and horizontal communication. (Horizontal communication is between people of comparable status and also between management and union.)

The lines of communication should not be too long, for if they are, those people who have to take action on the information may not, in fact, receive the exact message intended. Many readers will be aware of the children's party game called "Chinese whispers", in which a message is passed round a number of children. The message is always altered out of all recognition in this way. We should remember that short lines of communication help to ensure that the information is not distorted in its passage from one person to another.

The lines of communication to be discussed in this chapter are line management, joint consultation, suggestion schemes, and horizontal communication.

LINE MANAGEMENT

By line organisation is meant a vertical line organisation where one rank is clearly below another to which it is directly related (*see* Fig. 10).

The value of line management

There has been much discussion about functional and staff management. This has tended to overshadow the importance of line management, and some observers on communications have given the impression that the main techniques used to solve the difficulties

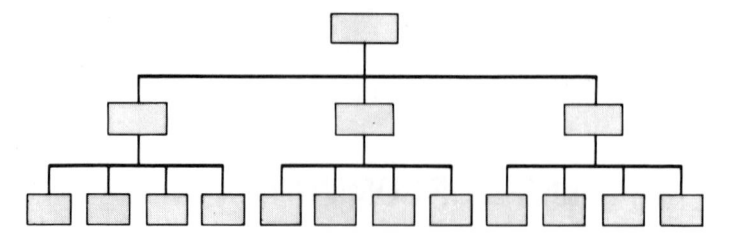

Fig. 10. *Line organisation.*

which inevitably arise are joint consultation, suggestion schemes, works magazines, and attitude surveys. The last are sometimes used by organisations to find out the attitudes, problems, and thinking of employees. The printed questionnaire is commonly used in the USA for this purpose. Another method employed is the interview survey.

Whichever method is used, the survey is often carried out by outside bodies who have the specialised knowledge required to obtain the most truthful answers. Having obtained truthful answers, the specialist survey firm may present an organisation with a difficult problem. We may assume that the consent of the workers to the survey has been obtained by the normal joint consultation machinery. If the survey reveals widespread criticism of management, should the survey be published? Suppression could endanger suspicion of management; publication could lead to loss of confidence in management.

Our experience and the many discussions we have had with managers in organisations of all types confirm the view that the normal lines of authority should be encouraged for communications purposes. For example, workshop problems, such as those involved in workshop reorganisation, are vitally important. Consultation on an informal basis between the supervisor and his team is fundamental and extremely helpful in reducing the risk of conflict. A major cause of conflict between managers and their subordinates is the absence of a clearly established set of objectives for the working group to achieve. Management by objectives attempts to remove this cause of managerial ineffectiveness.

Management by objectives

In brief, management by objectives is a systematic approach to management which includes setting objectives for the organisation and for the individual; control and review; and management development and appraisal.

This idea was originated by Peter Drucker and developed in his important work *The Practice of Management,* published by Pan

II. LINES OF COMMUNICATION

Books, which should form part of every executive's library.

Management by objectives (MBO) has been put into practice in this country in many different types of organisation—including Smiths Industries, Glaxo Ltd and the National Coal Board. It has also proved possible to introduce MBO successfully in firms with fewer than one hundred on the payroll. Thus there are no intrinsic reasons why even the smaller companies should not be able to apply management by objectives.

This technique has flourished in manufacturing industries because results there tend to be easier to quantify and measure. MBO has also worked well in banking and other service industries, and has been widely adopted by the civil service.

It will be clear, therefore, that the introduction of MBO may be part of a systematic approach to management training and development, and that this kind of approach will require from management a carefully drawn up action plan covering the following aspects:

1. specific assignment of responsibility within the company for management development;
2. the analysis of managerial jobs;
3. assessment of present and future needs;
4. recruitment and selection;
5. personal records and appraisal.

Most firms which introduce MBO want to improve the performance of managers in their present jobs. In management-development schemes there is now more attention being given to developing the average performers rather than the few "high fliers".

Other popular reasons for starting management by objectives have been to clarify responsibilities, to improve management structure, to establish "profit centres", to spot talent for promotion, to improve the appraisal system or to establish training needs.

Management by objectives is not a once-and-for-all technique. It must be seen as a continuous process. Once results have been evaluated, it is necessary to determine how far the plan was achieved and how it failed. In this way the plan can be reorganised, if necessary, and objectives reassessed.

The key is to ask how far are the organisation's objectives being achieved. The objectives will change and this, in turn, will have an effect upon the individual. It will show how far the individual has been successful in achieving objectives and what requirements are needed in training to help him develop.

The time needed for the implementation of MBO is often greater in practice than is first anticipated.

The plan may be drawn up on the following lines.

II. LINES OF COMMUNICATION

1. ESTABLISH OBJECTIVES

The main purpose of the business should be formulated. The purpose should be stated as a general intention at the top.

This requires the establishment of corporate objectives covering every significant area of the business together with a belief in long-range planning for profit and growth.

In a recent survey of firms who had adopted this technique, over 50 per cent did not have written corporate objectives before the introduction of their management-by-objectives scheme.

One objection is the security risk. It is now thought that this is often more imaginary than real. It is particularly important that middle managers should have a clear idea of the company's plans if they are not to become department rather than company minded.

If we are "in the picture" we shall put much more effort into our work.

2. ASSIGN OBJECTIVES

Next, the objectives—quantified and timed—should be stated. There is the need for sound organisation before assigning objectives.

Objectives should first be broken down into action to be taken by specified units and managers, by agreed times. The quantified results and targets to be achieved should also be set out.

The means of monitoring performance at all levels should then be considered.

Job evaluation should be carried out and job descriptions should be agreed between manager and individual. Many firms do not already use job descriptions before the introduction of MBO.

The job-holder should be allowed to play a big part in creating his own job description. Help by a consultant, either internal or external, is also a possibility.

3. AGREE ACTION

The subordinate should write down his own objectives for himself and for all the resources that he controls. The objectives the manager would like the subordinate to accomplish should then be listed.

The subordinate's objectives should next be reviewed in detail with him and suggestions offered.

A final written agreement should be made. The subordinate should be helped to overcome any obstacles.

All of this is good management practice, the only difference being the formal final written agreement.

4. TAKE ACTION

Having committed himself to fulfilling part of a plan, a subordinate should have found out what is expected of him as the job objectives change to meet the changing objectives of the organisation.

The position of the subordinate is demanding and challenging. He will know what he is expected to achieve and can develop himself to provide the skills his company objectives demand.

The subordinate should know whether or not he is succeeding and become aware of his shortcomings. This helps to set up controls to predict and measure results by the subordinate and keep him informed.

5. REVIEW PERFORMANCE

From the performance review it can be seen how the job was carried out. The potential in terms of future possible development can also be ascertained.

There is always a great deal of criticism of conventional appraisal schemes by both line and personnel managers. Indeed, an official two-year study of six companies and 1,440 manager appraisals was conducted a few years ago.

Three main conclusions were reached:

1. appraisers are reluctant to appraise;
2. interviewers are even more reluctant to interview;
3. the follow-up is inadequate.

In this phase of the operation there are certain points to watch. For example, performance review should not be linked with salary review. One of the longer-term implications of using MBO is a thorough overhaul of the concern's salary structure.

It is important to encourage genuine participation. We are all suspicious of the usual type of performance review. On the other hand, we are more ready to accept reviews under MBO. Here the review is concerned with measuring the manager's success against an understood and agreed base which he had a share in creating.

It may be useful to summarise the benefits which can arise from the introduction of management by objectives.

1. The company has a better understanding of an employee's needs, by allowing him to participate. The employee is also able to see where he should develop within the company.
2. The company can ensure an adequate supply of trained managers for the future.
3. Middle management is able to play an ever-increasing part in decision-making. If the manager at this level is to make the right decisions, a wider and fuller knowledge of objectives of the company is essential.
4. Cash benefits will accrue to the company from suggestions made by individuals.
5. The company should enjoy better internal communications.

With the growth of management by objectives, an improvement can be expected in the climate within which the individual can develop.

Finally, from the foregoing it should be clear that management by objectives is not a gimmick. It has, indeed, been called the distillation into a practical system of the best practice already followed by managers.

The working of management

FUNCTIONAL MANAGEMENT

As industrial organisation grew more complex it became necessary for those who were operating at a high level to delegate some of their authority to others. The principle of the division of labour (or specialisation) has therefore been applied to management. In this way people are made responsible for the specialised functions of management, e.g. development, selling, production, finance, or personnel relations. In turn, these functions are further subdivided to enable people to become more efficient. This system is far more satisfactory than making people responsible for a miscellaneous collection of jobs. Responsibility and authority are then delegated to the specialists who discharge these functions. It is, however, necessary to consider the manner in which the specialists carry out their duties. The principles to be employed here are covered by what is known as the span of control.

SPAN OF CONTROL

This principle, particularly important in large organisations, has been established by the experience of managers. It provides that no leader can effectively deal directly with more than five or six subordinates for whose activities he is responsible. Management principles no longer enjoy a ready acceptance among management theorists, but there is obviously a limit to the effective control of an executive with a growing number of subordinate managers to supervise. This principle may also be modified within certain limits for supervisors having mainly technical rather than managerial duties, and a leader may be greatly assisted where staff appointments are in force.

STAFF APPOINTMENTS

Good communications can be preserved by staff appointments. They are general or specialist assistants to a higher manager. Those who hold these posts will usually have designations such as "personal assistant", "training adviser", or "personnel officer". Staff appointments have been described as the extension of the leader's personality. The person who occupies a post of this type is merely a personal assistant to the higher manager and has no authority in his own right.

II. LINES OF COMMUNICATION

PRINCIPLE OF AUTHORITY

One of the tried and tested principles of scientific management is the principle of authority which lays down that the lines of authority should be clearly defined. Nobody should be accountable to more than one superior, who must be held responsible for the acts of those subordinate to him. Nevertheless, experiments are frequently being tried with forms of organisation which do not allow the conventional line management communication to operate without modification. A matrix structure of schools and divisions is common in colleges and is based on the assumption that a more effective service for students will result if course designers and supervisors are organised into schools, and teachers are organised into divisions based upon disciplines. The teaching divisions are led by appointed or elected academics with acknowledged reputations for scholarship and teaching ability. Teams are often used in industry for solving problems, changing membership according to the nature of the problem to be tackled. In Japan this practice has long been used at shop-floor level, where supervisors act as "trouble-shooters" in support of a highly productive work force. Job enrichment programmes may modify the application of the principle of authority in any organisation. The lines of authority and responsibility may, however, be suitably shown by organisation charts.

ORGANISATION CHARTS

Organisation charts showing lines of authority and responsibility in a company can be of great assistance to management in improving the communication system. Some companies have issued the organisation chart as part of their house journal. A well-known international oil company has also printed the pictures of the men by the side of their names on the chart, thus stressing the personal aspect of management. A very simple organisation chart is shown in Fig. 11.

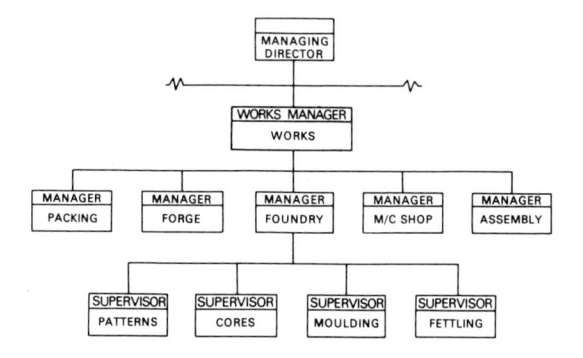

Fig. 11. *Organisation chart: horizontal organisation.*

The task of preparing an organisation chart enables every unit to be brought under review and the relationships of the units to one another to be assessed. Moreover, it ensures that the management considers the necessity of delegating to each employee the necessary authority to permit him to carry out his responsibilities. Each man should know his job, and the scope of all new jobs should be laid down.

With the increasing size or activity of an organisation the effectiveness of management may be reduced if the senior men are not freed for more important work and the more junior men prepared for future responsibility. Managements should ensure that any scheme of delegation is accompanied by adequate co-ordination of activities.

Organisation charts are thus an aid in many aspects of management. Where these charts do not exist they should be prepared as soon as possible. It must be emphasised, however, that it is necessary for the organisation structure to be flexible enough to allow adjustment when the basic circumstances change.

Organisation charts are useful tools in management, not only for the large organisations but also for the small ones. Most businesses today are still small ones. The principles of sound management need to be applied as much in the companies employing one hundred workers as in giant nationalised industries and multinationals.

JOB DESCRIPTIONS

We shall sometimes be required to write a job description. The object of describing the job in detail is to establish clearly its work content and requirements for its satisfactory execution. In this way subsequent evaluations are not based on assumptions, hearsay or inadequate appreciation of the job, but on the facts in each case.

A typical format for a job description follows.

1. Job summary: ideally this should not exceed a sentence or two and should indicate to whom the person filling the post is accountable.
2. Job content.
3. Job requirements:
    (a) skill requirements,
    (b) responsibility and mental requirements,
    (c) physical requirements and job conditions.

In collecting information about a job, account is normally taken not only of the content of the job but also of wider considerations, such as the purpose of the job; any limits of accuracy that are necessary to its proper performance; environment and conditions; tools and equipment; necessary relationships with other people; and supervisory responsibility.

Job descriptions may be required to establish clearly the roles of members of an organisation; to provide the basis for systematic training; to enable management to install management by objectives; and sometimes to ensure that applicants for new posts are not under any misapprehension about the responsibilities and duties of the posts for which they are applying.

When a manager compiles a job description to be used for the purpose of selecting staff he needs to make a profile of the sort of person he expects to be able to carry out competently the tasks which have been identified: we call this profile the man (woman) specification. The man specification will include the personal qualities, experience, and qualifications required by applicants.

JOB EVALUATION

In preparation of earlier editions of this book the authors decided to introduce material which was relevant to the task of the manager in the context of British membership of the European Economic Community. Equal pay is a requirement of British law but it is also a requirement of the European Community at large. Job evaluation is a means by which discrimination (in pay) against women may be satisfactorily removed on the shop floor.

The nature of job evaluation

Job evaluation is a systematic method of measuring the relative worth of jobs and relies on the standards derived from the content of the jobs themselves. Like so many enlightened concepts in management and industrial relations, job evaluation originated in Sweden in the late 1940s and was designed to overcome deficiencies in the existing payment systems. We must remember that the Swedes were looking for a system suitable for their industrial relations pattern based on industrial unions. Job evaluation was considered appropriate for plant- or industry-based negotiations but there was and continues to be some opposition to the concept in Britain with its multiplicity of bargaining units. British Leyland and other large organisations have, however, in recent years been successful in reducing the number of bargaining units. Moreover considerable progress has been made in the civil service and in local government in using job evaluation to determine the gradings and hence the pay of white collar workers.

Objectives of job evaluation specialists

We may find ourselves increasingly led to examine the job evaluation alternative to collective bargaining in determining a structure of wages and salaries.

Primarily our objective should be to create a climate of opinion within the organisation so that teams of employees are prepared to accept a systematic wage structure. We should attempt to show that job evaluation is:

1. fair because it can produce differential rates of payment independently of the prejudices of the persons normally assigned to assess the work and value of others;
2. helpful in enabling management to decide how to use its manpower effectively;
3. valuable in providing management with the evidence for changes to be made in the payments system;
4. a useful aid to supervisors and managers in their administration of wages policy.

The fundamental point for managers to remember is that the introduction of a job evaluation programme poses a major communication problem. Unless the staff are not only consulted but convinced of the value of job evaluation, the exercise could result in a greater feeling of grievance that that which existed under the original payments system.

We shall usually find it necessary to establish committees to introduce the system. A "steering committee" may be needed to understudy and eventually to replace the specialist job evaluation adviser. The table of standards produced by the steering committee will be needed by the "job evaluation committee" which will embrace the steering committee, management specialists such as the production engineer, and employee representatives. Job evaluation would form an appropriate matter for consideration by the "works councils" proposed by the European Economic Commission.

JOINT CONSULTATION

The term "joint consultation" has two meanings. In the first place it is used to cover the principle that workers should be notified of changes in policy, especially aspects of labour relations. Joint consultation also refers to the framework of committees by which labour and management are brought together to discuss those matters of common concern which do not fall within the scope of the negotiating machinery.

The various bodies which are used in joint consultation provide employees with an opportunity for expression, and thus fulfil a useful purpose in communication.

Yet a word of warning is necessary here. Most of us know of companies and other organisations where the machinery for joint consultation is extremely good but where, despite this, there is a great deal of industrial unrest. It does not follow that after designing a sound joint consultation procedure we can be complacent. It is essential for the dry bones of joint consultation to be clothed with flesh of good communication.

Procedures for consultation, efficient though they may well be, can never take the place of good management, which is a vital, living thing.

Joint consultation in the electricity supply industry

The Electricity Act 1947 made provision for consultation within the supply industry of Great Britain. Under the Act, the central authority was required to make agreements with the appropriate trade unions for the establishment and maintenance of machinery for:

> The promotion and encouragement of measures affecting the safety, health and welfare of persons employed by Electricity Boards and the discussion of other matters of mutual interest to the Boards and such persons, including efficiency in the operation of the services of the Boards and for providing facilities for the training and education of employees.

In the result, the industry set up machinery for one comprehensive system of joint consultation to cover all employees. Under the Electricity Reorganisation (Scotland) Act 1954 the supply industry has resulted in two separate systems of joint consultation, one for England and Wales and the other for Scotland (*see* Fig. 12).

The system in England and Wales was introduced as the result of an agreement dated 7th March 1957 with all the unions in the industry. It is based on advisory councils and committees on three different levels: national, district, and local. The matters that come within the purview of these advisory councils and committees are broadly as defined in the Acts of 1947 and 1957, namely, safety, health, welfare, education, and training and efficiency. No attempt was made to specify in detail the matters coming within these broad terms of reference, for it was considered that experience in the working of the machinery would eventually be the best guide. The only subjects having a bearing on the progress of the industry and the well-being of employees which are excluded from their terms of reference are those which relate to negotiation of wages and conditions of employment. Details of the system for dealing with these items in the industry are given later in this chapter.

At the national level there is the National Joint Advisory Council. The Electricity Council and electricity boards' members on the national council sit side by side not only with full-time officers of the trade unions but also with employees who have themselves been elected as representatives of their local advisory committees. The contributions made by these elected employees on the national council are a valuable means of bringing the opinions and views of employees at all levels directly to bear on important problems

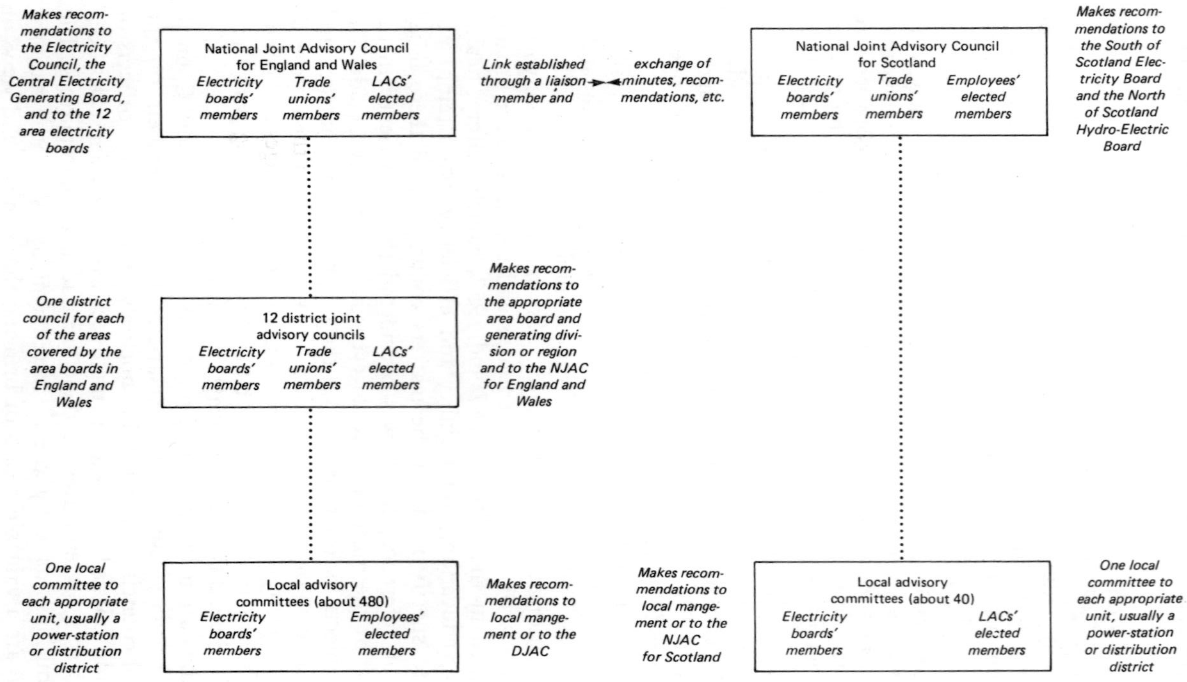

Fig. 12. Joint consultative machinery for the electricity supply in Great Britain.

affecting the industry's future or the working lives of people engaged in its service. Because it is representative of all interests, the National Joint Advisory Council provides a representative forum for management and employees of the whole industry. It is being increasingly used as a discussion ground for the many matters of national importance to the industry which arise from time to time. Each year the national council issues a report on the operation of the whole system of joint consultation within the industry.

Each district joint advisory council covers the whole of the territory of an area board and the corresponding section of the generating board. It comprises representatives of the electricity boards and of the trade unions, together with elected members of local advisory committees. District councils deal with matters in their own sphere in a similar way to that adopted in the national council in considering matters common to the industry as a whole. They may make recommendations to the boards or to the national council.

The local advisory committees are at the foundation of the system for joint consultation. It is their work which most directly and decisively affects the quality of human relations in the industry, and on their successful operation depends the health of the system generally. There are now about 480 local advisory committees in England and Wales, nearly all of them identified with a single local management unit, usually either a distribution district or a powerstation. They comprise representatives nominated by the boards together with directly elected representatives of employees of all grades working in the locality.

The electricity supply industry has encountered similar communication problems to those experienced by companies in the private sector of the economy. The first difficulty is that of passing on information to the shop-floor workers. An attempt to resolve this issue has been the use of informal departmental meetings at powerstations. The chairmen at these meetings are the departmental heads, and the supervisors and local advisory committee representatives are present. Although notice of the meetings is given some days in advance, there is no formal agenda, and any matters may be discussed, except those relating to the negotiating machinery.

Some districts have designed an improved form of local advisory committee agenda for posting on notice boards and have circulated leaflets describing the functions of the committee. Others have arranged district conferences and courses for local advisory committee secretaries and these, together with the national course held at the Horsley Towers Training Centre, have helped to remedy weaknesses and to improve the general standard of secretarial work.

The second problem is that of the by-passing of the supervisor in formal consultation machinery. The South-Western District Council has placed special emphasis in its discussions on the need to improve communication. As a result of the recommendations made by the council, the area board invites the district industrial relations officer to district managers' meetings, where full reports on current advisory and negotiating developments are given. After these meetings information is passed down by the district managers to all junior management. The district industrial relations officer is also invited to address junior management and supervisors in localities throughout the area board.

All apprentices are now receiving lectures on industrial relations procedures and developments, and similar lectures are given to all new entrants in a number of distribution districts. A further development has been to encourage senior staff in control of groups of employees to hold informal meetings of these groups, with the LAC representative in attendance. The objects of these meetings are to explain board policy as it affects the group and to discuss the agenda of forthcoming LAC meetings and other matters of interest.

The system in Scotland is essentially the same, with a National Joint Advisory Council for Scotland supported by local advisory committees, numbering about forty. There are, however, no district councils. A close liaison is maintained between the system in England and Wales and the system in Scotland.

Readers interested in obtaining further information about joint consultation in the electricity supply industry should consult the annual reports of the industry's National Joint Advisory Council.

The following paragraphs on collective bargaining in the electricity supply industry have been included so that readers may be able to distinguish the items covered by consultation machinery from those covered by negotiating machinery.

Negotiation of wages and salaries in the electricity supply industry

Since the nationalisation of the electricity supply industry a single system has been established for dealing with negotiation or "collective bargaining". This continued the principles of negotiation established in 1919, and comprises five national negotiating bodies:

1. National Joint Industrial Council, for industrial staff;
2. National Joint Board, for technical engineering staff;
3. National Joint Council, for administrative and clerical grades;
4. National Joint (Building and Civil Engineering) Committee, for building and civil engineering workers; and
5. National Joint Managerial and Higher Executive Grades Committee.

Virtually all employees are covered by agreements on a national basis.

The national negotiating bodies are composed of representatives of the employers, namely the Electricity Council and the electricity boards, and of the appropriate trade unions. The decisions arrived at through the negotiating machinery, appropriately endorsed, are executive decisions; there is an obligation on the part of the employing boards to observe them.

There is district machinery for each of the negotiating bodies with the exception of the Managerial and the Building Trades committees, which are small. These district bodies cover areas coinciding with the territories of the area boards of England and Wales and of the two Scottish boards.

At local level there is machinery covering the industrial staff, i.e. the works committees, and the clerical and administrative workers, i.e. staff committees. These local committees are mainly concerned directly with the application of the terms and conditions of employment after these have been negotiated nationally, and functions of the works committee (and those of the staff committee are very similar) include dealing with such things as meal-breaks and how the hours are to be worked (including shift-work arrangements). If any worker has a grievance or if there is a difference on either side of the works committee the dispute may be referred to the district council. Likewise the district council may refer the difference to the national council, and if the national council cannot resolve the matter they may refer it to arbitration.

The National Consultative Council for the Coalmining Industry

The notes which follow outline the constitution of the National Consultative Council for the Coalmining Industry and some of the topics discussed by the council.

CONSTITUTION AND RULES

1. *Title and Commencement.* The National Consultative Council for the Coalmining Industry (hereinafter called "the Council") shall be deemed to have been established on the Twenty-seventh day of November, 1946.

2. *Scope.* The Council shall have within its purview all the undertakings in the Coalmining Industry vested in the National Coal Board (hereinafter called "the Board").

3. *Function.* The function of the Council shall be to provide a regular means of consultation between the Board and organisations appearing to them to represent substantial proportions of persons in the employment of the Board, or any class of such persons, on:

(a) questions relating to the safety, health and welfare of such persons;

(b) the organisation and conduct of the operations in which such persons are employed and other matters of mutual interest to the Board and such persons arising out of the exercise and performance by the Board of their functions;

provided that questions relating to terms and conditions of employment shall be excluded from consideration by the Council.

4. *Membership of Council*: The Council shall consist of twenty-nine members of whom eight shall be appointed by the Board, nine by the National Union of Mineworkers, two by the National Association of Colliery Managers, three by the National Association of Colliery Overmen, Deputies and Shotfirers and seven by the British Association of Colliery Management. In the event of any member being unable to attend a meeting the organisation he represents may appoint a substitute to attend in his place.

5. *Officers.*

(a) The Chairman of the Board shall act as Chairman of the Council and the other organisations represented thereon shall each appoint a Deputy Chairman. In the absence of the Chairman, one of the Deputy Chairmen shall preside at all meetings of the Council.

(b) The Board shall appoint a Secretary to the Council who shall keep Minutes of the proceedings at each meeting.

6. *Meetings.* Meetings of the Council shall be held initially at monthly intervals, but if occasion arises, special meetings will be held in the intervening periods. Wherever possible, not less than seven clear days' notice of each regular meeting, together with a statement of the business to be transacted thereat, shall be given to members and to the Secretaries of the organisations represented on the Council. As long notice as possible shall be given of special meetings.

7. *Attendance at Meetings.* Members of the Council may bring advisers with them to meetings, but these will not be entitled to participate in the proceedings except at the invitation of the Chairman.

8. *Committees.* The Council may appoint from its membership committees for such purposes and with such powers as the Council may determine. The Council may appoint to such committees or authorise committees to co-opt persons with special knowledge or experience not being members of the Council.

9. *Procedure.*

(a) Both the Board and the other organisations represented on the Council shall be free to submit items in writing for the Agenda of any meetings, provided that (save in the case of special meetings) such items are submitted in time for the Agenda to be circulated wherever possible seven clear days before the date of the meeting.

(b) The opinion of the Council on all questions shall be reached as far as possible by mutual agreement and so recorded. But, so that the Board may receive the most useful guidance from the Council, the views of individual members will also be recorded where appropriate.

10. *Finance.* The expenses of members attending meetings of the Council shall be met by the organisations they represent and the general expenses of the Council shall be met by the Board.

11. *Amendment of Constitution.* The Constitution of the Council may be amended only following consideration of the proposed amendment at a

II. LINES OF COMMUNICATION   33

special meeting of the Council called for the purpose. At least twenty-one days' notice shall be given outlining the proposal for amendment of the constitution.

SUBJECTS DISCUSSED AT SOME OF THE RECENT MEETINGS

First meeting

Safety and health:
    Self-rescuers
    Periodic X-ray scheme
    Legislation
    Research
    Annual Reports
    Etc.
Minutes of Recruitment, Education, and Training Committee:
    Apprenticeship scheme for mechanics and electricians
    Procedure for obtaining second class certificates of competency
Output, manpower, and distribution
Long-service certificates
Composition of divisional councils

Second meeting

Self-rescuers
Large capacity exploders
Second class certificates of competency
Composition of divisional councils
Review of the industry's performance:
    (i) Results
    (ii) Mechanisation
    (iii) Manpower
    (iv) Distribution

Coal magazine

Third meeting

Accident at Cortonwood Colliery
Self-rescuers
Composition of divisional councils
Minutes of the Safety and Health Committee:
    Stone dust barriers
    Prevention of fires and explosions
Minutes of Recruitment, Education and Training and Welfare Committee:
    Second class certificates of competency
    National apprenticeship scheme for engineering draughtsmen
    Training of deputies and shotfirers
    First class certificates of competency
    Day release for clerical workers

The Financial and Economic Obligations of the Nationalised Industries
—government white paper
Labour supply, wastage, and turnover

Fourth meeting
Certificates of competency
Financial and economic obligations of the national industries
Minutes of the Safety and Health Committee (periodic X-ray examinations, etc.)
Progress and prospects
Disposals
Productivity
Manpower
Mechanisation

Prospects for next year
Allowances for members of colliery consultative committees
Scheme for awards for inventions in the technical field
Medical examination of re-entrants and young persons

The Ford Motor Company's procedures

JOINT WORKS COMMITTEES

We are very grateful for the help which has been given by the Ford Motor Company in the preparation of this part of the book. Set out in Fig. 13 is a summary of the procedures for dealing with grievances and disputes in the company.

A few notes are set out below to amplify the information contained in the diagram.

A joint works committee is established at all but the very small plants of the company. At the company's main locations at Dagenham there are five such committees. The maximum number of members of a committee is eight from each side. The employees are represented by shop stewards, who are elected from among their own number. Thus, employee representation is by indirect election. The employers are represented by what the Ford Motor Company calls middle to senior management, each of whom probably has responsibility for more than a thousand workers. These include production managers, superintendents, and other managers *who are normally in contact with the industrial workers.*

Joint works committees in the Ford Motor Company are not concerned with wage payments, which are the province of the National Joint Negotiating Committee. The function of these joint works committees is the discussion of essentially local problems affecting employees in that particular area. They meet regularly and additional sessions may be held to consider urgent questions.

II. LINES OF COMMUNICATION

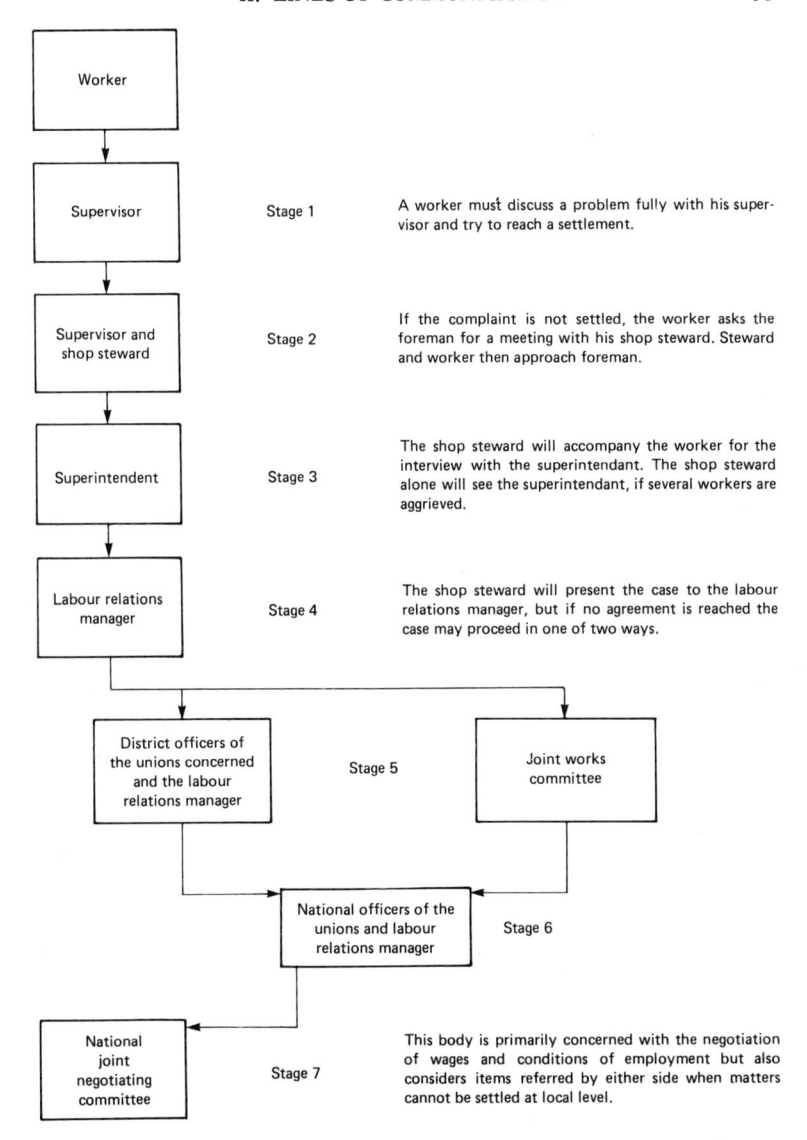

Worker → Supervisor	
Stage 1	A worker must discuss a problem fully with his supervisor and try to reach a settlement.
Supervisor and shop steward	
Stage 2	If the complaint is not settled, the worker asks the foreman for a meeting with his shop steward. Steward and worker then approach foreman.
Superintendent	
Stage 3	The shop steward will accompany the worker for the interview with the superintendant. The shop steward alone will see the superintendant, if several workers are aggrieved.
Labour relations manager	
Stage 4	The shop steward will present the case to the labour relations manager, but if no agreement is reached the case may proceed in one of two ways.
District officers of the unions concerned and the labour relations manager / Joint works committee	
Stage 5	
National officers of the unions and labour relations manager	
Stage 6	
National joint negotiating committee	
Stage 7	This body is primarily concerned with the negotiation of wages and conditions of employment but also considers items referred by either side when matters cannot be settled at local level.

(Courtesy of the Ford Motor Co.)

Fig. 13. *Ford Motor Company summary of the procedures for dealing with disputes and grievances.*

The following are some of the items which have been discussed at the Chassis Group Joint Works Committee, Dagenham, Essex, recently:

1. lighting, heating, and ventilation of various sections;
2. transport to the plant and car-parking space;
3. car sales to employees;
4. new pension scheme and representation on the panel of trustees;
5. canteen prices;
6. application of special allowances for particular jobs;
7. the prospects in the motor industry and, in particular, the prospects for the company;
8. short-time working arrangements;
9. punctuality and discipline;
10. departmental allocation of merit payments above the agreed basic rate;
11. medical facilities for night-shift workers.

The joint works committees of the Ford Motor Company are excellent examples of the principle of industrial communication, since they enable management to receive and pass on information. They are used, for example, to explain to the shop stewards the reasons for the short-time working, such as the failure of the supplier of an important component to provide the quantities required to maintain production. It is interesting to note that education and training are not discussed at joint works committees; nor does there appear to be any discussion on apprenticeships.

The constitution of joint works committees at the Ford Motor Company is as follows.

1. A Joint Works Committee shall be set up at any of the Company's factories where agreed by the National Joint Negotiating Committee.

2. The numbers appointed to each Joint Works Committee shall be related to the number of Employees at the factory concerned, but in no case shall any such Committee consist of more than eight representatives of the Company and more than eight Shop Stewards.

3. The Shop Stewards constituting the Employees' Side of the Joint Works Committee shall be elected by, and from, the whole of the Shop Stewards of the Unions in the factory concerned.

4. The Shop Stewards elected to the Joint Works Committee shall, subject to re-election, hold office for not more than twelve months.

5. The Company shall nominate its representatives to each Joint Works Committee and from such representatives shall also appoint a Chairman for each Joint Works Committee.

6. Each Joint Works Committee in respect of the factory it represents shall deal with any matter referred to it under the agreed procedure.

7. In addition, each Joint Works Committee may consider the application and interpretation of such wages matters as are a domestic issue capable of settlement within the factory and any other matters affecting Employees other than those which are the rightful function of Management, the Unions or the National Joint Negotiating Committee.

8. Either Side, party to each Joint Works Committee, is empowered to

place appropriate items on the Agenda for consideration.

9. There shall be Joint Secretaries of each Joint Works Committee, one of whom shall be appointed from the Employees' Side of the Joint Works Committee and shall be known as the Convener, and one from the Company Side. Their duties shall be to prepare Agenda for circulation at least three days prior to the meeting and to prepare an agreed report of the proceedings of the meeting and its decisions. Joint Works Committees may issue statements concerning any item of particularly important business conducted at their meetings for publication on Works Notice Boards. These statements must be mutually agreed by the Joint Works Committee and will be issued above the signatures of the Joint Secretaries.

10. Should any Joint Works Committee have for consideration any matter concerning a Department or Departments having no direct representation on that Committee, the Joint Works Committee may, as regards that question, co-opt a Shop Steward or Shop Stewards for the Department or Departments concerned.

11. Should any question fail to find a solution in the Joint Works Committee, such question may be referred by either side to the District Official or Officials for the Union or Unions concerned.

12. Joint Works Committee meetings shall be held at least once a month.

13. The Company and the Unions shall recognise only the duly authorised Joint Works Committees.

SUPERVISORS' JOINT CONSULTATION COMMITTEES

In the Ford Motor Company there are two kinds of consultation: that resulting from the procedural agreements made with unions—supervisors are represented by the Association of Scientific, Technical and Managerial Staffs; and that initiated by the company on a plant basis. Plant supervisors' committees vary in size from six to eight members including representatives of both managers and supervisors. The chairmen of these committees are the plant managers. Frequently occurring items at plant supervisors' committees are:

1. car-parking and other facilities;
2. car sales to employees;
3. plant manager's report: a survey of company plans and results; plant targets and achievements;
4. pensions and fringe benefits;
5. training programmes;
6. employee relationships.

Each plant supervisors' committee sends delegates to the annual conference where matters of common interest to supervisors throughout the company are discussed with senior managers. Reports are made to the plant supervisors' committee on the action taken as a result of the discussions at the annual conference.

BRIEFING GROUPS

In addition to the supervisors' consultative machinery the company has established a system of informal communication called briefing groups. Briefing groups were introduced in 1970 with the help of the Industrial Society whose director, John Garnett, has successfully established the system in more than 200 companies. Significantly, the Ford Motor Company was the first large company to mount a briefing group exercise so that it could effectively overcome the harmful results of the grapevine communication network.

Briefing groups are simply the means by which each level of management seeks to inform a lower level on any matter which is important to the company and its employees. The briefing groups system scores over other methods in that it is speedy and confirms the authority of managers and supervisors. Employees find the system an advantage because they have the opportunity to ask questions on aspects which they do not understand. However, debate is avoided because there are other channels for consultation and discussion.

When a plant manager has a message which he wishes to be passed on he calls a meeting of his departmental managers and general superintendents to give them the information. These managers in turn hold meetings with their superintendents, general foremen and staff supervisors, and when these groups have been briefed, pass on the information at meetings of their line supervisors. Finally, the supervisors hold briefing meetings for their work groups.

Despite the fact that briefing groups are time consuming the company is convinced of their value in ensuring that important information is effectively passed on to employees. Ford is under no illusions that briefing is an industrial relations panacea: they accept that basic conflict is inevitable. Briefing does, however, help to reduce the conflict resulting from misunderstanding or the absence of authentic management messages. Ford believes that a lack of management communication is the most fertile ground on which the destructive grapevine flourishes.

Joint consultation in the Marconi-Elliot Avionic Systems Company, Basildon

The pattern of joint consultation varies widely from industry to industry and from company to company within each industry. In April 1972 the Marconi Company was reorganised and assumed the new name of Marconi-Elliot. Among the many changes which followed the regrouping was the establishment of a single consultative committee to take the place of the original staff advisory and works committees.

Membership of the advisory committee consists of the chairman (personnel manager), works manager, plant engineer and a senior divisional representative (alternately from the Aeronautical and Electro Optical Systems divisions), one supervisor on rotation and fifteen elected members representing the various areas on the site. The consultative representation is by direct election and for that reason differs from that operating in many companies where indirect representation by shop stewards is the rule. The method of selection is similar to that used by works councils in the Federal Republic of Germany and in a modified form may be the basis for the election of worker directors in British companies if the government eventually agrees to legislate for industrial democracy as envisaged by the European Commission.

The advisory committee of the company make extensive use of committees and sub-committees to help them in their work. Some important items dealt with recently are set out below:

1. traffic problems (sub-committee report);
2. canteen prices;
3. output and budgetary information;
4. new equipment to be produced;
5. safety (sub-committee report);
6. loss and damage (good housekeeping);
7. lay-out changes;
8. exhibition (sub-committee report);
9. suggestions and inventions (committee report).

As with the Ford Motor Company, the negotiation of wages and conditions of service lies outside this procedure.

Further information about the use of committees by the Marconi-Elliot Company is given in Chapter IX.

Joint consultation at Van den Berghs and Jurgens Ltd

Another interesting example of joint consultation occurs at the Purfleet factory of Van den Berghs and Jurgens, a member of the Unilever Group.

The factory council was established in 1919, and it is significant that this margarine factory has been free of serious labour trouble.

A revised system of consultation was recommended by a working party and was inaugurated in January 1972.

It provides for monthly departmental meetings between departmental managers and the shop stewards of their departments. These meetings are followed one week later by others at which the twenty-one hourly paid union representatives combine to form the works committee and together with management representatives the health and safety and catering committees. Two weeks later in the same month the joint works council meets to discuss problems which are common to the site as a whole. The representation at the joint works council comprises the works general manager, the chief engineer, the personnel manager, the industrial relations manager and departmental managers representing management and the works committee.

The three other groups, who meet separately each month, managers and assistant managers and office staff, are also represented at the joint works council.

The object of these changes was to produce a situation in which departmental problems were resolved at that level leaving the joint works committee to deal with matters affecting the whole plant.

Industrial democracy

When Britain joined the European Economic Community, the original six members were already aware of the European Commission's views on industrial democracy as set out in the Fifth Directive. British company structure was seemingly incompatible with the supervisory boards and management boards of the German model and an official committee of enquiry (the Bullock Committee) was appointed to examine proposals for the introduction of worker participation in the control of industry. The Bullock Committee reported in 1977 but the Labour government was unable to introduce legislation implementing the main recommendations, although it had undertaken to do so.

As long ago as 1968 the British Steel Corporation introduced appointed employee directors and have found the presence of these directors helpful at the level of policy making and corporate planning, although the participation is at the group board rather than main board level. A recent and interesting account of the experience of British Steel's employee directors is given by John Bank and Ken Jones in *Worker Directors Speak*. Further involvement of the workers in the consultative process takes place at local level through "local lump sum bonus schemes". The corporation have made no moves to revert to the composition of the conventional British board, unlike British Telecom, who discontinued their experiment with employee directors in 1980.

British employers remain largely hostile to the concept of worker directors and particularly opposed to being compelled to adopt the principle. Moreover, many have argued that the Bullock requirement that only union nominees would be acceptable is basically undemocratic, when half the working population do not belong to trade unions.

Although it has been argued that implementation of the Bullock proposals would merely give to British workers what German workers already have, there are significant differences. Firstly, Germany has thirty years' experience of co-determination and co-decision; secondly, German company structure enables policy to be separated from day-to-day management by means of the two-tier board system; and thirdly, German industrial democracy involves the election of worker directors nominated by works councils elected in turn by the workers as a whole and not merely by union members.

Works councils

Although the concept of works councils based on the German principle of election by the workers as a whole, regardless of union membership, has been gaining in popularity — e.g. the SDP/Liberal Alliance endorses the principle — many managers favour a less structured approach involving consultation at the shop floor operational level. Nevertheless, despite the general opposition of trade unions some works council agreements have been concluded by companies which already enjoy good relations with their employees. Even where they have been established the composition is different from the German model but it is useful to examine the structure of a British example at the London factory of the Glacier Metal Company, a company with a deserved reputation for innovation in personnel and industrial relations policies.

THE GLACIER METAL COMPANY'S WORKS COUNCIL SCHEME

Glacier's works council was established as a result of an agreement made in 1969 by the company with the unions concerned with negotiations, both nationally and locally, on behalf of employees at the factory. These unions were the Amalgamated Union of Engineering and Foundry Workers, the Transport and General Workers' Union, the Electric, Electronic, Telecommunication and Plumbing Union, and the Draughtsmen and Allied Technicians' Association. At present the scheme provides for a council of up to fifteen members, comprising the management member, one supervisory member, who need not necessarily belong to a trade union, and thirteen members elected from the works committee composed of shop stewards and representatives from shop and office committees.

The scope of the discussions enables any reasonable subject to be considered, but nationally agreed wage rates and conditions may be altered only in accordance with a procedure approved by the appropriate trade unions.

When the constitution was drawn up it was agreed that the works council should have three principal functions.

> 1. To decide the principles and policies within which the management and members of the London factories area shall operate in the light of opinions, both of those whose conditions will be affected by the policy and of those who will have to implement the policy; and taking into account total Company policy and the policies of trade unions signatory to this agreement, and the interests of the Company and its customers.

2. To revise, up-date and clarify, where necessary, existing policy in the light of the opinions and interests mentioned above.

3. Recognising that its decisions and policies are binding upon all members of the London factories area, to take whatever steps may be appropriate from time to time to ensure that they are implemented and observed.

Much of the work of the council is undertaken by committees, of which the most important is the steering committee which operates virtually as an executive committee in that it may refer matters to committees in between the monthly meetings of the council. Both the steering committee and special committees have no power of co-option, but appointed committees may include members who are not also members of the council.

An important appointed committee is the health and safety committee established to meet the requirements of the Health and Safety at Work Act 1974. The composition of this committee is as follows.

1. Nominated by management:
    the chairman;
    the safety officer;
    the medical officer;
    a senior technical specialist;
    a senior personnel specialist.
2. Nominated by the trade unions: six representatives from amongst the employees appointed by the signatory trade unions.

Additionally this committee may co-opt members with specialist knowledge to help it in carrying out its function.

SUGGESTION SCHEMES

Suggestion schemes can be one of the chief ways of making sure that the bright ideas of all members of an organisation are considered. They are used for office workers as well as for those whose employment is in factories. Many such schemes have been in use for a great many years. One firm with fifty years of existence has been operating suggestion schemes throughout that period of time. Nearly 60,000 ideas have been yielded in this way.

In preparing this we are indebted to the work of the Nottingham and District Productivity Association, the executive committee of which formed a sub-committee to survey and stimulate suggestion schemes in the Nottingham area, with particular reference to local conditions and requirements. A number of companies were represented on the sub-committee, and the schemes which they operated were examined in a booklet entitled *A Study on Suggestion Schemes*. As the result of this painstaking work, certain principles of a recommended suggestion scheme were evolved. Variations were made to suit the individual requirements of different industries, and provision was made for principles which could be applicable to small as well as to large companies.

The aims of suggestion schemes were considered, and the sub-committee came to the conclusion that the primary aim of any scheme of this type must be to increase productivity. They also recommended that this should be stressed at the very start in the published outline of any scheme. In their admirable analysis of suggestion schemes and productivity the sub-committee came to the conclusion that "the suggestions scheme is, therefore, a first-class means of bringing the worker and management together in a congenial day-to-day manner, thus greatly improving personal relations in industry".

Preparation of the scheme

The sub-committee next considered the features which should receive study before a scheme is installed. These principles were taken to be eight in number, and we have included one or two brief notes about each.

1. *The terms of reference.* These should be published in such a way that everyone has access to them when necessary. Subsequent amendments must also be published.

2. *The secretary.* He should have constant management support. On the committee he should be without powers to vote.

3. *The committee.* The number of voting members must not be less than three, and must at all times be an odd number.

4. *The scale of awards.* The aim should be to provide awards which will encourage the submission of further ideas.

5. *Eligibility.*

(*a*) Staff and factory employees (excluding technical personnel), up to and including chargehands, assistant foremen, and assistant managers, should be eligible for all awards.

(*b*) Managers, foremen, and executives below director level should receive awards when the suggestion is considered to be outside their normal duties.

(*c*) Technical personnel should receive awards only for suggestions outside the scope of their normal duties.

The Industrial Society's guide for determining the suggestor's normal duties considers that it is outside the scope of normal duties: (*i*) if the suggestion needed the approval of a technical or development department; (*ii*) if the suggestor could not be reasonably criticised for failing to implement the suggestion himself.

6. *Status of the scheme.* The scheme should be not only accepted but welcomed by workers and management at all levels. It should

be regarded as an integral part of the company's activities.

7. *Management attitude.* The management has a duty to show continual interest in the scheme.

8. *Anonymity.* This should be maintained up to the point when the final award is to be paid. Only at that point, provided the suggestor agrees, can the award and identity be revealed.

Working of the scheme

It should be possible for practical contributions to be made in this way, particularly if the workers are skilled in technical fields.

We set out below in abridged form the report which was prepared by the sub-committee of the Nottingham and District Productivity Association laying down the essentials for an efficient scheme.

EFFICIENCY AND SPEED OF ACTION

A scheme will be successful and remain so only if it is consistently run on an efficient basis; in addition, the fact that it is efficient must be patent to both workers and management.

This is always made obvious by the speed of action in dealing with the suggestor's idea, by which is meant the quickness with which the suggestor receives an acknowledgment of his idea and the urgency with which it is subsequently dealt with at all stages of progress.

When ideas take a long time to mature the workers gain the impression that a scheme is dilatory and inefficient and therefore a waste of time. This can be overcome if the secretary always conveys an atmosphere of urgency to whoever is dealing with any aspect of the suggestion scheme, particularly when the development of a suggestion is concerned. It cannot be over-emphasised that efficiency and speed of action are all-important.

PUBLICITY

Good publicity constantly maintained, but varying in presentation, is of vital importance to create, stimulate, and retain interest in suggestion schemes.

The unanimous opinion of the committee is that the most effective way of achieving this is the publication, in the fullest possible way, of the payment of a major award. Rarely is a recipient too shy to accept the gentle persuasion of the secretary to have the presentation of his award made known to all concerned, as it gives him a sense of pride. Where reasonably practical, the actual presentation ceremony should be photographed and used along with "the story" in the works magazine, on the billboards within the factory, and on leaflets. Almost always the local press are delighted to print a "story", particularly one with human interest and generally accompanied by a photograph. It is the secretary's duty always to make an endeavour to secure the aid of the press.

Fullest use should be made of reporting in the works magazine, if such exists, all interesting matters and stories centred on the suggestion scheme. Another method of stimulating interest is to include a leaflet in the employees' wage packets, from time to time, but again its presentation should vary.

Attractive posters strategically placed in the factory and offices are a vital adjunct to any suggestions scheme. Posters should preferably be colourful, and changed monthly. If a firm has an advertising or publicity department, full use should be made of its services and skill to help the scheme.

A note on competitions

The committee cannot recommend the use of competitions for stimulating interest, however ingenious or attractive they may seem. It is always extremely difficult to decide which is the best suggestion, and the danger exists that the committee's choice could cause ill-feeling, particularly if there are a number of suggestions of equal merit. The tendency would always be to choose the suggestion with the highest financial value to the company; thus the merit of the intangible suggestion would tend to be overlooked.

A better way of stimulating interest is to present small articles for all suggestions received during a particular month or period (usually an off-peak season is chosen). These can be ball-point pens, lighters, notebooks, and similar items, provided the whole exercise is covered by publicity. However, any method of stimulating interest does increase the amount of staff work.

The smaller firm can with advantage institute an annual dinner or dance at which people who have submitted award-winning ideas are freely entertained, and during which the opportunity can be taken by the managing director, or other high executive, to present outstanding awards.

As we indicated at the start of this section, we have found the publication *A Study on Suggestion Schemes* extremely valuable and we have drawn freely upon the material in this report.

Two typical suggestion schemes are illustrated in Figs. 14 and 15. Figure 14 shows the procedure followed by John Player & Sons, while Fig. 15 shows a leaflet distributed to workers at the former Ericsson Telephone Company, which now forms part of the Telecommunications Division of the Plessey Group of companies.

The "instructions" referred to in Fig. 15 are set out on the back of the form as follows:

II. LINES OF COMMUNICATION

SUGGESTOR

SUGGESTION BOX

FACTORY MANAGER OR DEPARTMENT MANAGER

PROCESS RESEARCH COMMITTEE

1. SUGGESTION RECORDED
2. PRELIMINARY CONSIDERATION BY COMMITTEE
3. INVESTIGATION BY SUB-COMMITTEE
4. RE-CONSIDERATION BY COMMITTEE
5. IF NOT ADOPTED – PROCESS RESEARCH DEPT. WILL REPLY GIVING THE REASON
6. IF RECOMMENDED FOR ADOPTION WITH AWARD

FACTORY PRODUCTION COMMITTEE FOR CONFIRMATION AND DIRECTORS' APPROVAL

AWARD WITH REPLY TO SUGGESTOR

SUGGESTION PUT INTO USE

PROCESS RESEARCH DEPARTMENT FOR ACTION

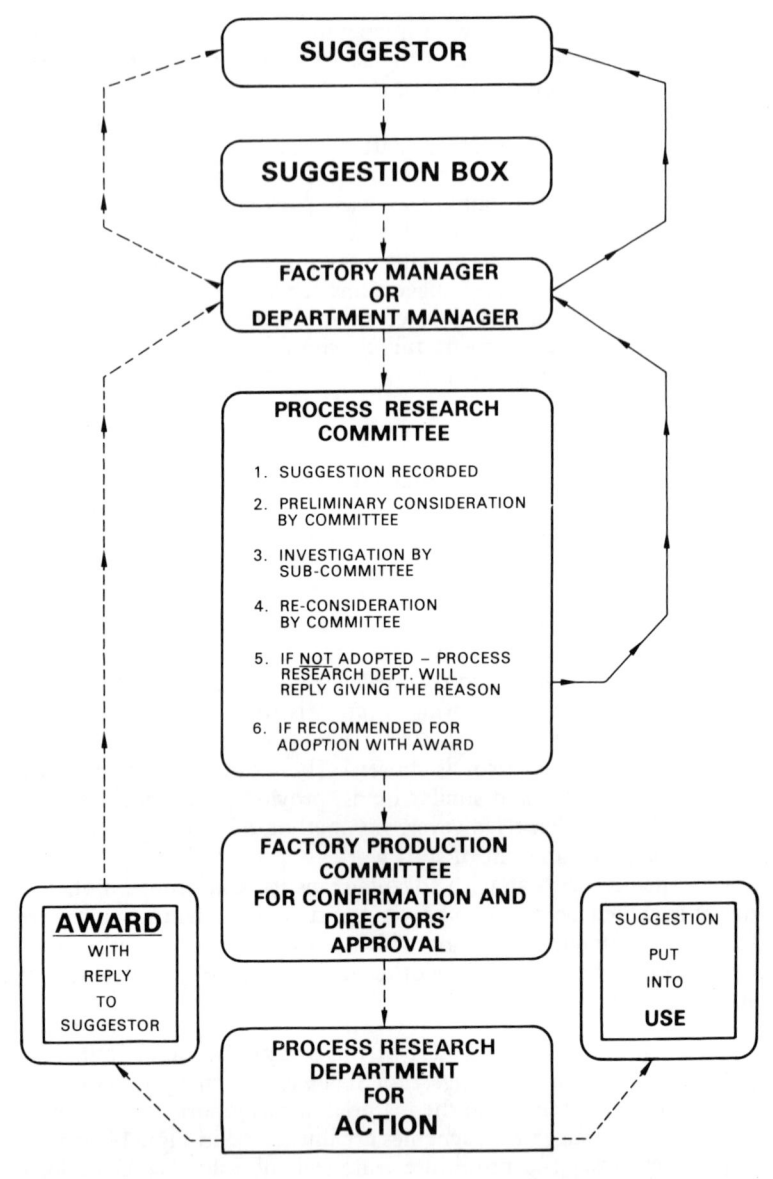

(Courtesy of John Player & Sons)

Fig. 14. *Diagram of the suggestion scheme run by John Player & Sons. This scheme provides for consultation with line managers both before and after a suggestion is submitted to the process research committee.*

II. LINES OF COMMUNICATION

```
┌─────────────────────────────────────────────────────────┐
│               ERICSSON TELEPHONES Ltd                   │
│               SUGGESTION SCHEME                         │
│                                                         │
│   DATE RECEIVED              SUGGESTION NUMBER          │
│   (LEAVE BLANK)              (LEAVE BLANK)              │
│                                                         │
│   ........................  ........................   │
├─────────────────────────────────────────────────────────┤
│   PLEASE READ INSTRUCTIONS ON THE BACK BEFORE YOU       │
│                WRITE YOUR SUGGESTION                    │
├───────────────────────────┬─────────────────────────────┤
│ IF YOU NEED MORE SPACE OR │ My SUGGESTION WILL AFFECT   │
│ ARE PREPARING A SKETCH    │ ...................DEPT     │
│ USE SAME SIZE PAPER.      │ TOTAL PAGES.............    │
├───────────────────────────┴─────────────────────────────┤
│   SUGGESTION                                            │
│                                                         │
│                                                         │
│                                                         │
│                                                         │
│                                                         │
└─────────────────────────────────────────────────────────┘
```

(Courtesy of Plessey Group)

Fig. 15. *Suggestion scheme of Ericsson Telephone Ltd (now part of the Telecommunications Division of the Plessey Group of Companies).*

INSTRUCTIONS
TYPES OF SUGGESTIONS PARTICULARLY WELCOME

Save

Labour
Material

Improve

Quality of product
Processing methods
Storage, packing or shipping
Tools or machinery
Service to customers
Working conditions
Method of maintaining company property

Eliminate

Waste of every kind
Safety hazards in work or property
Unnecessary records, data, materials or equipment

All suggestions must contain specific recommendations in order to be accepted.

Complaints about the lights, ventilation, etc., should be registered with your supervisor.

Suggestions will be accepted, from all employees, under the above headings but for obvious reasons an award will not be made to an employee for a suggestion which he ought to make as part of his normal routine duty.

An illustration will make this rule clear. Assume that a particular stationery form in general use can be improved and much clerical labour thereby saved. An award would not be made to the person whose job it is to devise such forms nor to his supervisor whose job it is to see that the most suitable forms are in use, but an award would be made to anyone else making a suggestion which was accepted.

HOW TO MAKE YOUR SUGGESTION

1. Write your suggestion on the opposite side of this sheet in the simplest way you can. If possible set it out as follows:

A. MY SUGGESTION IS....................
B. I BELIEVE IT SHOULD BE DONE BECAUSE....................
C. IT IS NOW DONE AS FOLLOWS....................
D. MY SUGGESTION CAN BE ACCOMPLISHED BY....................

2. You may, if you choose, include sketches, samples or models and it is not required that you limit your suggestion to this one page.

3. Review your suggestion to be certain that you have expressed the idea you intended.

4. Number each sheet of your suggestion and show the total pages in the space provided.

5. Place your suggestion in the envelope, and write your name and department inside the flap. Seal the envelope, and send to the personnel manager through the shop clerk or through the works post.

6. You may make as many suggestions as you wish, but each must be in a separate envelope.

WHAT HAPPENS TO YOUR SUGGESTION

1. It is sent in a plain envelope for investigation.

2. Your suggestion is reviewed by a committee after investigation.

3. Your name will be withheld during both the investigation and the review.

4. You will be notified on the factory notice boards if your suggestion is accepted or rejected.

5. If accepted, a voucher for cashing on Wednesdays only will be obtained from the personnel manager's secretary.

6. If rejected, you may write to the personnel manager, who will give the reason on request.

HORIZONTAL COMMUNICATION

Horizontal communication means communication between those of comparable status (for example, departmental head to departmental

II. LINES OF COMMUNICATION   49

head). It also includes relationships between management and trade unions. This is contrasted with downward communication (from superior to subordinate) and upward communication (from subordinate to supervisor).

There are a number of methods which can be used to bring about good horizontal communication within an organisation and to secure improved co-ordination. These methods include both written and oral devices, but we wish to stress the value of face-to-face meetings wherever possible.

Letters, memoranda, and reports are well-tried methods of horizontal communication. Forms are another method. The telephone and other intercommunication systems are both important; meetings and interviews also have their place. Most of these methods are considered in detail elsewhere in this book.

Failure of horizontal communication is common, and continuous attention must be paid to this aspect. The lines of communication—both formal and informal—must be readily available to meet the many problems which may arise.

Good communication is especially important between specialist and line supervision, where misunderstandings have an unfortunate habit of occurring and causing difficulties on the most unexpected occasions.

Methods of horizontal communication which are based on personal contact, for example, committee meetings, will generally be found to be more effective than others.

QUESTIONS

1. What do you understand by joint consultation? Comment on its contribution to good personnel management.   (NEBSS)

2. Summarise in diagram form the procedure for dealing with disputes in the organisation in which you work or in any other organisation with which you are familiar.

3. Compare the suggestion schemes of three firms in the area in which you work. Discuss the difficulties which may be encountered in the administration of suggestion schemes.

4. Discuss the view that if the lines of communication are well defined the factory or other place of work will automatically be well managed.

5. What is "horizontal communication"? Discuss the main methods used to facilitate horizontal communication.

6. "Even if workers have a few ideas, ours are better." Discuss this criticism of suggestion schemes, assumed to have been made by a group of supervisors.

7. It is becoming accepted increasingly that adequate communication of information in large concerns is necessary to promote and sustain high morale. Discuss the kind of information that ought to be communicated and whether

the responsibility for its communication should rest on line staff or a separate department or both.

8. Some companies have many strikes, while others in the same industry are almost entirely free from strikes. Discuss the managerial implications of this fact.

9. Discuss the implications of the introduction of a code of practice in connection with industrial relations. (NEBSS, *modified*)

CHAPTER III

THE SPOKEN WORD

The best evidence any aspiring manager can display of his ability is the capacity to present his thoughts and conclusions clearly. Communicating by word of mouth is especially important, because this method takes up so much of the manager's time.

We usually communicate orally when we give orders. Face-to-face discussions, interviews, conferences, and meetings are other ways in which two-way communication of thoughts and ideas is possible by word of mouth.

Much of the modern manager's time is spent at committee meetings, and Chapters IX and X have been devoted to the committee as a means of communication. Committees will, in addition, be discussed elsewhere in the book.

Another method of communicating by word of mouth is by the telephone. Because this is an important aspect of external communication and can do a great deal to make or mar the reputation of any organisation, we have dealt with this separately (*see* Chapter XI).

In communicating in any way there are three interpretations:

1. what the writer or speaker meant to say;
2. what he did say;
3. what the person receiving the message thought was said.

We should all try to ensure that 1 and 3 are identical. This is especially important with oral communication, because we are often required to say things on the spur of the moment. We shall return to this point from time to time in this chapter.

CLARITY AND BREVITY

Most of the instructions given by managers are still by means of the spoken word. It is an axiom that anyone who has to give instructions should modify the language so that the message he is trying to put across is delivered with maximum effect. Because of this, careful attention must be paid to the way in which the instructions are communicated. Clarity of expression must be the aim at all times. On this question of clarity we may find it instructive to consider the following quotations taken with permission from *The Times*:

> LORD KILLEARN "May we take it from the statement that has been read that the Government have definitely decided on the construction of a *tunnel*?"
> THE EARL OF DUNDEE "No, My Lords. We have decided *en principe* as the French say, on the construction of a tunnel; that is to say the two Governments will now have discussions in order to work out the details."
> LORD KILLEARN "My Lords, I understand French fairly well. *En principe* is a phrase I know of old. It is all very well to decide *en principe* with somebody but have the Government decided they wish to support the construction of the tunnel?"
> THE EARL OF DUNDEE "My Lords, the reason why I use the term *en principe* is because I think it is generally recognised that things that are agreed *en principe* do not always take place."
> VISCOUNT AMORY "My Lords, as we are all getting very Continental, would I be right in thinking that the rough interpretation of *en principe* would be 'in principle'?"
>
> (*Hansard*, House of Lords, 6th February 1966)

As *The Times* aptly commented, "Words ought to mean what they say."

Next to clarity must come brevity. There is a strong tendency for speakers to over-communicate in both face-to-face and group situations. We can rarely hold attention for more than twenty minutes, and we should make our points, which should be few in number, long before this period has expired. The spoken word has a decided advantage over the written word, because the communicator can on the spot deal with difficulties of comprehension and interpretation. However, this advantage should not encourage the speaker in inadequate preparation.

Whenever we are giving a job instruction, conducting an interview, or addressing a meeting we should prepare ourselves to communicate with conviction. If we do not know our subject-matter we shall succeed in communicating little more than our inadequacy.

BE PRECISE

Although the machinery of communications may be adequate, it is necessary to ensure that the material itself is expressed well. It is not enough that the joint consultation procedures should be efficient if the people concerned are inarticulate. The formal lines of communication do not, of themselves, guarantee the smooth working of the machinery. The American Constitution as a formal document does not, and cannot on its own, guarantee freedom of speech. Some of the more important aspects of the American system of government rest rather on agreed custom than upon legal sanctions.

Similarly, the formal lines of communication do not guarantee that the necessary instructions will be issued effectively and carried out or that the employees' exact views on any particular topic will automatically become known to the management.

In our speaking and writing we should always try to use precise words and to indicate quantities. It is better to say "about 750" than "hundreds of". Where we are aware of the percentage we should quote it. "About three-quarters" is more helpful than the "majority of".

Different words convey different impressions to different listeners. Words should be clearly defined for the purpose of communication. "This must be finished by two o'clock" is better than "this is urgent". But, as with all instructions, we should give explanations wherever possible. The reason the job must be finished by two o'clock should be given. The listener should not be left to infer that it is merely because you are the boss and he is not.

A NOTE ON VOCABULARY

The Americans say that it pays to increase our word-power. The implication of the word "pays" is a financial one in this context. In other words, if we extend our vocabulary we shall be able to increase our earnings. It has been emphasised elsewhere in this book that to consider the necessity of paying attention to communications purely as a means of making more money is to take too limited a view of a vital and up-to-date study.

Nevertheless, it is necessary to stress the need of trying to assimilate into our speech a rather wider range of words than most of us possess.

A recent authoritative estimate put the number of words used by the average person at between four and five thousand. The vocabulary of a person with a good command of words would, on the other hand, amount to four or five times as many. It is a great advantage, even for business purposes, to be able to convey fine shades of meaning.

Many of us, for one reason or another, have not been able to take full advantage of opportunities which were available earlier in our lives. Some people who have not been able to receive a good basic education have adopted a positive policy of learning the meaning from a good dictionary of any new word they come across and of adding it to their vocabulary. We are aware of one very well-known professional lecturer and writer who in his early days used to keep a copy of Roget's *Thesaurus*, the dictionary of synonyms and antonyms, by his side so that he could quickly find the exact word he needed. He even used to say that he wore out more than one copy of this admirable book by frequent use.

This is not to say that we should pepper our speech and writing with words which are not within the average person's vocabulary. We should, however, try to increase our vocabulary, provided that the new words can be used naturally in speech and writing.

COMMUNICATION BY SILENCE

Although this chapter deals with communication by the spoken word, it is important to remember that we also frequently communicate by our silence. If we say nothing when things with which we disagree are happening and if we do not criticise when criticism is called for, we are, nevertheless, communicating. In these ways agreement, indifference, lack of concern, and apathy can be communicated.

PUBLIC SPEAKING

Most managers find it necessary to speak in public from time to time. To those of us who have not a great deal of experience of public speaking it is an ordeal. The main rules of public speaking are therefore summarised in the headings of this section, and each will be amplified as we proceed.

Most of us are self-conscious in our early attempts to speak in public. Even skilled speakers admit they are still apprehensive before they rise to address an audience. But even the most modest person gains fluency with experience.

Experienced speakers constantly tell us of the difficulties they encountered in their earlier days. We cannot all be orators, but even the greatest orators of our time have found it necessary to practise their art and to keep on practising it.

It is possible to attend classes for speech training, for general speech and voice production, which are held at centres throughout the country. These are particularly valuable to those who enjoy the spoken word and also those who wish to pursue drama studies.

We have referred elsewhere to the useful but inexpensive publications of the British Association for Commercial and Industrial Education of 16 Park Crescent, London W1. Their booklet on speaking called *Tips on Talking* should be on every supervisor's bookshelf. Even managers with some experience of public speaking will find the hints useful.

III. THE SPOKEN WORD

The preparation of speeches

KNOW YOUR AUDIENCE

Before preparing any speech it is helpful to know who will comprise the audience. We can then deliver our message to the greatest effect if we bear in mind all the time the composition of the people who will be in front of us.

It is a great advantage to be aware who they will be, their probable number, their likely attitude, how much they know already about the subject, and also their capacity for absorbing fresh material.

The subject of the audience has been dealt with first because it is an axiom of good instruction that we should *teach the students and not the subject.*

KNOW YOUR SUBJECT

The next point to decide is the purpose of making the talk. It is vital to be clear about the object it is desired to attain.

If possible it is wise to let the idea simmer for a few days. If a notebook or a sheet of paper is kept to hand a note may be made of any ideas that may occur *when* they occur. It is then simply a matter of arranging the material.

The methods of collecting the material are many and various. Some people put book-marks or slips of paper in the various books and publications. Others put their ideas on separate slips of paper or cards. It is essential to jot down all the ideas which come to us. Most speakers find that it is a sound idea to use separate pieces of paper so that the *order* of the ideas can be rearranged without much trouble. For this reason it is better to write on one side of the paper only.

Information for a talk can be obtained from a number of sources. Most of us know a certain amount about many subjects. Our own knowledge and experience are thus the first sources of material. Often we have friends or colleagues who are very conversant with the subject and are able to fill in any gaps in our own knowledge. A discussion with them either personally or over the telephone will thus provide further information. In this way, too, we are often able to clarify our views and obtain possible alternative lines of thought.

Sometimes we have notes which we made when we attended courses. These notes may be of considerable assistance to us in gathering material.

A great deal of very useful information can be gathered from published material. These days most organisations try to build up their own files of matter which may prove of value. Public libraries, especially their reference sections, are also excellent sources of information to which we may need to refer occasionally.

The other sources of such data are very numerous and vary according to the industry and the purpose for which they are required. The publications of HM Stationery Office and the various trade associations will be found to be particularly helpful. They represent inexpensive ways of obtaining valuable information and statistics not only for speeches but for reports too.

A good newspaper, read regularly, will also provide good source material. This presents one not only with an opportunity of keeping up to date but also of taking cuttings on matters of a more permanent significance.

PREPARE HEADINGS

Experienced speakers emphasise the importance of limiting strictly the number of points to be put over in a talk. This is because the span of comprehension is limited. Most of us can assimilate only a small amount of new information at any one time. Inexperienced speakers usually try to cram their talks with information; if any time is left for questions the audience is generally so dizzy with ill-digested material that the reaction is poor. Yet question time should be the most valuable part of any talk because the audience is truly participating in the activity.

The material should be arranged into three groups for use in the beginning, in the body, and at the end of the talk. Headings should then be prepared of the main points it is wished to make. It will, of course, usually not be possible to use all the information that has been gathered for the talk. Much of it can be retained and used for other purposes.

The presentation of speeches

FACE THE AUDIENCE AND AVOID MANNERISMS

When making the speech face the audience and speak to all members of it. Avoid excessive mannerisms because they distract the attention of the audience from what is being said. In particular, avoid looking out of the window while speaking. Do not pace up and down, or juggle with chalk. Do not create a barrier between speaker and audience by, for example, placing a briefcase on the table.

SPEAK—DO NOT READ ALOUD

The best speeches are spoken, not read. Although advice has been given on the preparation of headings, it should be remembered that there is nothing more disconcerting to an audience than a speaker who is reading from detailed notes and who, more often than not, manages to lose his place.

VARY THE PITCH OF THE VOICE

The speech should be delivered naturally and should be as clear and audible as possible. The pitch of the voice should be varied to avoid boring the audience and sending them to sleep. Listeners in the back row should be able to hear every word spoken.

USE VISUAL AIDS

Visual aids should be employed to enhance the value of the talk. Audiences, whether they are large or small, more readily understand information which is presented to them visually. These aids are important, because the more senses which we use in putting our material over, the more effective the message will be.

Chapter I deals briefly with charts, diagrams and posters, films, film strips and videos. In Chapter XII there is a discussion of the visual methods employed in teaching. Experienced speakers use blanket boards, blackboards, and models. All visual material used should be clearly visible to the audience and should not distract them. Visual aids should add to, and emphasise, the points made by the spoken word. For example, in the course of a short lecture it is very disconcerting to have two sessions of film strips which may involve plunging the hall into darkness.

LECTURETTES

Anybody who has responsibility should be able to communicate his thoughts effectively by word of mouth. The authors have found it of great help to themselves and also to their students to have experience in giving lecturettes, which are short talks on a given topic.

One of the great advantages of exercises of this type is that the performance of students can be criticised by their colleagues and also by their teachers or instructors. Great value is obtained from preparing and delivering a lecturette.

Readers will be aware that this system is used extensively at universities, and at teacher-training colleges. It is also an integral part of the training of officers and non-commissioned officers in the armed forces as well as in management training.

The preparation of a lecturette should follow similar lines to those for public speaking. We should be particularly careful to avoid cramming too much material into the short space of time allowed.

ORAL INSTRUCTIONS AND ORDERS

Lecturettes demand careful preparation but they are not an everyday executive activity. However, managers may be called upon daily to give instructions to members of their work group; careful preparation is just as important for this more routine means of communication. We must be sure that the order is the right one for the particular situation which we face. The employee must know exactly what he has to do and the kind of results we expect from him.

For the best results we should take care in selecting the person most likely to carry out our orders well. We should be confident and calm when we issue instructions. Finally, we should make a practice of checking that our instructions are carried out at the time and in the manner we lay down.

It may be necessary for our instructions to be repeated to avoid misunderstanding. The employee should have the opportunity of asking questions if he is still not clear as to what we want. Many supervisors use a more positive approach and question the employee to ensure that the instruction is fully understood.

INTERVIEWING

Interviews are employed by management for a number of purposes. An outstanding example is selection interviews. Here it is necessary to have full information about the job, and to find out as much relevant information about the applicant as possible. The next step is to match the best applicant against the known demands of the job to ascertain whether he is suitable or whether the post should be readvertised.

There are, however, other valuable applications of interviews. An induction interview is conducted so that the new employee can be eased gently into his new employment and given details of the job and of the proposed training plan. After the interview the newcomer is often shown round the works or department and introduced to his fellow employees.

Progress interviews are conducted so that employees may be given suggestions on how to improve their performance. From time to time employees will have grievances, and the manager will try to remove the causes of the friction and to restore the earlier good relationships.

Another cause for interviewing will be to deliver a reprimand. In this case, too, the manager will try to avoid destructive criticism and attempt to show the employee how he can improve.

But whatever the reason for interview, a systematic approach will ensure that the conclusion reached is the most satisfactory one in the circumstances.

The interviewer should always have a plan. Firstly, he should be clear about the purpose for which the interview is being conducted. Secondly, adequate preparation should be made, so that as much data as possible is available. Often, because the matter is confidential, the interviewer will himself have discreetly to collect this information.

The third stage is vital and deals with the conduct of the interview. Adequate time must be allowed for all the stages of the interview and for each interview. Privacy is usually essential, so that the person being interviewed can be put at ease. The questions or point of view of the interviewer should be put clearly and concisely. The interviewee should be encouraged to speak. Sometimes an irrelevant question can achieve that objective. Attention should be paid to what is said and also what is left unsaid.

Since we also communicate by our attitude, the interviewee should be observed throughout the interview to reinforce impressions made by the spoken word. Notes should be made unobtrusively. Before the interview ends a check should be made to ensure that all the necessary information is available. Where it is possible to make a decision there and then, this should, of course, be done. Otherwise the interviewer should explain what is to be the next step and ensure that this takes place. The interview should then be ended.

The fourth step on interviewing procedure is to ensure that the results are checked. For example, an induction interview may follow a selection interview. Opportunity may occur for an informal chat; or a check can be made on the work of somebody who has earlier been reprimanded.

A great deal of the work of the manager is concerned with the conduct of interviews. Thus, it is wise for us to ensure that in this work we do, as far as possible, achieve the object which we set out to attain.

ADVANTAGES AND DISADVANTAGES OF THE SPOKEN WORD

It may be of help if we list the advantages and disadvantages of communicating by means of the spoken word, since over a wide range of situations it will serve as an alternative to the written word.

Advantages

1. Face-to-face contact is often the best method of communication. In this way it is possible to secure the desired co-ordination and sense of common purpose which are now so essential because organisations have grown in size and complexity. The written word can easily cause our relationships to become cold and formal: the spoken word introduces humanity.

2. We can elaborate where necessary. Even with a large audience an experienced speaker can sense when he is not achieving the desired end. Since the amount of new information we can absorb at any one time is limited, a speaker can emphasise his points when this is needed and give examples to underline the points he is making.

3. With the spoken word we can put right any mistakes the moment they are made. If we are called upon to make a formal speech we should be able to reduce the possibility of error by careful preparation.

4. Agreement is easier to reach with spoken rather than with written words. We can thus achieve the intended purpose more quickly than we can by corresponding with the other party. We assume here, of course, that the parties enter into discussion in a spirit of wishing to reach agreement.

Disadvantages

Among the disadvantages which are usually quoted against communicating by the spoken word are the following.

1. It does not in itself provide the speaker or the listener with a permanent record of the message. Usually, the speaker will not be sure exactly what he said. Moreover, as the span of comprehension is limited, the instructions may not be carried out as efficiently and effectively as would be possible with written instructions.

2. Senior members of the management find that oral communication makes great demands on their time. In large organisations it will be necessary for them to travel to various factories to address meetings of employees about the company's proposals for development and similar topics. A great deal of time is also spent interviewing employees individually and in small groups.

3. People usually take less care when speaking than when writing. This can easily cause friction and other difficulties in an organisation.

4. Spoken announcements and instructions are often less precise than written ones.

5. The spoken word is always less concise than the written word. Often the exact point the speaker is trying to make is lost in a mass of words.

LISTENING

We have stressed at several points in this book that communication is a two-way process. It has been estimated that we spend up to forty per cent of our working day listening, yet half of any oral message is forgotten by an untrained listener within eight hours. Listening is not the same as hearing. It is not merely a passive skill: the listener is a partner in the communication process. Unless somebody listens to the message and understands it there is no communication. Good listening does not come naturally to us but requires training. We have to work hard at being a good listener, but such effort is worth while. The supervisor who is a good listener can often predict what changes are needed or will occur.

Because we do not listen well messages have to be put in writing. Permanent records of messages require more staff, more equipment and bigger budgets than would be necessary if the listening were more efficient. Improved use of listening skills will usually save an organisation more money than the cost of the training.

As listeners we should concentrate on what is being said. A conscious effort should be made to check the points and to ensure that each has been understood. We should ask for clarification of any points about which we are not clear. It is useful to restate a point in our own words to check whether this is how it was meant to be received.

Notemaking

Notemaking is part of the skill of listening. Notes should be accurate, brief and concise. Notes are an aid to concentration. As listeners we are forced to understand what is being said, so if notes are being taken the communicator is aware that he is achieving the desired end. Moreover, notes serve as a record to which reference can later be made.

ORAL EXAMINATIONS

Despite the disadvantages of the spoken word as a means of communication the oral examination is being increasingly used to supplement the conventional written examination. It is essentially a test of self-expression. For example, in the oral test for the Diploma for Personal Assistants conducted by the Royal Society of Arts Examinations Board there is included a test on the use of the telephone. This aspect of communications is covered fully in Chapter XI.

Another typical oral test is conducted in groups of about six persons. Each group is given approximately one hour, the duration of the test to be flexible and at the discretion of the college. Each candidate in turn is required to develop some aspects of his extended essay or project and other candidates of the group may be called upon to comment in a general discussion. Alternatively, or additionally, a candidate may be asked to speak briefly upon some topic within the framework of the examination in question.

The Association of Medical Secretaries also includes an oral examination which is internally assessed and set by the college. There is no prescribed form. Candidates may be examined in groups or as individuals. It is suggested that the length should be not less than ten minutes for individuals or more than thirty minutes for groups. Candidates are assessed on quality, fluency and accuracy of expression. The test should not be one of formal elocution.

The sound principle to be followed by a candidate for an oral examination may be stated thus: preparation is the basis of success. It is certainly foolish to regard an oral examination as of less importance than the more formal written test: in some respects the oral examination is a more searching method of finding both the strength and weakness of a candidate.

III. THE SPOKEN WORD

QUESTIONS

1. As a member of the works joint council you consider that an improvement in the canteen facilities is long overdue. You have been asked to present the case to the employer's side at the next meeting of the council. Draft your opening and closing paragraphs and outline the main points you intend raising in the body of your case.

2. List twelve words or phrases which have a similar meaning to the word "important".

3. You are a member of the personnel department. One of the chargehands is coming to discuss with you in five minutes the view that staff vacancies should be advertised throughout the works and all local applications considered first before the post is advertised elsewhere. This is contrary to company policy. Invent any details necessary and deliver a short speech justifying the policy.

4. Prepare a talk on one of the following topics and assume that you have approximately ten minutes to speak.
   (a) Shop stewards and their functions.
   (b) How products are made in my factory (department).
   (c) The duties of a supervisor.
   (d) The qualities required for management.

5. Draft a questionnaire to be completed by candidates for the position of cashier and assistant accountant.

6. Discuss critically the advantages and disadvantages of communicating verbally.

7. Prepare notes for a short talk to a group of employees about the possible effects of automation on their job. (NEBSS)

8. What fundamentals should be observed when giving an oral instruction to a subordinate? Under what circumstances would a written instruction be preferable? (NEBSS)

CHAPTER IV

THE WRITTEN WORD

CORRECT ENGLISH

In every place of work it is one of management's responsibilities to arrange for notices to be displayed. Correctly worded notices give a favourable impression of a firm's efficiency; badly worded notices like the one shown in Fig. 16 give a most unfavourable impression.

> **NOTICE**
> THIS ROAD IS CLOSED TO ALL VEHICULAR TRAFFIC EXCEPT GOVERNMENT VEHICLES AND THOSE BELONGING TO PERSONS HAVING BUSINESS AT PIRBRIGHT AND DEEPCUT CAMPS AND NOT EXCEEDING 12'6" IN HEIGHT WHO MAY USE IT AT THEIR OWN RISK

Fig. 16. *Sign at the entrance to Pirbright Camp, Surrey (quoted in the* Daily Telegraph).

There are no words in this notice which will be outside the average man's vocabulary, yet the author has managed to ensure that his message will be misunderstood by most readers. His greatest folly must surely be an inability to see the need to place close together those words which are associated in thought.

Short sentences are the key to effective communication. They reduce the risk of grammatical error and solve most punctuation problems. Difficulties may, of course, still arise, as the following short notice illustrates:

WANTED:
MEN TO KNOW ALL ABOUT MACHINES, ALSO GIRLS.

Correctness and clarity do not always go hand in hand, but correct sentences will generally be more easily understood than incorrect sentences. This poses the question: what is an incorrect sentence? Incorrectness can occur because a wrong word has been used or because the grammar is poor. There are, of course, differences of opinion about correctness, because English is both a living and a changing language. Expressions valid two centuries ago are no longer acceptable; others have changed their meanings; entirely new words have entered the language as world communications have become more effective and our knowledge has grown greater.

The safest plan for the manager to adopt when he is writing instructions or letters is to use those words which are still acceptable and those grammatical constructions which have not been discarded. Aggressive managements may try all kinds of innovations in production and selling to secure a market for their goods; they should think twice before they improvise with words. The aim of the writer should be to see that he is fully understood; he should seek the rewards of effective communication rather than those of literary merit.

UNNECESSARY WORDS AND PHRASES

Quite

In *The Complete Plain Words* Sir Ernest Gowers analyses the conclusions of writers on the use of certain words, and it is a surprise to find that he does not deal with "quite". "Quite" has been making steady progress during the last twenty or so years, and it is interesting to note that Fowler, in *Modern English Usage*, does not cover the modern usage—or misusage—of "quite"; his section on this word deals with the excessive use of "quite" and with the now established practice of using "quite" for "I agree". Yet "quite" as an adjective has become so respectable that it can introduce a *Times* leading article. Even in this eminent journal the word does little to add to the meaning of the imprecise word "number" which it qualifies in the phrase "quite a number".

It should be clear from the discussion of this word "quite" that there are words which the writer must use with care if he seeks to have his message understood. The best rule for the purposeful writer to follow is: use those words which have meaning or add to meaning; avoid superfluous words.

The elimination of unnecessary words should readily appeal to the manager. He daily seeks to reduce costs and to save time. He should follow the same principle in communication. Effective communication results from the use of simple language unencumbered by meaningless adverbs or adjectives like "quite". We shall now discuss other words which have become the literary adornments of the instructions which emanate from official and commercial desks.

IV. THE WRITTEN WORD

Definitely

Television viewers can always be sure of a "definitely" when the questioner asks the trade unionist for his opinion of the value of the strike weapon. It is strange that this word is always uttered with conviction. Perhaps one day we shall be lucky enough to hear an "indefinite" person respond. Meanwhile we should be on the alert lest this word should find its way into our way of writing. Let us now consider a typical, though imaginary, management notice.

ALL THE TECHNICAL STAFF MUST DEFINITELY WEAR WHITE COATS IN THE LABORATORY

The word "must" surely indicates that the instruction may not be ignored. Would the notice lose any meaning with the omission of "definitely"? The writer of this notice could be relied upon to reply: "Definitely!"

Comparatively, relatively, unduly

These words are often thought to be essential to a sentence if the aim is to impress the reader. There are other adverbs which are just as vague like "very" and "so", and the only merit possessed by "comparatively", "relatively", and "unduly" is length. Short words should always be preferred to long ones.

Unfortunately not only are these words long; they are usually wrong. When we are asked for the attendance at our union's annual general meeting we find it "relatively" easy to reply: "Comparatively few, but the executive are not unduly worried."

These words are useless unless there is some standard of measure. If we say: "The dismantling of the new gear cutting machines was a difficult process, but the job of reassembly was relatively simple," we have drawn a comparison. "Comparatively" could be substituted for "relatively". When we examine "unduly worried" we may wonder how much more worried (or less worried) we should be if we were unduly worried rather than just plain worried. All worry is undue because it retards recovery in patients and action in businessmen.

Hopefully

Kenneth Hudson in his amusing book *The Dictionary of Diseased English*, insists that the battle to prevent "hopefully" from gaining a foothold was lost long ago. Nevertheless, the manager in his letter and report writing should beware of ambiguity resulting from the use of "hopefully", especially as a shortened version of the phrase "it is hoped".

IV. THE WRITTEN WORD

Collective prepositions

Adverbs are not the only means of avoiding brevity. Others include phrases which do the work of "about". "About", like walking, has lost status; it does not pack the horse-power of "with regard to", and it is in the veteran class if we compare it with "in so far as concerns". Yet if we have another look at "about", and also at other neglected prepositions like "with", "to", and "on" we shall find that these words can adequately and modestly do the work of all the collective prepositions given in the examples below.

People who would never consider saying, "The number of rose blooms varies *in relation to* the severity of pruning", would be only too eager to write this sentence. These people are impelled to use collective prepositions where excellent single ones would serve. They also feel the need to use these important-sounding phrases to introduce new paragraphs. New paragraphs do not require introductions; their purpose is to deal with new topics or different aspects of a topic.

The following examples show the common use of collective prepositions.

> The secretary of the safety committee issued a report *with regard to* [on] the stacking of completed containers.
>
> All employees must obey the regulations *in respect of* [about] smoking.
>
> He spoke *with respect to* [of] the country's need to increase exports.
>
> *So far as concerns this company* greater productivity would result from an improvement *in regard* to industrial relations.

(This last sentence should be rewritten as: "Greater company productivity would result from an improvement in industrial relations.")

Jargon

It will be noted that the last example of the use of collective prepositions requires complete rewriting, mainly because of the use of *jargon*. Unhappily many managers who are aware that the most efficient office and factory systems are the simple ones are not aware that simple language produces the best and quickest response from their staff and customers. Examiners in management subjects, too, are easily led into jargon, as the following question will illustrate.

> What are the basic principles to be observed in *relation to* planning in connection with business management?

The need to avoid jargon is covered in the section on letter writing (Chapter VI), but it will do no harm to emphasise the need to use a simple style in our communications. One of the worst offences of letter writers—and, remember, we are all letter writers—is to use ready-made phrases borrowed from official or legal documents. We, alas, enjoy sounding important.

> In the majority of instances firms employ a personnel officer to deal with the recruitment respecting staff. [Most firms employ a personnel officer to recruit staff.]

> A number of cases have arisen where firms have not co-operated with the Department of Employment. [Some firms have not co-operated with the Department of Employment.]

Equally important is the need to avoid phrases popularised by observers of the political and industrial-relations scenes on television. One much-loved phrase is "at this moment in time" instead of which we generally write the simple word "now".

"No way" has become an established phrase for indicating a negative response to a request, or for attempting to reinforce such a response, thus: "No way will I accept the committee's decision"; or "I will not agree to the committee's decision — no way!"

It is arguable whether these constructions are an improvement on the straightforward "I will not accept the committee's decision."

Indecisive decisions

Sometimes we think that it is unkind to be direct. We therefore use phrases which soften the harshness of the word "death". Our friends have "passed on" or "passed away". In official writing we hesitate to say "no" if we have a choice of "decision softeners", and we may tell (probably "inform") our customer:

> We regret that we are unable at this juncture to see our way clear to accede to your request.

The direct approach would have been:

> We are sorry that we cannot, at present, grant your request.

Pompous language

There may be an excuse for "decision softeners" because they represent an attempt to be polite; however, there is no excuse for using pompous language. High-flown phrases add to the length and weight of the letter; they add nothing to the meaning.

Consider this ponderous minute:

> Consideration was given to the question of the possibility as to whether the Authority continue to pursue the policy of subsidising the repertory company at the Atlas Theatre.

There are several criticisms which may be made. Firstly, the heavy pompous passive construction has been used. Even in formal records we could profitably use the active. Secondly, the question of the possibility is surely an extension of Parkinson's law to words (words increase in number to fill the quantity of paper available for them). Thirdly, "as to" is not only another ugly prepositional phrase, it is superfluous. "As to" is never needed with "whether"; it is, indeed, seldom needed in any context.

If we use an active construction we produce a minute which is no more important sounding than any other piece of prose. The minute has been completed by a decision.

> The committee considered the annual grant to the repertory company at the Atlas Theatre and decided to give the company £1,000 for the current financial year.

Unnecessary new words

Knowledge is growing fast and continuously. For this reason we need new words and our language grows. Many modern words are scientific and indicate the ever-increasing importance of science in our lives. "Radar" is barely forty years old, and "electronics", with which it is associated, has come into common use with the rise of a new industry producing equipment for the home, industry, commerce, and the armed forces. The introduction of new technical terms is inevitable in a nuclear age: but we must be watchful of the use of ugly terms which seek to overthrow existing words.

It is difficult to imagine how arrangements ever became completed before the emergence of "finalise". But then the "finalisers" were not to know that railways could be brought up to date—that they could be "dieselised".

The following letter, reproduced by permission of the *Sunday Times*, gives an extreme example of the use of ugly terms.

Americanisation

> Sir, Correspondents on the mutilation of English will be interested in the following extract from the minutes of a meeting of the American Electronic Engineering Committee:
>
> ". . . in the interest of easierly reaching internationalistic agreementation on a standardizationalized endocificationalization."
>
> I think that our American friends would regard this as "an all-time high".
>
> J.L. Maitland
> Farnborough, Hants.

Ugliness is not confined to "ise" words. We must, it seems, now follow simple verbs like "face" and "check" with "up to" and "up on". Not many readers will gain more from "We must face up to our responsibilities" than from "We must face our responsibilities".

The investigation is not more thorough when we have "checked up on", rather than checked. Compare the following:

All visitors to the firm had their credentials checked at the main gate.

All visitors to the firm had their credentials checked *up on* at the main gate.

There are, of course, many constructions involving the use of prepositions after verbs, and these have their place in our language; but too many prepositions together tend to form an ugly construction. Where a construction has become fully established we should, however, be chary about dropping prepositions. Let us take the example "look up to". This expression may indicate an invitation to raise our eyes or to respect a superior. If we omit "up" we are left with "look to", but "look to" means take care of; if we omit "to" we may mean find, or improve.

We should always try to express ourselves clearly, and we should avoid unnecessary words. It is odd that the United States, where scientific management is so highly valued, should be the exporter of "face up to" and "check up on". This may, to some extent, explain the provision, in that country, and at home, of quicker reading courses.

USE WORDS THAT WILL BE UNDERSTOOD

We should now remind ourselves of the purpose of communication: to send messages effectively from one person (or group) to another person (or group). Failure occurs when we cease to be effective. One cause of failure is the selection of words indicating the breadth of *our own* vocabulary, not the narrowness of the reader's. If we are addressing a learned society we may find satisfaction in the use of "esoteric" rather than "secret". As managers and supervisors we are normally employed in giving instructions, orally and in writing, to workpeople of ordinary education. We should use simple words.

One important rule we ought to observe is: avoid the use of foreign phrases. It should be appreciated that even those children who leave school with some knowledge of a foreign language quickly lose their slight grasp. We should therefore communicate in English, which does contain, of course, many foreign words now fully accepted as part of the language.

It would be ridiculous to suggest that firms should in future call chauffeurs "managers' drivers". Most people will readily understand the word "chauffeur", but trade-union speakers will probably find that they are understood better if they talk of a "trouble-making spy" rather than an *"agent-provocateur"*. The aim of the user of foreign phrases is sometimes to practise an indifferent accent (in oral communication) and sometimes to impress the reader. Unfortunately, antagonism is the most likely result.

Even when we limit our communication to the English language, we find a large number of tempting words we may use to try to impress the reader. Sir Ernest Gowers, in his first edition of *Plain Words* (published by HMSO), lamented the rise of "unilateral". It is clear now that the victory of "unilateral" over "one-sided" is complete; for the most uninformed people now use it with the ease with which they use "nice" and "definitely". We may, however, question whether these "unilateralists" or the people to whom the remarks are addressed know precisely what the expression means.

Diplomats and economists may yearn for multilateral agreements, compromise on bilateral agreements and deplore unilateral abrogation of both multilateral and bilateral agreements; but ordinary people are unlikely to understand this political jargon, even if they have some interest in international co-operation. Where an agreement has been broken by one side the obvious course is to tell this to the readers. Thus:

> The other side has ended the agreement without our approval.

Consider the following examples.

1. *Unfamiliar:* "The 1939 Non-Aggression Pact between Russia and Germany was unilaterally repudiated by Germany in 1941."
Familiar: "The 1939 Non-Agression Pact between Russia and Germany was broken by Germany in 1941."

2. *Unfamiliar:* "The Opposition does not favour unilateral renunciation by the British of nuclear weapons."
Familiar: "The Opposition does not agree that Britain should alone refuse to use nuclear weapons."

More pompous words

1. ANTICIPATE

We have a good word "expect" which is normally the one we need. Anticipate means to take action to counter an expected move. For example:

> The tennis champion anticipated her opponent's attack and ran towards the net for a volley. [Correct use.]

2. MINIMAL

This word is becoming increasingly popular with letter writers to *The Times*. Numbers are never *small*, but are very likely to be minimal. Economists, instead of talking of a *slight change* or *little effect*, will tell us of "the repercussions being minimal".

3. PARTAKE

"Partake" should be used to indicate the consumption of food and drink, and not the taking part in an activity. If people join in the selection of records during *The Jimmy Young Show* they are taking part in (not partaking of) the programme.

4. TERMINATE

Terminate is a word well loved by personnel departments, who think, perhaps, that they are helping discharged workers by using this dignified word in the letter of dismissal. "Terminate" does not wound less than "end"; so there is no point in using the longer word when the shorter word "end" will suit.

5. TRANSPIRE

This word is preferred by those who think that it is superior to "happen". The superiority lies not in its length, but in the subtle difference in meaning it has from "happen". "Happen" can always be used in the place of "transpire" when the intention of the writer is to convey that something has occurred. If the writer wishes the reader to understand that something quite different has occurred from what has previously been believed, "transpire" is the right word to use.

Compare the following examples.

> A small explosion may occur when the safety valve is allowed to close. If an explosion transpires [happens] operatives must turn off the main gas supply.
>
> Most people believed that, during the 1939/45 war, Bomber Command succeeded in destroying a large part of German industrial plant: it is now apparent that what transpired during the thousand bomber raids was a temporary set-back to the German war effort.

As we are dealing with "happen" we may make a plea for not using it merely to add to the number of words in the sentence. Thus:

> I happen to be [am] the mayor.
>
> He happens to be [is] the president.

We give no more information, nor make the meaning clearer, when "we happen to be", rather than when "we are".

Avoid the vague word

Sometimes what we write is not clear because we have used words which do not have a precise meaning. These words include "nature", "situation", and "position". Whenever we use these words and others like them we should ask ourselves whether we could reword the sentence to make clearer our intentions or requirements. We are not being very helpful when we ask:

> What is the coal position?

We do not make clear whether we are talking about the stock of coal, its delivery, or its cost. Examples of questions using concrete words are:

> What are our stocks of coal?
>
> How much coal is left in the bunker?
>
> What is the current price of coal?
>
> How long does the merchant take to deliver coal ordered in January?

Critics of books on communication often argue that a manager is a busy man and that jargon is unavoidable because it enables him to deal quickly with correspondence. If he thought of new phrases each time he wrote a letter he would have no time for other managerial duties. The authors accept that managers have limited time for correspondence, but cannot accept that writing simple English is time consuming. Scientific management is a set of principles requiring a change of the manager's attitude; communication no less is an art demanding attention to the presentation of information. With practice, writers will find no greater difficulty in writing jargon-free prose than they did in putting together cliché-ridden phrases.

For many routine matters managers often have a scheme of standard letters. This scheme should periodically be reviewed to ensure that it is being fully used. Time saved by this means may profitably be used for careful thought about less-simple written communication. The writer of the following instruction may have been too busy to think about the meaning of his message.

> NOTE:
>
> After completion of this form duly completed should be placed in the envelope provided which should then be sealed and either left by hand at the office from which the form was issued, or enclosed in another envelope and sent by post to the officer by whom the form was issued as shown on the envelope provided.

A NOTE ON TROUBLESOME WORDS

The notes given below are intended to draw the reader's attention to those words which are often confused.

> *advice* (noun). This word has two meanings. First it means an opinion, especially a legal opinion; secondly, it means information given.

IV. THE WRITTEN WORD

advise (verb). Similarly, the verb means to give an opinion or recommend, but it may also be used as a synonym for "announce".

complement (noun). In grammar this term indicates the words necessary to complete the meaning of the verb, e.g. the furniture looks *cheap*; it means the establishment of a ship; and finally it means the deficiency of an angle from 90°.

compliment (noun). According to the *Oxford Dictionary*, this word means "a polite expression of praise". In the plural it may have the special meaning of *greetings*.

(verb). The verb means to offer polite praise: "I compliment the school on its excellent scholastic record."

council (noun). As assembly: the *Oxford Dictionary* gives the word full treatment.

counsel (noun). As a noun this word may mean advice or consultation, but it may also be used to describe a barrister.

(verb). As a verb the word means to advise or to recommend.

draft (noun, adjective, and verb); *draught* (noun, adjective, and verb). The history of these two words is interesting (*see Shorter Oxford Dictionary*), and the writer may be forgiven for confusing words which have been given alternative spellings in several centuries. Soldiers are sent on *draft* to Hong Kong (i.e. they are withdrawn from their camp for a special purpose). We may ask the bank to send a *draft* for fifty pounds, i.e. a cheque for this sum representing money withdrawn from our account. We may also *draft* (a verb) a reply. Here we are writing a letter in rough form so that alterations may be included in the final attempt.

Draught cattle are used for transport purposes in India (a cart is *drawn* by cattle). A draught represents a source of heat-loss. (Here the word means a current of air.)

"Flat-bottomed boats have a shallow *draught*" (displace a small quantity of water).

When we are unwell we take a *draught* (a dose of medicine).

illegible (adjective). This word is used to describe poorly formed words which cannot be read.

ineligible (adjective). We speak of lords being ineligible for admission to the House of Commons. (Here the words "ineligible for" mean "disqualified from".)

practice (noun). "This is another example of industrial restrictive practice." (Here the word means rule; indeed "working to rule" is a restrictive practice.) Doctors and lawyers have practices which represent their business. Thus a large practice is a large professional business.

practise (verb). "We must practise the art of listening if we are to be effective managers." Practise means to experience or perform;

it is used specially in medicine and law to represent the performance of professional duties. We practise medicine, but we are engaged in engineering.

principle is always used as a noun. Principle is concerned with the abstract; it means a general law or rule of conduct.

"Joint consultation is an example of the principle of democracy applied to industrial relations."

"He was a man of few principles."

principal may be used as a noun or an adjective. It means the sum of money (noun), the head of an organisation but particularly a college, or the person on whose behalf agents are acting. As an adjective it means chief.

"The principal (noun) of the college addressed the students."

"The principal (noun) outstanding on your mortgage is £20,000."

"A principal (adjective) cause of inflation is excessive government expenditure."

their. This word is a possessive adjective and has only one use—to indicate possession. "Their labour turnover was high." "Now productivity is their greatest problem."

there. Although this word has several uses, it remains an adverb. "Go there!" "It was there when the shop steward entered the workshop." "If it is not here, it will be there." "There are four principles involved in this theory."

stationery is a noun. It means "writing material". "Each year we are using more stationery in our offices."

stationary is the adjective meaning motionless. "The lorry crashed into the stationary car, whose driver was having morning coffee at a nearby café."

EXAMINATION TECHNIQUE

An examination answer paper is an exercise in communication. The person the candidate is communicating with is the examiner.

There are several ways in which, as examination candidates, we can considerably improve our performance. Careful attention to this section and to the relevant parts of the book will enhance the chances of every examinee.

We should obtain a copy of the regulations, syllabus and time table of examinations and several past examination papers in the subject and of the examining body we are taking. If possible, we should obtain copies of the examiners' reports on recent examinations. Preparation should cover the whole syllabus and practice should be obtained in answering typical examination questions. On the day of the examination we should allow plenty of time to get to the centre.

IV. THE WRITTEN WORD

In the examination room we should read the instructions at the top of the paper. The question paper should be read once through and we should spend five to ten minutes deciding which questions we are going to answer. Time should then be allocated to the required number of questions. Experienced examinees tackle first the questions which they know best. This builds up confidence.

We should plan our answer by setting down the main points and arranging them in their logical order before beginning to write in detail. Brevity and relevance are important. No marks are awarded for irrelevant material, however well it is expressed. At the end of the allotted time for a question we should go on to the next. We should attempt the right number of questions. The examiner will ignore any additional answers. Finally, we should read what we have written, correct as necessary and cut out anything which does not make sense.

In the next section we consider the problems inherent in the writing of essays for examinations.

ESSAY WRITING

The essay forms an important part of most examinations in English and Communications. Essays offer candidates opportunities to express themselves; these opportunities are often neglected or rejected. Yet aspiring managers should welcome the chance to express their thoughts. Certainly senior management will expect their subordinates to present fresh ideas on the company's methods, and the essay offers good practice in using an original approach to material intended to interest as well as to inform the reader. Essays should always be interesting; they should not be regarded as tests of knowledge. Many candidates think that technical knowledge is required to write an essay entitled "Oil" or "Coal". What is needed is the intelligent use of information provided by books, lectures, films, newspapers, radio, and television.

The general essay

Let us assume that we have to write an essay on oil. We could if we knew some geography and geology examine the distribution of the sources of oil, and give the scientific explanation for its existence. A good concise account together with a discussion of the uses of oil would probably earn us a pass in the examination.

However, we may know little of the geography and geology of oil. In this case we may be able to use and amplify what knowledge we do have, on perhaps one facet of the subject. Suppose we know nothing of the oil industry itself but have some knowledge of a producing area. For instance, Houston, the oil town of Texas, has grown rapidly and the citizens enjoy a high standard of living. Many people are murdered each year in Houston, and we could discuss the relationship between the incidence of violent death and oil wealth. We could describe typical citizens of Houston and contrast this dynamic oil town with the depressing contracting American coal-mining communities. Nearer home, North Sea oil presents similar opportunities for the development of interesting themes. Everyone likes the human interest story; examiners weary of inaccurate accounts of the uses of oil will be pleased to give credit for a fresh approach to the topic.

We shall now assume that we have been asked to write an essay entitled "The Circle of Our Relations". The secret of writing an interesting essay on this topic is the use of material obtained outside our family circle—our own family is unlikely to provide the characters we require. However, we may recall an amusing drawing-room comedy play in which the family always try to avoid these "friends". We can label them Uncle Fred and Aunt Emily, and they then become the subject of at least one paragraph in our essay.

Quality and not quantity should be our aim, but we must provide a minimum quantity to satisfy the examiner. We therefore need two or three further entertaining paragraphs if the essay is to be acceptable. We are fortunate in having friends who describe how they have to provide all kinds of services for their aged Aunt Matilda. She is at once immensely rich and mean. She runs a motor car and employs a chauffeur, yet in eight years she has not completed the mileage for the thousand miles service. Her house is large, dismal, and draughty; the plumbing is pre-Victorian, and every time the cook wishes to fill a kettle of water she is required to use an outside tap. We have now enough material for the body of our essay, but we need a conclusion.

Remember that the examiner must be left with a feeling of well-being at the conclusion of the essay, because it is at this point that he is going to award the marks. The essay is essentially a subjective test; it is the impression that counts.

A useful ending would be one that described the career of the member of the family who escaped from the closed family circle. Most of us have a family black sheep, and if with a little imagination we can allow him to run away to sea, win a fortune in a South American lottery, and settle in Brazil so much the better. We can conclude by congratulating this member who escaped the tyranny of "the circle of our relations".

Many readers may well be able to write the body of the essay but have difficulty in beginning. We should try to open with an arresting statement. If we cannot think of an appropriate quotation we can always use the shock treatment. We can, for example, begin with:

IV. THE WRITTEN WORD

I hate my family. By "family", of course, I do not mean my mother and father, but their brothers and sisters and a host of people who are covered by the generic term "relations".

If we are taking a paper in English as part of an examination in several subjects we have a store of information to use in the essay. We can possibly use this material to open. Thus a student of political theory could well begin:

> Political theorists tell us that the state differs from all other associations in that membership is compulsory. They are wrong: they have forgotten the family.

Another useful introduction could be:

> Marx has been accused of wanting to abolish the family. If he had a family like mine I can well understand his determination to end this institution. I am sure, too, that it was hatred for the family rather than a love of books that caused him to spend so much time in the British Museum.

The general essay presents few planning problems and may be the best one to choose in the examination.

The story

Some essay topics require us to tell a story. The story requires more planning than the general essay, and if we intend to tell a story in our examination we should read some short stories to see how experienced writers treat topics.

We shall need to know how our story is going to end, so that the events lead up to the ending quite naturally. We must preserve a unity of theme and avoid lengthy digressions about the family background of characters. The important point is that the reader should gain the impression that the story is complete.

The following extract is an opening paragraph of a short story entitled "Wet Night in London" which appeared in *The Times*.

> It was after 11 p.m. when a knock came on the door. The house was part of an east London settlement, so that late callers were not unusual. A short man of indeterminate age, with sparse sandy hair, came in, followed more hesitantly by a woman of perhaps 30 years of age and good looking in a conspicuously Irish way.

The opening sentence of this paragraph is typical of those used to begin stories. If we are asked to relate an incident which happened to us, we may begin:

> I remember well I had just begun breakfast when the television forecaster made his highly optimistic prediction for the day. Within minutes the skies blackened, and the thunderstorm broke, deluging the town — a prelude to a devastating flood.

It is useful to end any essay with a reference to the beginning. We may, therefore, end our essay on "An Exciting Personal Incident" with:

> I shall always be grateful to breakfast television because it helped to restore my faith in the British businessman's traditional insistence on carrying an umbrella, regardless of the forecasts of weathermen.

The argument type of essay

Some textbooks, and at least one professional body, advise candidates to present the arguments for and then the arguments against in any controversy. Impartiality leads to dull essays. And dull essays earn low marks.

We shall earn high marks if we present our point of view in an interesting and provocative manner. For most professional examinations we should adopt a style which is lively without being too familiar. If we wish to present opposite opinions we should be able to criticise these opinions intelligently. We may decide to use our opponents' views as a means of putting forward our own argument. Whichever approach we use, we must be able to provide evidence to support our case.

We shall find it useful to begin a discussion type of essay with an allusion to a current case or by means of a story. Our introduction should be short, because its only purpose is to stimulate the interest of the reader. For example, a discussion on "Police Powers" could begin with a reference to a recent trial.

Some writers are able to remember quotations for all occasions. Professional writers often have to do some research to obtain the right quotation. The following extract is taken, by permission, from the *Observer* and is a good example of introducing an article with a quotation:

COLLEGE FOR HALF A NATION?
by Thomas Pakenham

Take the 100 best universities in the world. You will find that many of them are American. Take the 100 worst and you will find that all of them are American.

(From an after-dinner speech at Harvard.)

While our universities shudder at the sight of the Treasury's axe, America is going ahead with university expansion on a vast scale, and in dazzling variety.

To pay for this the President has proposed $6,400 million Federal aid for scholarships. The alumni dig ever deeper into their pockets; for one part of Harvard alone they recently subscribed over $80 million.

Americans are now talking of having half the age group at university —compared with the 6 per cent planned here. New buildings are blossoming everywhere: among the mellow quads of The Ivy League: in the teeming campuses of the Great Plains and the Great Lakes—at Wisconsin, Michigan and Chicago: among the small and select liberal arts colleges in their aboretums around Philadelphia.

All over the country the college has become accepted as a status symbol. The best hamburger at a bar in New York is called "the hamburger with the college education".

Abstract titles such as freedom, democracy, justice, truth, and topics on economic problems like international trade, inflation, the budget, and location of industry are best introduced by a definition. The remaining statements of the opening paragraph should reveal the general trend of the argument.

Description

Descriptive compositions are of two main types: firstly, the technical description, in which the writer gives an accurate and detailed account of an object; secondly, the literary description, in which the writer seeks to give an impression of a subject.

Questions requiring technical description appear in many English examinations, and are designed to test the candidates' competence in lucid, concise writing. Normally the candidate is asked to describe in words only, but occasionally he is asked to draw a sketch.

The best plan to adopt in technical descriptions is to begin with a brief general definition of the object. Thus a description of a thermometer could begin:

> A thermometer is an instrument for measuring temperature.

The opening sentence should be followed by a paragraph indicating the main parts of the object and the materials of which it is composed. We should state in this paragraph the colour, shape, and size of the object.

We shall need another paragraph if our object functions. Thus our description of the thermometer could end:

> The liquid in the capillary tube expands and contracts with changes in temperature. A reading from the scale may be obtained by observing the height of the liquid.

The aim of literary description is to present an impression rather than a photograph of a scene or person. Literary description, like the artist's painting, is the better for being partial and selective. Certain aspects of the subject are emphasised; others are ignored. The photograph is unselective and may, for that reason, be dull.

A good example of literary description is contained in the following extract taken by permission of Penguin Books Ltd from Jack London's *The Mutiny of the "Elsinore"*.

> Hers was a slender-lipped, sensitive, sensible and generous mouth—generous,

not so much in size, which was quite average, but generous rather in tolerance, in power, and in laughter. All the health and buoyancy of her was in her mouth, as well as in her eyes. She rarely exposed her teeth in smiling, for which purpose she seemed chiefly to employ her eyes; but when she laughed she showed strong white teeth, even, not babyish in their smallness, but just the firm, sensible, normal size one would expect in a woman as healthy and normal as she.

Readers may wish to contrast this highly personal description with the following objective account taken by permission of Watford Corporation, from the section of the town guide dealing with its twin town — Mainz in West Germany.

> Mainz is situated on the Rhine, with a population of 180,000. Founded by the Romans in 38 BC, it was originally called Mogontiacum and its history spans centuries. This is depicted in its beautiful historical buildings, such as the thousand-year-old Cathedral, churches of Gothic and Baroque architecture, the Electoral Palace of the Renaissance period and the ancient Citadel, fortified castle of the Archbishops of Mainz. There are also splendid examples of modern architecture, notably the new Town Hall, the Rheingold Halle, and the Mainz Hilton Hotel, all on the Rhine river frontage. Birthplace of Johannes Gutenberg, inventor of movable-type printing; his principal work, the 42-line Bible, can be seen in the Gutenberg Museum, World Museum of Printing.
>
> Mainz is an important wine trade centre and is famous for its wine markets and also its gay Carnival at Fastnacht.

Essay writing is a technique, not a mystique. With practice we can all succeed in this exercise. Planning will help us to give our essay balance and authority, but remember that examination essays must be written within a time limit. We are marked for the finished essay, not the brilliant plan that did not materialise. If inspiration fails, we should use the can-opener method and apply these questions to the subject: How? When? Why? Where? Who? What?

The extended essay

Examination procedures are changing. Several examining bodies already require students to prepare extended essays on subjects relevant to their business and professional interests: other professional institutes are likely to adopt this practice.

We are sometimes asked to write about a project to give us a deeper understanding of a subject. The distinction between an extended essay and a project is often a fine one, but we must generally expect to undertake more personal investigation and experimentation if we are assigned a project.

The principles involved in the preparation of an extended essay do not vary with its length which will be laid down in the regulations of the examining body.

Usually we are unable to choose just any topic that interests us.

The subject chosen must be clearly connected with the course of study.

We should choose some aspect of a topic so that the subject-matter can be kept under control. It is a common mistake to select a subject that is too large; for example, industrial relations.

On the other hand we must first decide upon our field of interest and then limit the area in this field which we are going to explore thoroughly. What we finally choose to write about should represent a still further reduction of this area. In this way we know more about the subject than the part we are selecting for the extended essay.

Sometimes we are able to study a matter of local interest; for instance, a local industry about which little is known nationally. We shall thus be able to obtain our material first hand and this will be reflected in the quality of the work.

Often an extended essay is prepared under the guidance of a tutor.

The final draft should be a competent, logically arranged piece of prose. Some examining bodies like the extended essay to be in typewritten form.

We shall usually be given credit for acknowledging sources of information and we shall be wise to give a bibliography.

Assignments

The Business and Technician Education Council core module at National Award level has been based by BTEC on an assignment approach. An assignment should set a realistic situation which leads to a variety of tasks containing both communication and human relations elements.

The BTEC-published sample assignments have illustrated the intended approach. Further recommended books of assignments are indicated in the bibiliography.

ARTICLE WRITING

A rather special type of essay writing is involved in the preparation of articles for *publication*. With the growth of professional organisations there is an increasing demand for contributions to technical journals and we may expect at some time to be invited to write an article for our professional association or perhaps for our house journal. By writing an article we may contribute knowledge to our chosen field. Our own knowledge of the subject is often thereby improved. Sometimes, too, we may, by technical writing, help our firm, and also ourselves to gain prestige. It is also possible to obtain extra income by writing technical articles.

Many books have been written on the subject and most are worth consulting. But the business of the writer is to write. The advice given in this section should at least get the prospective technical writer started.

It is essential for the new writer to find suitable publications for his articles. For example, *Willings Press Guide* contains a useful index of class publications. If a writer wishes to specialise in articles on any subject, the names of the appropriate magazines are detailed in the *Guide*.

Another valuable publication for the would-be writer is *The Writers' and Artists' Year Book* (A. & C. Black). This book details the requirements of magazines, publishers and agents in Britain, the Commonwealth, the USA and South Africa. There is also a great deal of information on the preparation and submission of manuscripts, publishers' agreements, translations, and rates of remuneration. In addition, there are articles on copyright, writing for television, marketing a play, and a journalist's calendar.

The best procedure for a new writer is to study several copies of a magazine for which he wishes to write. He should then submit an *idea* for an article to the editor: he should also state his qualifications for writing the article and indicate the length proposed.

The aspiring writer should, on being told that the idea is acceptable, gather and prepare the material. The section on the preparation of speeches in Chapter III contains advice on this aspect of the work. There are also countless organisations from which we can obtain useful information. We find that it is vital to obtain copies of the London telephone directories and also the classified directories. We can obtain copies by applying to the local telephone area office.

The *Directory of British Associations* is another invaluable aid. This publication lists interests, activities and publications of trade associations, scientific and technical societies, professional institutes, learned societies, research organisations, chambers of trade and commerce, agricultural societies, trade unions, cultural, sports, and welfare organisations in the United Kingdom and in the Republic of Ireland. A letter or telephone call to one or several organisations can supply a great deal of up-to-date material.

We shall find it helpful to remember that any sentence which does not lend itself readily to reading aloud is usually unattractive in print.

When the article has been sent to the editor, the writer should make a start on the next project.

We should keep a record of ideas and of articles sent and ensure that we write regularly. A record of expenditure incurred should also be kept.

We should submit our article typed on single sides only. Double line spacing should be used so that the editor may make any amendments to the script.

Most writers keep an ideas book and write whenever they can. Although we shall find it profitable to concentrate on particular aspects of a subject, a bigger bonus, however, may be the increased prestige that writing brings.

There is a great advantage in writing in series. With the material assembled we may have the basis for a book on the subject.

QUESTIONS

1. Find simple alternatives for the following list of words: adumbrate, bellicose, concerning, contiguous, eliminate, inform, predilection, proletarian, terminate, unilateral.

2. Rewrite the following passage in a simpler form:

   Didactic materials are manifestly important for the pedagogue. If he utilises appropriate aids the results will be commensurate with the effort expended. Innovation should be carefully synchronised with the approved syllabus, so as to maximise the student's acquisition of knowledge. Literature should not be confined to classical works, but should include vernacular newspapers. Only by these devices will the educationalist help the progeny of the proletariat to achieve literacy.

3. Comment on the following sentences:

   (a) There has been relatively little improvement in the country's economic position.

   (b) In the majority of cases vaccination is efficacious.

   (c) The shortage of skilled craftsmen is one of the greatest bottlenecks in industry.

   (d) Inflation is quite a problem.

   (e) So far as the nuclear power point of view was concerned, the government was investigating the situation with a view to seeking multilateral agreementation respecting this subject.

4. (a) First explain carefully the meaning of the following words (if possible giving their derivation), and then write appropriate sentences containing them: aboriginal, metropolis, culture, philanthropy, antiseptic.

   (b) Write sentences to bring out clearly the meaning of: entomology, liquidate, identification, deficiency, buttress, optional, quixotic, evoke, spontaneous, arbitration. (ICSA)

5. (a) First explain carefully the meaning of the following words (if possible giving their derivation), and then write appropriate sentences containing them: dilapidation, automatic, inspiration, potential, bilateral.

   (b) Write sentences to bring out clearly the meaning of: informal, credentials, referendum, consecutive, nominal, coroner, benefaction, delegate (verb), premium, refute. (ICSA)

6. Write an essay on the following subjects:

   (a) The Common Market.

   (b) Technical developments since the Second World War.

   (c) Municipal libraries.

(d) Social responsibility in industry.
(e) Apprenticeship training.

7. Write an essay on one of the following subjects:
    (a) The rights of minorities.
    (b) National health services.
    (c) Nature, man's friend and enemy.
    (d) Modern youth: its strength and weakness.
    (e) "No man is well educated today who has no knowledge of economics."
    (ICSA)

8. Write about 350 words on one of the following subjects:
    (a) Modern children.
    (b) The chief problem facing the government of your country.
    (c) Projected improvements in the transport systems of some country known to you.
    (d) Does education make people happier?
    (e) Should there be uncontrolled competition between rival transport undertakings? (Inst. of Trans. Grad.)

9. Write an essay on one of the following subjects:
    (a) The affluent society.
    (b) Export markets.
    (c) Education in the years ahead.
    (d) The foreman as part of management.
    (e) The developing countries.

10. Write an essay on one of the following subjects:
    (a) The world in the year AD 2000.
    (b) Emigration.
    (c) Is village life decaying?
    (d) The virtues and vices of ambition.
    (e) The place of the arts in this age of technology.

11. Write about 350 words on one of the following subjects:
    (a) Modern advertising.
    (b) Have adults any obligations towards their parents?
    (c) The early days of one branch of transport.
    (d) The role of the United States in the world today.
    (e) Do you believe that the branch of transport with which you are associated should be subsidised (or should it continue to be subsidised) from public funds? State the argument which could be brought forward for and against your point of view. (Inst. of Trans. Grad.)

12. Write an essay on one of the following subjects:
    (a) Advertising.
    (b) Redundancy in industry.
    (c) The supervisor's problems.

13. Write an essay on one of the following subjects:
    (a) On being a spectator.
    (b) Monopolies.

(c) Chairmanship.

(d) The value of "do-it-yourself".

(e) "Where there is much desire to learn, there of necessity will be much arguing, much writing, many opinions". (ICSA)

14. Write about 350 words on one of the following subjects:

(a) What arguments would you advance for and against allowing corporal punishment to be administered in schools?

(b) Modern women.

(c) Steps which could and should be taken in order to reduce traffic congestion in towns.

(d) The chief virtues and failings of your countrymen.

(e) Give an account of recent developments in travel by land or sea or air in such a way as to make your meaning clear to readers who have no specialised knowledge of the subject. (Inst. of Trans. Grad.)

15. Write an essay on one of the following subjects:

(a) Road safety.

(b) A book you have recently read.

(c) "My job".

(d) Discipline in industry.

CHAPTER V

MIND YOUR Ps, Qs, and COMMAS!

A LOOK AT GRAMMAR

There are many excellent works which deal with the niceties of grammar. In this book we are primarily concerned with effective communication; and we shall therefore deal with those constructions which may give rise to vague or ambiguous communication. To some readers a further attempt to tackle the so-called "common errors" will be tiresome, but the authors think that most readers will find the effort worth while.

The misrelated participle

The misrelated participle has been chosen because it can cause confusion in the mind of the reader. This must always be avoided.

The following extract from a circular letter will illustrate how the effectiveness of communication is reduced by a misrelated participle.

> Being a disabled ex-serviceman, *you* will readily understand how difficult it is for *me* to obtain employment with an employer.

At the first reading we must surely understand that we, the readers, are being labelled disabled ex-servicemen. Upon re-examination of the sentence we come to the conclusion that the writer of the letter is disabled.

In the example we have given, the misrelation of the participle occurs when the writer changes places with the reader. Sometimes the error occurs because an object is given human characteristics. Thus, we may not say:

> Going up the stairs, the bathroom is on the right.

The simplest rule to follow to avoid the dangers of the misrelated participle quicksands is: always use a finite construction. An example will indicate the advantages of this advice.

WRONG
> Having prepared a detailed account for head office, the general manager asked me for three additional statements.

CORRECT
> After I had prepared a detailed account for head office, the general manager asked me for three additional statements.

Fused participles

Fused participles cause less concern than misrelated participles, and indeed have been upheld by some grammarians. The problem does not really arise with pronouns, as the following example will show.

FUSED PARTICIPLE
> The foreman objected to *him having* a half-day's leave of absence to attend the local technical college [*him having* is regarded as one word—a fused participle].

ACCEPTED CONSTRUCTION
> The foreman objected to *his having* a half-day's leave of absence to attend the local technical college.

If we accept that "having" is a verbal noun, then we cannot allow a pronoun to qualify it. Our solution is to convert "him" into a possessive adjective. When the pronoun is replaced by a noun the problem is less convincingly solved. Let us consider the following example.

FUSED PARTICIPLE
> The council were unwilling to accept responsibility for the plan, owing to their *committee being* divided on this issue.

ACCEPTED CONSTRUCTION
> The council were unwilling to accept responsibility for the plan, owing to their *committee's being* divided on this issue.

We have a verbal noun "being" and we should be consistent in making "committee" into the adjective "committee's". Fowler is adamant in rejecting the idea of a fused participle which combines the participle with the associated noun. The amended version above can be faulted for being clumsy, and a better solution is to avoid the participle construction altogether. Thus, if we apply the formula to our previous example we obtain:

> The council were unwilling to accept responsibility for the plan, because their committee were divided on this issue.

The drawback with the fused-participle construction is that it tends to emphasise the person rather than the action being described. In our example the non-acceptance of responsibility is not really due to the committee, but to the division of the committee.

Number agreement

Errors in the number often give rise to confusion in the mind of the reader. The authors propose here to limit discussion to errors which result from the use of a wrong pronoun or verb. Pronouns are useful in enabling us to avoid the unnecessary repetition of a noun. But when a pronoun is used in a sentence which follows the sentence containing the noun for which it stands, ambiguity may result.

> Accidents sometimes occur in factories in which all reasonable precautions have been taken. It may occur because they have problems of staff co-operation or they may be due to external influences.

Errors in number agreement really come under the "saying what you mean" heading. In our example we have invited the reader to accept "it" in place of "accidents" although "accidents" is a plural noun. We should certainly use a plural pronoun; but we have already used "they" as a substitute (presumably) for "factories". Nor is this all. We have used "they" a second time, and on this occasion we have expected the reader to perform a smart mental turn-about in order to cope with this pronoun as a substitute for "accidents".

An alternative construction would be:

> Accidents sometimes occur in factories in which all reasonable precautions have been taken. These accidents may occur because there has been a failure to obtain staff co-operation or they may be due to external influences.

Pronouns should not be needlessly avoided. Civil servants will often go to any length to omit a pronoun, and in doing so produce an ugly sentence containing the word "such".

> Instructions will be posted on the notice board each week and *such instructions* [they] will be signed by the departmental heads.

Number attraction

This error is similar to the previous one; number is involved. Let us examine the following sentence.

> A list of the supervisors who have been elected have been pinned on the notice board.

We find that we have given the verb "have" a plural form because "supervisors" is plural, but we have the wrong relationship. The subject of "have" is "a list" which is singular. We must ensure that verbs agree with their correct nouns. These are not always the nearest ones.

V. MIND YOUR Ps, Qs and COMMAS! 89

Word arrangement

Our last comment in the previous paragraph is a useful introduction to the last error to be discussed. Words connected in thought should be placed as near to one another as possible. Wrong arrangement of words is the greatest cause of ambiguity. If we cannot grasp any of the finer points of grammar we must understand this principle. An example will demonstrate how ambiguity can arise from a poorly constructed sentence.

> The maintenance of good communication in industry is recognised to have a profound effect on production by the government.

The government is apparently having an effect on production, but our writer presumably intended to convey that the maintenance of good communication in industry would affect production.

We must think clearly before we write—clearly. If we again remind ourselves to write simple sentences we shall be less likely to make this error. Complicated sentences are generally long sentences, and long sentences are very susceptible to ambiguity. Short, simple sentences lend themselves to clarity of expression.

PUNCTUATION

The avoidance of grammatical errors, by correct sentence structure, helps to improve the effectiveness of our communication. Good punctuation adds to the effectiveness. Many organisations now expect their staff to adopt an open punctuation policy based upon the omission of all punctuation marks in business correspondence, except those which would be required in the body of the letter. Examples of closed (traditional) and open punctuation—either of which, if consistently followed, are accepted by professional examining bodies—are given in Chapter VI.

Remember to stop

The aim of communication is the transference of ideas from one mind to another. If we do not stop to allow the customer time to digest what we have written in our letter we must not be surprised if he gives up and seeks satisfaction from one of our rivals. Punctuation provides the necessary pauses.

The comma

International tension has been raised by an offending comma. Lawyers wisely ignore the comma in their contracts, and we should try to follow their example. Yet we must punctuate. We shall reduce the need for commas if we write short sentences. Further, we shall remove the need for almost all punctuation except the all-important full stop.

The following is a disguised extract from a trade-union journal.

> By being recognised at Polbiddle Distilleries in 1980 Polbiddle Branch Committee were faced with on of their greatest problems, to have 450 members one week and to find themselves with a possible 4,000 members the next, it appears to them to be like an army with long lines of communication, one false move . . . .

This article went on for 170 words before coming to a halt. By contrast a *Daily Mirror* paragraph seldom exceeds 40 words, and a sentence is usually 10 or 12 words long. Only the most loyal brother would have pursued the paragraph in the union journal to its tedious conclusion. The point is this: the writer cannot help the reader to understand what he is saying by liberally sprinkling his work with commas. Indeed, the modern writer tends to punctuate lightly.

The comma does have uses, and we shall now describe them. Firstly, it can be used to mark off the items in a list as follows.

> The safety committee dealt with the fencing of machinery, the risk of fire, the stacking of board and the handling of raw materials.

Secondly, the comma may be used to separate the introductory words from the rest of the sentence.

> Members of the committee, I must ask you to give special consideration to this problem.
>
> Moreover, we shall try to expand our exports. However, the productivity of the factory has increased.

Thirdly, the comma is used to mark off the clause which merely makes a comment (non-defining clause): the comma is omitted from true adjectival clauses. The following examples will illustrate the correct use of commas.

> The company dismissed the staff, who were on unofficial strike last week. [Non-defining clause.]
>
>   The company dismissed the staff who were on unofficial strike last week. [Adjectival limited clause.]

In the first sentence the "who" clause passes a comment on the staff, all of whom were dismissed. The second sentence indicates that the company *limited* the dismissals to those members of staff who struck.

Some writers use commas for statements in parenthesis, but brackets are more suitable for this purpose. Moreover, statements which are inessential to the sentence do not belong in business communication.

V. MIND YOUR Ps, Qs and COMMAS!

The full stop

Commas may be lightly used. Full stops must be liberally used. Every sentence must end with a full stop. Since we have emphasised the need for short sentences in business communications, we must also emphasise the need for full stops. Provided we have written a group of words which makes complete sense we must punctuate with a full stop. The important point to remember is that the sentence must contain a finite verb.

The full stop is often used after an abbreviated word and after an initial letter that stands for a word or name. The important rule to observe is: Do not duplicate the full stop if the sentence ends with an abbreviation.

> Among the candidates was one who was exceptionally well qualified; the qualifications were M.A., Ph.D., C.Eng., M.I.E.E., M.I.Mech.E.

In modern English usage, abbreviations are often written without full stops. Full stops are not usually written in a group of letters that are pronounced like a word, e.g. NATO (North Atlantic Treaty Organisation).

Semi-colon

In most business communications the full stop and comma will be adequate. Sometimes, however, it will be advisable to use a semi-colon. The semi-colon may be used whenever we wish to join two sentences closely related in thought. We can still observe our rule about short sentences. An example will illustrate its use.

> All workers must begin work at 8.0 a.m.; they must first stamp their time cards.

The semi-colon may also be used before a conjunction if we wish to make the stop longer than that indicated by a comma. We can often emphasise a point by using the semi-colon.

> Employees under the age of twenty-one years may attend at a technical college on one day a week; however, they must study subjects which will lead to a qualification approved by the company.

It is useful to remember that "also" is not a conjunction and that it therefore may not be used to join sentences. We may be forgiven for using "also" in this way in everyday speech, especially when we have after-thoughts. Careful writers, especially those preparing reports, should, however, collect their thoughts before committing themselves to paper.

"So", "therefore" and "then" may be used as conjunctions, although many writers feel that these words need strengthening in this capacity by the assistance of a semi-colon or another conjunction.

> All employees will be supplied with protective clothing, and therefore will be given a locker to store their personal belongings.
>
> The chairman spoke for ten minutes without interruption; then uproar broke out among the disappointed shareholders.
>
> Industrial accidents are caused mainly by carelessness, but also, on occasion, by inadequate systems of plant maintenance.
>
> The production manager was anxious to increase output during the summer months; so he negotiated with the shop stewards for an extension of the overtime stipulated in the local agreement.

(A comma would, however, be acceptable in place of the semi-colon used before "so" in this sentence.)

Committee secretaries will need to use semi-colons to mark off clauses in a long resolution. The following example shows the use of semi-colons for this purpose.

> The committee resolved:
> *(a)* that the branch officers be asked to report, at the next meeting, on the dispute at Black's Foundry;
> *(b)* that headquarters be asked to send a national officer to the foundry to seek an early meeting with the employers;
> *(c)* that other unions be requested, meanwhile, not to handle goods from the Foundry.

Some writers like to use the semi-colon to link two constrasting statements.

> Last year the country had a favourable balance of payments; this year the country has an adverse balance.
>
> Sole traders have unlimited liability; shareholders in companies have liability only for their shareholding.

Colon

A colon may be used instead of a semi-colon or a full stop if there is a fundamental break in the sentence: it has, however, special uses. It may be used if we have already joined several sentences by means of semi-colons and we wish to join a further sentence which demands a longer pause. If we use the colon for this purpose we break our rule about short sentences: we should therefore hesitate before using a complex sentence structure. Comprehension may suffer.

> After the meeting, the secretary dined with the committee members; he outlined the new scheme for improving the office administration: no one could detect from his outward appearance that he was seriously ill.

The colon is often used in place of the word "namely" to give further information on a subject introduced in the sentence preceding the colon.

There were several reasons for the unofficial strike at the factory: firstly, the company did not honour its agreement with the union; secondly, the supervisors had received no formal training and were ill-equipped to handle employees; thirdly, the union members were apathetic and seldom attended union meetings; fourthly, the professional officers of the union were unable to obtain the support of the union membership; and lastly, the militant shop stewards were excessively powerful.

The colon may be used to introduce a list of words, phrases, or clauses.

> The management carefully considered the shop stewards' suggestions and decided:
> (a) that the price of canteen tea should be reduced to ten pence a cup;
> (b) that the lunch break should be extended to one hour;
> (c) that tea breaks should be limited to ten minutes in the morning and in the afternoon; and
> (d) that strong disciplinary action would be taken against employees who abused the tea-break concession.

Some writers use the colon to introduce all quotations, but the accepted practice is to restrict the use of the colon to the introduction of lengthy quotations. The following is an example of how *The Times* uses the colon:

> Mr J.E.D. Williams, managing director of Euravia (London) Ltd, said today: "We are greatly impressed with the enthusiasm Luton Corporation has shown over the airport. They are the sort of landlord we want."

Like the semi-colon, the colon may be used to join two contrasting sentences.

> I like the man: I despise his politics.
> Surpluses bring happiness: deficits bring misery.

The remaining uses of the colon are best explained by the following examples.

> Taylor evolved principles of scientific management: these principles, however, were to Taylor less important than a scientific attitude of mind.
>
> The insurance company paid in full the amount shown on the policy: in the circumstances they could hardly do otherwise.
>
> It was a strange accident: yet I have known stranger ones.
>
> We must succeed: and we shall.

Dash

To some people the dash is the answer to all punctuation problems: the dash should, however, be used with caution. It may be used before and after a statement in parenthesis, but in business communications we should try to avoid this type of construction, which is more suited to rhetoric than to reports.

> If we look to the future—and that is where we should be looking—we shall see indications that the economic weather will be brighter.

Writers often use the dash to collect a rambling subject. For example:

> To supervise the employees in the department; to be responsible for the maintenance of safety regulations; to ensure a smooth production flow; to prepare reports for senior management—all these and more, are the functions of the production supervisor.

The dash may be used when the writer wants to amplify a previous statement.

> The jet engine was a great invention—the greatest in the short history of the aeroplane.
>
> Supervisory and management training can make an important contribution to increased productivity—perhaps the greatest single contribution.

Sometimes the dash is used to introduce a humorous or unexpected remark, but it should not be used for this purpose in the normal letter or report.

> Unkindly, he suggested that the country had made but one important invention—the mouse-trap.
>
> The claims of what the president calls a common-sense solution are still so much more attractive—and inevitable, one might almost say.

The dash is often used with the colon, especially after "as follows", to introduce a list or a quotation in typed reports.

> The causes of the wartime inflation were as follows:—
>
> *(a)* Shortages caused prices to rise.
> *(b)* Unemployment ceased with the expansion of arms production and labour shortages ensued.
> *(c)* Members of the armed forces and munition workers were paid wages, but their efforts did not increase the supply of goods required by domestic consumers.

Parenthesis ("brackets")

The true parenthesis is normally separated from the remainder of a sentence by ( ). Whether the writer uses a pair of parentheses, dashes, or commas is to some extent a matter of personal preference. However, Eric Partridge, in *You Have a Point There*, has suggested a table of smoothness of interruption beginning with parenthesis and ending with colons. Both parentheses and dashes are not true marks,

and the punctuation of parenthetic statements should be dealt with as if the parentheses or dashes were not shown.
A few practical examples should help.

To France (she has, after all, most to gain), the Common Market represents an important step towards a United States of Europe.

Building Societies (mortgage banks on the Continent) play an important role in gathering small savings.

In his book, the author discusses (he does no more!) the economic problem of the North and South and, in the third chapter (pp. 121-185), he examines the causes of high unemployment in the North East (Yorkshire, Durham and Northumberland).

Industrial training should be given first priority by any government which works to improve both the quality and mobility of labour. (I have referred to management training in Chapter I.)

Exclamation mark

Exclamation marks have little use in business communication. Primarily the marks follow an interjection; but they are used with emphatic remarks. Exclamation marks should be used sparingly to preserve their value. The following examples illustrate their use:

Alas!
Good Heavens!
What a design!
Mind the step!

Question mark

This stop is used after direct questions only. Pedants would insist that it should be used after the polite request: "Would you please let me have a reply by return?" Normally the subject appears after the verb in a question, but in conversation surprise is frequently suggested by intonation. Thus:

You are going tomorrow?

In report writing indirect speech must be used, and both exclamation marks and questions marks should be excluded.

Direct speech	*Indirect speech*
"Are you a member of the Transport and General Workers' Union?" asked the personnel officer.	The personnel officer asked the employee whether he was a member of the Transport and General Workers' Union.
"Good Lord!" exclaimed the manager.	The manager uttered a mild oath. [An alternative construction would be: The manager swore mildly.]

Quotation marks (inverted commas)

Quotation marks serve several purposes. Firstly, as their name indicates, they are used to quote the statements of speakers.

> "I intend to recommend your promotion to departmental foreman," said the works manager.

Secondly, the marks are used to enclose the titles of songs, chapters in books, essays and articles in magazines. They are also used for the titles of books, plays and films, when the work is not being undertaken by a printer (*see* the section on italics below). For example: "Raiders of the Lost Ark", "Jesus Christ Superstar", "Hamlet", "Nicholas Nickleby".

Thirdly, quotation marks are needed to show the unusual or derisive use of a word or phrase.

> We had a very "interesting" lecture.

> The Duke of Windsor returned to the French battleground during the period of the "phoney war".

As will be seen, single quotation marks are used for a quotation within a quotation.

The punctuation of passages including quotations does cause some difficulty. Some grammarians advocate this rule: put the stop outside the quotation marks if the entire sentence is not a quotation. For example:

> (1) A Katanga statement described the talks as "very cordial", and Mr Brian Urquhart, United Nations Representative in Katanga, told reporters they were "excellent, sensible, and businesslike". [Quoted from *The Times*.]

> (2) A meeting of the council of Leeds Chamber of Commerce today would have tended to agree with their president Mr R.H. Braine, who said that at first it appeared to be "a bit of a leg pull". [Quoted from *The Times*.]

The following examples give the punctuation for a complete quotation.

> (1) "As it's practised now, it's a farce," Mr Evans said.

> (2) "Plenty of people in Crewe are giving more for goods in part exchange than they were worth, and that, to my mind, is price cutting." (Quoted from the *Observer*.)

> (3) "Rustling which had previously been known only through the *Virginian* TV series and John Wayne, was becoming a matter of increasing concern.
>
> "Mr Hamilton (Lab., West Fife) said amid laughter: 'Rustling is probably the major growth industry now in Scotland.'
>
> "Earlier Mrs Peggy Fenner, Parliamentary Secretary, Agriculture, said that the penalties which could be imposed were substantial. She was not aware of any need to increase them." (Quoted from the *Daily Telegraph*.)

Italics

Printers can avoid some of the problems of the punctuation of quoted passages by the use of italics. Italics are valuable to indicate the titles of books, films, and plays; they are also useful to show that a word has been used in a special sense. Some publishers use italics for foreign phrases, thus:

> When the secretary addressed the meeting of party workers, he warned of the need to be watchful of the activities of a notorious *agent provocateur*.

Apostrophe

Punctuation, like the alphabet, has its reformers. Some years ago the *Observer* contained correspondence from supporters of the abolition of the apostrophe. The reformers based their argument on usage—or rather non-usage—of this mark. It is true that department stores and local authorities have almost given up the struggle—departmental stores have their "mens department" and local authorities label their conveniences "gentlemen". However, we can still defend the apostrophe, because it does prevent ambiguity.

Sometimes goods are owned in common. If we omit the apostrophe we do not tell the reader whether the goods are owned by one person or several persons.

APOSTROPHE OMITTED

> The dispute was referred to the employees union.

APOSTROPHE INCLUDED

> (a) The dispute was referred to the employee's union.
> (b) The dispute was referred to the employees' union.

In the sentences given above we have ambiguity in the one where the apostrophe is omitted. We can distinguish between a union representing one employee and a union representing several or perhaps all employees when we include the apostrophe.

The apostrophe is required for three purposes. Firstly, it is needed to show possession. The general rule is that the apostrophe is placed before the *s* for the singular possession and after the *s* for plural possession. The number of things possessed does not affect the rule. Thus:

> The shop steward's attendances were noted by the committee. [Correct for one shop steward.]

> Each firms' products were carefully examined. [Incorrect.]

When the possessive word is a plural ending in -en, for example, men, women, children, and oxen, the apostrophe *s* is placed thus:

> The men's representative.
>
> The women's protective clothing.

Secondly, the apostrophe is used to show the omission of letters from words which originally belonged to speech, but which are now increasingly regarded as suitable for formal writing. Thus: can't, don't, won't, it's, I'll, and wouldn't.

Many people, in error, convert the pronoun *it* into *it's* to make a possessive construction. The following example shows the grammatical use of both *it's* and *its*.

> It's simple to calculate the area of a rectangle: multiply *its* length by *its* breadth.

Another common error arises from the misuse of *ours, yours* and *hers*. These absolute possessivees do not take the apostrophe and may not be used as substitutes for *our, your,* and *her*.

> This is *yours* [incorrect] and our home.
>
> Ours [incorrect] and your relatives have been friends for years.
>
> Her [correct] and our views, on training for shop stewards, are identical.
>
> My income and hers [correct] are treated separately by the Inspector of Taxes.

Thirdly, apostrophes are used by a few people for the plurals of figures and letters, although this can be avoided by the use of the apostrophe for figures by writing all numbers below one hundred in words.

> Why do you write your 4's so badly?
>
> Line up in alphabetical order! A's here, B's here and C's here, and so on.
>
> The crowd eagerly awaited the arrival of the crews for the rowing eights race.

If the apostrophe is omitted from the plural of the letter *a* the word could be taken for *as*.

Correct punctuation is important—Eric Partridge puts punctuation before spelling. Yet it must be admitted that much of what is written on both punctuation and grammar comes under the heading of style, rather than grammatical correctness. *The Times Educational Supplement* prints *l.e.a.s.* as the abbreviation for local education authorities. Other publishing houses prefer to print *l.e.a.'s*. Some writers drop hyphens; others insist on *ize* rather than *ise* word endings. Provided that a writer is consistent in his punctuation and vocabulary habits, his readers are unlikely to be confused.

Mr Jackson, in his interesting and amusing book *The Examination Secret*, tells us that Mark Twain's solution to the punctuation problem was to invite the publisher to allocate, as he thought fit, the marks enclosed with the manuscript. This practice is no doubt adopted by many executives when dictating to their luckless secretaries. The responsibility remains with the writer, and we may wonder how the problem is solved when the secretaries are absent.

QUESTIONS

1. Punctuate and make any alterations you think are necessary to the following letter which appeared in the *Observer*.

   Sir,—why cannot we all follow the example of the logically minded child who along with the apostrophe, is prepared to abolish the capital letter, colon, semi colon, hyphen, question mark, bracket, quotation mark—everything, indeed except the full stop and the comma.

   "if we do as we are told, say he, and write in short concise sentences, the full stop and the comma satisfy our every need.

   "if, he adds, dickens and jeans and that lot had been confined to the full stop and the comma, how much happier would our comprehension periods be."

2. Insert the punctuation removed from the following extract.

   Apprenticeship is a good thing for producing skilled workers but unfortunately it often happens in practice that on the apprentice completing his period of training he is sacked as he has become entitled to the wages of a skilled worker an unscrupulous employer might save a good deal on his wages bill by training apprentices for skilled work as rapidly as possible accordingly it is fair that apprentices should be reasonably remunerated there may be need eventually to curtail welfare schemes on the ground of cost or are they an essential expense like planned advertising super showrooms and the like but the time may well come when the employment and the welfare of labour will be a top heavy item then will come the wedge of the old exploitation of labour especially if there are many workers applying for every job owing to more and more businesses closing down high wages and high costs resulting therefrom may well cripple our export trade.

3. Insert the punctuation required by the following extract, which should give the reader good practice in the use of the colon and semi-colon.

   A scheme of this kind would 1 enable the bec awards at ordinary and higher levels to be established with industry 2 avoid excessive competition for well qualified business staff 3 give time for business studies departments to acquire mini/micro computers and associated software 4 place the first degree award business studies babs on a comparative footing with the well established bsc in engineering.

4. Put apostrophes where necessary in the following phrases.

   The BBCs television service; its unnecessary to write long sentences; the governments policy contradicts its election manifesto; four days pay; womens welfare; the workers pay packets; Brother Smiths remark; the Swedish Employers Association; its always possible that MPs will be interested.

5. The following sentences contain errors: rewrite the sentences in their correct forms.

V. MIND YOUR Ps, Qs and COMMAS!

(a) Looking at the question logically, the answer was obvious.

(b) A complete list of the members names is placed on the notice board.

(c) Production is higher than last year.

(d) The departmental manager sent a memorandum to the general manager in a temper.

(e) When he telephoned the personnel officer it was answered by the secretary.

(f) At the works committee meeting, the management asked the employee's representatives to consider a longer working week within forty hours.

(g) When the committee were asked for it's decision, they decided to defer the matter until it's next meeting.

(h) The apprentice asked whether he could attend a weeks refresher course, but the management would not agree to him going.

(i) Referring to your letter of the 12th January, the generator will be delivered before the end of this month.

(j) Everyone should accept their responsibility for the dispute.

CHAPTER VI

BUSINESS CORRESPONDENCE

In previous chapters we have discussed the value of correct English. We now examine the use of English in business letters. We again emphasise that there is no need to use outdated "commercial English".

THE IMPORTANCE OF SOUND BUSINESS LETTERS

When we visit a home for the first time we are often impressed by the exterior decorations and general external state of repair. Similarly, we are impressed, favourably or otherwise, by the external communications of a business. We shall deal with the importance of the telephone in Chapter XI, and we shall, therefore, confine our discussion here to the letter. Even when we do use the telephone it may sometimes be necessary to confirm the results of the call by letter.

Business correspondence can give a firm a good name in one of several ways. First, a prompt reply will usually indicate that a firm is efficient. If a firm is efficient in the office it is likely to be efficient in other departments. Secondly, if the letter is well set out the recipient will probably be disposed to think that he is dealing with a tidy-minded organisation. Thirdly, if the reader can understand what has been written he may express his gratitude tangibly by placing his order with the writer's company. What is equally important is that he may tell his friends about this, apparently, highly efficient firm.

It is perhaps this "good name" aspect of business letters which first induced jargon into commercial correspondence. There can be little doubt that jargon has succeeded in creating an entirely wrong image of most firms. Lawyers are always being criticised for using what seem to be unnecessarily complicated constructions: businessmen cannot afford to have the same criticisms levelled at them.

VI. BUSINESS CORRESPONDENCE

THE PURPOSES OF BUSINESS LETTERS

According to the pamphlet *A Guide to the Writing of Business Letters*, published by the British Association for Commercial and Industrial Education, a business letter has two main purposes. Firstly, it enables business arrangements to be made without the need for the parties to meet. Secondly, it enables both parties to have a permanent record of these arrangements.

We should note carefully that the prime purpose is to remove the need for personal contact. It is a strong indication of the failure of such business correspondence if a meeting is necessary to remove misunderstanding. A letter is successful if the writer achieves his object. Before the letter writer begins his letter he must understand what his object is.

When the writer is clear about this object, his writing and the presentation of the writing should enable this object to be reached. The language should be simple and clear. Pompous jargon and foreign phrases have no place in business communication. Sometimes we are required by the subject-matter to use technical terms. We may use technical jargon provided we are certain the recipient will understand the terms; otherwise we must explain ourselves in non-technical language.

Simple language will help to get our message over, but we should remember that simple language alone will not solve our problems. We have our object to achieve, and we must therefore make sure that we include all the details necessary to give our reader a clear idea of what we require of him. We must also remember that businessmen are by definition busy men who do not wish to waste time on irrelevant material. Avoid ungrammatical and insincere concluding sentences like "Assuring you of our best attention at all times."

We can fail in our purpose through grammatical errors and careless spelling. The following example taken from a reader's letter in the *Daily Telegraph* illustrates this point.

> We have pleasure in informing you that your shoes are *not* available.

No doubt the writer of this letter would argue that he left the spelling to his secretary, who typed "not" for "now". The responsibility for faults in letters cannot be shifted; it remains with the writer. If the writer finds that his dictation is not taken down correctly he has several solutions. He can, for example, start by listening to his own dictation on tape. If the dictation is coherent he can try the excellent management exercise of training or retraining his secretary.

LETTER CONSTRUCTION

Members of Parliament who do their homework make effective speeches. Managers who do their homework write effective letters. Effective letters cannot be written without some preparation. Brief notes should be written in the margin of letters to be answered. If we are starting the correspondence and the material is in the least complicated we should also prepare a few notes. This latter preparation is particularly needed when we dictate letters, rather than prepare drafts for the typing pool. Remember that if we do not know what to say and in what order it should be said our letter will provide a challenge, not information.

If we have prepared our letter we shall know how much space we shall require to present our request or information. This is important, as the good physical appearance of a letter does much to communicate the idea that our organisation is efficient. Setting out the letter is the typist's task, but it is our responsibility to ensure that the letter helps to achieve its own purpose. Letters which have not been paragraphed should be retyped.

THE FORM OF THE LETTER

Addressing the letter

The modern approach to business communication is helping to relax the rigidity of commercial correspondence, but conventions dictate that certain forms of address shall be used. We should address business letters to firms rather than to individuals, unless we are invited to do otherwise. Many of the prestige advertisements for senior staff in the "quality" daily and Sunday newspapers do ask us to address our applications to the personnel manager or to some other named official. Moreover, letters to government departments, local authorities, nationalised industries, and banks, among others, are normally addressed to the senior official of the department. Thus a letter to a local authority about the rate demand should be addressed in either of the following ways:

CLOSED PUNCTUATION	OPEN PUNCTUATION
The Director of Finance,	The Director of Finance
Council Offices,	Council Offices
Old Field Square,	Old Field Square
BRIDEWALL,	BRIDEWALL
Loamshire,	Loamshire
IG5 OAA	IG5 OAA

Normally, however, letters should be addressed to the company, thus:

VI. BUSINESS CORRESPONDENCE

CLOSED PUNCTUATION	OPEN PUNCTUATION
Co-operative Bank P.L.C.,	Co-operative Bank PLC
5/7 Market Street,	5/7 Market Street
WATFORD,	WATFORD
Herts.,	Herts
WD1 7AB	WD1 7AB

Because companies often prefer letters not to be addressed to employees, some writers try to obtain special treatment by writing on the envelope "For the attention of . . ." It may occasionally be helpful to use this device, but the letter reference heading should be adequate. Indeed, *For the attention of . . .* is an implied criticism of the efficiency of the company receiving the letter.

"Messrs" should not normally be used for corporate bodies: its use should, in any case, be restricted to businesses whose titles contain personal names. Partnership names take "Messrs" thus:

CLOSED PUNCTUATION	OPEN PUNCTUATION
Messrs Smith, Green and Co.,	Messrs Smith Green and Co.
Haloway Chambers,	Haloway Chambers
LONDON,	LONDON
WC1E 7HS	WC1E 7HS

Layout of letters

In the example given above, the address is shown with successive lines beginning in the same position as the first line. This practice is often adopted for the whole letter so that paragraphs are not indented. Moreover, companies may, in order to save secretarial time, decide to eliminate punctuation in the address, salutation and complimentary close, and at the ends of lines.

The fully blocked system may look unattractive to some readers, so a compromise may be used, e.g. the conventional position may be adopted for the date, address, salutation, and complimentary close, but the remainder of the letter is blocked at the left hand margin.

Salutation

Letters to firms require the salutation *Dear Sirs*. If the letter is addressed to an officer the form is *Dear Sir*. We assume that company officers are masculine, unless we know them to be feminine. There is therefore no need for the device *Dear Sir or Madam*. *Dear Madam* has no plural, and Fowler tells us that *Ladies* is the substitute for the plural form. The correct salutation for a letter type of report from a company secretary to a board with both men and women directors is *Ladies and Gentlemen*.

Sometimes we wish to refer to the addressee by name, if, for example, he is an old customer of the company. Thus we may write:

VI. BUSINESS CORRESPONDENCE 105

Dear Mr Smith or *Dear Miss Jones*. Letters from senior executives to their subordinates are often written in this way. Subordinates, of course, should not adopt the familiar form of address in their correspondence with superiors.

The heading

If we have thought out carefully what we want to say we should be able to summarise the letter in a heading. This is not to say that a heading is always necessary. For very short letters headings are sometimes superfluous. However, it is courteous to give a heading when our letter is a reply to one in which a heading has already been given. We should naturally use the same heading.

Building Societies like to quote the mortgage account numbers in correspondence with their members. Thus a typical heading would be:

B.126593
Arrears of Subscriptions

Garage-proprietors, when writing about their customers' cars, like to quote the model and the registration number. For example:

FORD GRANADA XYZ 123
Major Engine Overhaul

It is helpful in a reply to quote an order number in the heading. Thus:

Non-delivery of angle iron (Order No. 135/YZ)

We shall often find that we can shorten the length of our letters with headings. This particularly applies to requests. For example:

Dear Sir,

Appointment of Work Study Officer

Will you please let me have the details of the position?

Yours faithfully,
T. Brown.

We shall write many letters to which there will (or should) be no reply. For these letters headings may be unnecessary. We shall, however, find it useful to give a heading for letters which may be the beginning of a file of correspondence.

Finally, we should remember that headings are intended to help the reader. The following extract from *The Times* illustrates the danger of having a heading with does not agree with the subject-matter:

MOST MORRIS CARS TO BE ASSEMBLED IN BELGIUM

BRUSSELS, Feb. 23—All makes of Morris cars, with the exception of Riley and Wolseley, will be assembled in Belgium from the early summer. Morris cars are now imported fully-built or from assembly plants in Holland. The Belgian firm, Beherman-Demoen, already holding similar contracts for Standard-Triumph and Borgward, will assemble the cars at Wilrijck, near Antwerp, under a contract which provides for delivery to begin on August 1.

Meanwhile, in Birmingham, a BMC spokesman confirmed that these Nuffield products were to be assembled by Beherman-Demoen and added that the corporation looked upon the new contract as a further step in its efforts to build up Common Market trade.—*Comtelburo*.

Beginning the letter

Many letter writers have difficulty with the opening sentence of their letters. This even applies to those correspondents who have done their homework. We should have no problem if we start the sequence of correspondence. The best plan to follow is the direct approach. For example, if we wish the reader of our letter to send us pamphlets on his firm's central-heating schemes we may begin:

> Will you please send me the pamphlets on your firm's central-heating schemes?

Nothing more need be said. Of course, if we want estimates of installation costs we must clearly say so. It is certainly not necessary in a general enquiry to give elaborate explanations of the reasons for writing the letter.

Much of our letter-writing time will be spent answering letters. Our correspondents will be expecting a courteous reply, and this gives a clue to the way we may begin. We shall often be able to begin:

> Thank you for your letter of 13th February.

If we intend to write a short letter with no heading we should mention the subject-matter of our correspondent's letter. Thus:

> Thank you for your letter of 13th February about the new superannuation scheme.

Notice that we have avoided vague terms like "communication" and "enquiry". If we have received a letter there is little point in calling it another and longer name.

Sometimes we receive letters which cannot be answered with a "thank you". Perhaps we have been admonished for failing to meet an order on time. One way to begin would be:

> We have received your letter of 15th March and we are sorry that our packing department has been unable to let you have your order.

We should thank customers who tell us about our mistakes. We may find from an indignant customer that our postal department did not enclose the stamped addressed envelope we mentioned in our letter. This useful, if painful, letter from the customer may lead us to examine the methods for the despatch of mail.

We should try to avoid using the familiar "With reference to your letter . . ." to the exclusion of other phrases. If we do use "With reference to . . ." we must be careful to follow with a phrase indicating the person making the reference.

> With reference to your letter of 21st January, we are pleased to tell you that our company have agreed to allow in full your claim for fire damage.

If we do not follow this plan we may write an absurdity.

> With reference to your letter of 21st January, your claim for fire damage will be met by the company in full.

In this example "your claim" is apparently referring to "your letter".

We must also avoid writing only:

> With reference to your letter of 21st January.

This is a long phrase, not a short sentence.

Some writers, despite Sir Ernest Gower's warnings in *The Complete Plain Words*, persist in using "I have to inform you that . . ." Sir Ernest described this construction as "undefined compulsion". The authors know at least one office where the compulsion was, for many years, not undefined, because the staff were instructed to begin all letters and memoranda in this way.

We no longer have any excuse for following "In reply to" and "With reference to" with "I have to inform you". If we can satisfy the customer we can say "We are pleased to tell you", and if we cannot satisfy him we can say "We are sorry to tell you". Whatever we have to say we should keep our opening sentence short. The following example taken from the *Daily Telegraph* illustrates how we can ruin a letter with a long sentence.

> Referring to the final paragraph of our letter of the 22nd August, to you, concerning a letter of yours dated the 14th June, we have now received your letter of the 18th August, with which is attached a copy of your letter of the 13th June, which apparently is the letter to which reference should have been made in your previous letter.

This letter from a civil servant was received by a Malvern reader of the *Daily Telegraph*. We can only assume that *The Complete Plain Words* was not available in the civil servant's department.

The opening sentence is important; it should be brief and courteous. All paragraphs should preferably be short. Short paragraphs enable the reader to grasp the message we are trying to give him.

Moreover, business letters are often read by people in more than one department. If we break down the letter into short paragraphs the paragraphs may be specially marked by the official who opens the post. If our letter follows the familiar pattern of introduction, explanation, and the request for instructions we shall not need an ending. Occasionally long technical letters dealing with specifications may need summaries. But these letters are exceptions.

Consider the following example:

PARAMOUNT INSURANCE COMPANY
Paramount House Mount Place London SW15 4JF

Telephone:
01 752 1234
  Ext 24

Our ref HA/JHT Your ref

10 December 19 . .

Mr D J Smith
24 Old Street
WESTLON
Kent
WS10 0NP

Dear Sir

Thank you for your letter of 8th December about fire insurance for your house.

The premium for fire insurance is normally 10p for each one hundred pounds of cover, but if your house is constructed mainly of wood you will have to pay at a higher rate.

I enclose an application form and a copy of our leaflet giving details of fire insurance, and other perils householders usually insure against.

Yours faithfully

H B ROBINSON
Manager

This letter finishes quite naturally with the indication of the next step to be taken—the completion of the form. Mr Robinson could have added another *sentence*.

> Please let me know if you would like further help.

Mr Robinson should not, however, have concluded with purposeless *non-sentences* such as follows.

> Trusting this explanation has been satisfactory. [An ungrammatical expression of the writer's lack of confidence in his ability to communicate.]

VI. BUSINESS CORRESPONDENCE

Assuring you of our best attention at all times. [A clearly worded, prompt, and helpful reply is assurance enough.]

Technical letters are sometimes written with numbered paragraphs. This practice is quite useful for correspondence between technologists, and certainly gives letters a tidy appearance. But this military precision may be decidedly unhelpful for correspondence between a company and a private person. We should try to humanise our letters: thus the customer expects our company to have a soul as well as a computer.

The signature

We shall usually find that we can close our letter with "Yours faithfully". Some writers like to end with "Yours truly", which is suitable to use with both "Dear Sir" and "Dear Mr ———". "Yours sincerely" is the ending for letters which begin "Dear Mr ———". American writers often invert the order of the words for the close to give, for example, "Sincerely yours". In this country the inverted form is not acceptable, although film-stars like to use "Sincerely yours" when autographing photographs.

"I am, Sir, your obedient servant" is seldom used, except by civil servants and correspondents to *The Times*. Even these special groups are gradually dropping this highly formal close.

After the subscription we must put our signature. Some companies insist that the signature must be preceded by the name of the company. This practice is not followed by banks, insurance companies, and most commercial companies, but it is widely adopted in industry. There seems little point in it, because the letter heading boldly announces the origin of the letter. Moreover, nobody really believes that the board of directors considers every letter sent from the company. The absurd custom of placing p.p. or per pro (*per procurationem*) before the company's name is dying, though p.p. is commonly used by a person such as a secretary signing on behalf of someone else.

By the time we have reached managerial status we have probably developed an affected scrawl for our signature. We should, therefore, have our name typed under the signature. If we hold a designated appointment in the organisation we should have the designation typed under the signature.

In some organisations the letters are always sent out under the signature of a senior executive. If we sign the letters we should add our initials. The authors think that it is a better plan for management to allow the writer to sign his own name "for production manager", "for personnel manager", and so on.

Inside address

The inside address of the recipient should be placed on the left of the letter, immediately below the date, or immediately below the signature. If the letter is to be placed in a window envelope the postal town of the address should be typed in capitals. If the letter is to be placed in an ordinary envelope a check should be made to see that the address on the envelope agrees with that on the letter. Remember that the recipient sees the envelope before the letter, and he may easily be upset by a misspelt name.

Telephone extension number

Many organisations still do not insist that letters are sent with the telephone extension quoted. The result is that much valuable time is wasted by customers in conversation with the operator and other employees not interested in the purpose of the call. Customers telephoning small firms, and those firms where writers sign their own letters, may not be seriously inconvenienced. This cannot be said of customers telephoning large organisations where letters are sent under the signature of the chief officer, as in local authorities. To omit the telephone extension is both bad manners and bad business.

Reference

If our correspondent has given a reference we should quote it in the top left corner above the inside address. This will enable the clerks opening our letter to mark the letter for the correspondent. It will also help the filing section at our correspondent's firm.

We should, of course, ensure that our own reference is given on our letter.

BUSINESS JARGON

In Chapter IV we examined the principles of written communication. These were:

1. use short simple words rather than long words;
2. use familiar words rather than unfamiliar words;
3. use concrete nouns rather than abstract nouns;
4. use short sentences.

Now that we have dealt with the construction of the letter we should remind ourselves of these principles. Indeed, we should remind ourselves whenever we have letters to write. The use of business jargon is contrary to the principles of effective communication. We would not say:

What is the position in regard to the time?

We would omit "the position in regard to". This is the sort of nonsense we should omit from our letters. The simple straightforward words of everyday speech are the right words for business letters.

Here are some typical examples of jargon with the corresponding English equivalents:

adverting to	referring to
assuring you of our best attention	(omit)
deem	think
enclosed please find	we enclose
favour	letter
majority, the	most
a percentage of a proportion of	some
same, the	it
substantial (sum)	large
ult., inst., prox.	(use the name of the month)
we beg to acknowledge	we have received
yours to hand	thank you for your letter

Before we use a long word we should ask ourselves whether we can use a shorter word. Before we use an unfamiliar word we should try to find a suitable familiar word.

Readers may find the following list of long and unfamiliar words a useful guide:

Long/unfamiliar word	Short/familiar word	Long/unfamiliar word	Short/familiar word
acquaint	tell	proceed	go
adumbrate	sketch	purchase	buy
assist	help	request	ask
commence	begin	reside	live
concur	agree	state	say
consider	think	sufficient	enough
despatch	send	terminate	end
inform	tell	transmit	send
initiate	begin	unilateral	one-sided
materialise	happen	utilise	use
peruse	read		

A word on costs

We should try to reduce the cost of producing letters and try to make them more effective. In addition to the advice given elsewhere in this book, there are several other ways in which the cost can be kept down.

We should consider the use of forms, i.e. standardised letters, as these save the time of the dictator. Dictating machines are also useful time-savers, because they can be operated at any convenient time. Thus representatives and managers can often use one of the excellent small machines when they are spending a period away from the company.

One of the most important aids to reducing typing time has been the introduction of the word processor. Word processing represents the application of microchip computer technology to typing. In effect the typist can type a letter to be shown on a visual display unit in front of her and this affords her the opportunity to make all corrections before committing the type to paper at very high speed. Additional error-free copies of the text can be provided from the information stored on a "floppy disc". The great value of the word processor is that it obviates the need for retyping of amended drafts as the machine can be operated to adjust for all corrections whilst retaining the uncorrected material. For small companies not wishing to purchase word processors, bureaux now operate a word-processing service similar to that on offer for photocopying.

Typing time can also be saved by the use of window envelopes. Many organisations install franking machines to increase speed and efficiency as well as to improve security.

Moreover, the Post Office has powers to require that, at a future date, only the Post Office preferred (POP) range of envelopes will be accepted at the lowest postage rates.

Finally, because of the mounting cost of sending correspondence we should always ask ourselves "Is it really necessary to send this letter?" It is well known that continental executives are not so addicted to letter writing as their British counterparts who will always confirm a telephone conversation rather than regard it as a substitute for a letter.

In determining the method of communication to be used we should consider the cost of the possible methods.

Brevity

We end this section with a strong plea for brevity in business letters. As an example of how long letters may ruin public goodwill, we reproduce by permission of *The Times Educational Supplement* a letter sent by the Surrey County Council:

Dear Sir/Madam

Following the written examination taken by candidates on 23rd January, some children have now been selected by the Education Committee for a course of grammar education commencing in the autumn term of this year. The parents of those children have been informed of this. In the case of all other candidates, of whom your child is one, a final decision has not yet been made.

The next stage in the selection procedure will be the investigation of the cases of those candidates on the borderline for grammar education. You must not, however, assume that your child will necessarily be one of these children. Indeed, in the case of the majority of parents who receive a copy of this letter, their children will not be among the borderline group.

The investigation of borderline cases will be carried out by a number of panels specially appointed by the Education Committee for this particular purpose. These panels will visit the schools concerned to discuss each borderline case with the Head, to examine the school work that the children have been doing and then to interview them. This stage in the selection procedure will commence in March and will not be completed until, at the earliest, the end of May.

Within about two weeks following the visit to a school by an interviewing panel, letters will be sent to the Head of the School for transmission to the parents of all candidates apart from those already selected following the January examination. In the letter which you will receive you will either be informed that your child has not been selected for grammar education and that he/she will not be considered further under the Common Entrance Examination selection procedure, or you will be told that your child has been interviewed and is still under consideration and that the final decision concerning him/her will be made towards the end of June. In the latter case there will be enclosed a copy of the Form HS1, which the parent will be asked to complete and return through the Head of his child's school (except in the case of candidates attending schools not maintained by Surrey County Council, where the parent will already have completed one of these). If you receive this type of letter there will also be mentioned in it that a further communication will be sent to you towards the end of June, informing you whether or not your child has been selected for grammar education. If he/she is selected you will at the same time be told the name of the school where a place is offered.

It is fully appreciated that the parent of a child who has been interviewed will have to wait for a period before he receives the final letter telling him what has been decided concerning his child. This, however, is unavoidable due to the time that is required for a thorough investigation of all borderline cases.

Some of the comments of *The Times Educational Supplement* were:

An unfortunate letter.

The language of the letter itself is so inept, ambiguous and tortuous as to make reasonable parents wonder whether the writer himself would be able to pass the 11 plus in plain English, let alone the intelligence tests.

This would be a good public relations joke were it not that many parents are suffering from a piece of local administration which reveals a callous disregard for human feelings.

The design of forms

Forms may be used to save unnecessary correspondence, but forms are often introduced before it can be established that they are needed. The first question we must truthfully answer is therefore "Do we really require this form?" We may, for example, find that we are able to obtain the information we need by amending an existing form. Sometimes, too, the simple solution of using carbon paper to obtain copies will enable us to dispense with yet another form.

FORM LAYOUT

We shall not receive the correct response to our questions if we do not state clearly and concisely what we wish to know. We may be able to reduce the risk of spurious answers by the multi-choice answers technique. This will merely require the person completing the form to put marks in the boxes provided. If our answers are required as lists of figures we should make provision for totals in a clear position at the bottom right-hand corner of the form.

Managements are, of course, not only concerned with obtaining the correct information but with reducing administrative costs. For this reason we must give careful consideration to possible ways of producing and using the form economically. Thus we may be able to dispense with the use of envelopes by providing a special folding with an address position. We should, however, ensure that folding positions occur in places where the creases do not obscure the responses. The quality of the paper we use should be compatible with the amount of handling involved, the life of the form and the number of copies we need.

We should design our form to be cut from the smallest possible standard size of paper without waste, and to prevent the unnecessary transfer of detailed information from one form to another we should try to make our form do more than one job. Thus, we may be able to provide columns on the form for use by the receiving department.

We should try to avoid the use of different colours for copies and rely on symbols to identify copies required for different departments. We should remember, too, that some colours are not suitable for photographic reproduction. Finally, we may avoid unnecessary costs by giving the printer a clear and accurate draft of the form we require.

THE NEED FOR CONSULTATION

Although a form may be needed for the more efficient and effective management of the organisation we must remember that a form is completed by people for people. We should always encourage the users of forms to make practical suggestions about improvements. Indeed, it is by sensible consultation that we may come to the really important conclusion that we have no justification for introducing or continuing our form.

VI. BUSINESS CORRESPONDENCE

INTERNAL COMMUNICATION

Memoranda (memos)

Inside the organisation the memorandum will be the main method of written communication. Memoranda should be composed with as much care as the letters which are sent to other companies, since the prestige, reputation, and probably promotion prospects of the writer will depend upon the impression he creates. The principles of letter writing also apply to the writing of memoranda. There is, however, no need for a salutation, such as "Dear Sir", nor for a complimentary close, "Yours faithfully".

It is a sound rule to deal with one matter only in a memorandum. Some people think that paragraphing should not be used in memoranda, but the authors prefer to see short paragraphs used even in this form of communication. Reports prepared on the writer's own initiative are normally submitted to management as memoranda. These memoranda should be well paragraphed if they conform to the usual pattern of introduction, evidence, and conclusion.

It is always advisable to quote file numbers on all correspondence, including memoranda. It is also helpful in large organisations if the writer states his telephone number and extension.

Instruction manuals

The aim of the instruction manual is to ensure uniformity of procedure in a large organisation. Writing a manual is specialised work which requires the author to have an analytical and discriminating mind. He should also be able to work well with people so that he may be able to obtain information about the problems they face. He will be able to understand their difficulties only if he has a knowledge of methods study or some practical experience of the ground to be covered by the manual.

Most manuals are too long and too obscure, often due to the issue of amendments to cover rare difficulties. Revision will be needed, and the writer should keep the manual as short as possible. It may, however, sometimes be of advantage to give reasons for procedures so that the spirit of the regulations may be understood.

The instructions contained in manuals should be supplemented by oral instruction for new entrants and for all employees when there has been a revision. Instruction manuals should be regarded as an aid to, and not a substitute for, training.

FINDING AND MAKING AN APPLICATION FOR A JOB

With the recent increase in unemployment many of us have been forced to find a new job. The basic aim must be first to obtain an interview. The main routes, which should be attempted concurrently, are:

1. applying for posts which are advertised in the press or at job centres/Executive Register bureaux;
2. applying direct to an organisation which might have a suitable vacancy;
3. placing our name on agency lists;
4. advertising in the press, or even on local radio;
5. getting introductions through friends and contacts.

It is often necessary for us to draw up our curriculum vitae (c.v.) or career history. This should be designed to show the benefits the organisation will get in employing us. It is a vital form of communication. We should tailor the curriculum vitae to the post in question. We should never send a stencilled or photocopied c.v. Details should include:

1. personal details: *(a)* full name, *(b)* address, *(c)* telephone number (if possible day as well as evening), *(d)* date of birth, *(e)* marital status and family;
2. educational attainments including career-related training;
3. professional qualifications and membership of relevant organisations;
4. career to date;
5. special interests and skills;
6. names, addresses and telephone numbers of referees.

QUESTIONS

1. Write a letter to the appropriate authority making a specific complaint about the road or railway transport service in your district. Write also the reply.

2. Write a letter to your local council complaining about the state of the roads in your vicinity and write the reply.

3. Write an application for a vacant post which you have seen advertised. Choose the kind of post you know most about, and give your prospective employer all the information he would require about you. (ICSA)

4. A youth community centre is being planned by a committee of prominent local citizens. As honorary secretary of this committee, write a letter to the press to explain to the public the kind of activities proposed, and to appeal to members of the public for offers of voluntary services and gifts of equipment. (ICSA)

5. You have decided to emigrate and are resigning your job to do so. Write to your employer tendering your resignation and giving your reasons. (ICSA)

6. As secretary of your supervisors' association write to a large undertaking for permission for a party to visit the undertaking's main plant. Write also the reply.

VI. BUSINESS CORRESPONDENCE

7. As the works manager of a small engineering concern write to the principal of your local technical college inviting him to visit the works to discuss plans for day and block release training of technicians. Write also the reply.

8. Your board of directors has considered a request from the office staff association for an increase in their salaries. As secretary write a letter to their association setting out in detail the board's decisions and policy in the matter.
(ICSA)

9. Write a letter of application for the post offered in the following advertisement:

> Assistant works manager required by the North Loamshire Engineering Co. Ltd. Previous experience in a similar capacity in a light-engineering concern essential. Minimum educational qualification HND. Corporate Membership of the IMechE desirable. Commencing salary in the range £10,000 to £12,000 according to experience and qualifications. Applications to the Personnel Manager, North Loamshire Engineering Co. Ltd, Bidmouth, Wamshire, B15 4AA.

10. As secretary of a firm write a letter for general circulation among members of staff explaining that the directors have decided to open a canteen for the use of all employees. (ICSA)

11. Write a letter to a newspaper replying courteously to correspondents who have complained about recent increases in the cost of some branch of transport.
(Inst. of Trans.)

12. Write a letter to your employer or to some appropriate superior in your company respectfully asking that you be allowed an additional week's leave each year and giving reasons in support of your application (e.g. seniority, length of service, amount of leisure time devoted to study). (Inst. of Trans.)

13. You are secretary of a newly formed works social club: (a) write a letter to to your works manager, asking him if he will accept the office of president; and (b) assuming that he has accepted, write a letter thanking him.

CHAPTER VII

SUMMARISING INFORMATION

On the manager's desk the mountain of correspondence grows daily. For this reason junior and middle management have a special responsibility to ensure that their contribution to this mountain is restricted to *necessary* information. However successful we may be in limiting the supply and length of our letters and reports, many writers will, unfortunately, continue to be liberal in their consumption of words. We must expect, therefore, to be called upon to summarise lengthy reports for senior management.

The form of the summary will vary from one organisation to another; but essentially it will be a statement of the main points of the original communication. In formal examinations the summary (often called the précis) should not be tabulated, but should be written as a continuous narrative. Moreover, the précis should not normally consist of more than one paragraph, as the passages selected seldom deal with more than one topic. A manager may require a lengthy document to be summarised: a summary of this sort may run into several headed paragraphs. No difference in approach is needed whether the summary is required for an examiner or a manager.

THE METHOD OF SUMMARY

The theme

We shall not be able to summarise unless we grasp the theme of the passage which we are asked to summarise. However urgent the task of summarising, we must first tackle the problem of *comprehension*. In an examination we shall probably be unfamiliar with the material, so that we must read the whole passage before we attempt to reduce its size.

The title and the notes

Finding a title is useful in keeping our précis close to the theme. The title can usually be selected from a first reading of the passage, but we should not make notes until we have read the passage a second time. The notes should cover all the important facts, and these can often be listed under subtitles for each paragraph. If the passage is well written the subtitles should not be too difficult to obtain. A paragraph should be an elaboration of the topic sentence —the sentence which indicates the subject of the paragraph—and the subtitle should be based on this topic sentence.

The draft

From our title, subtitles, and rough notes we should be able to prepare, in our own words, a rough draft of the summary. If we work from our notes we shall avoid using the wording of the original. We should now check the rough draft against the original to ensure that we have not left out essential material. For management we shall be expected to produce a summary in the least possible number of words; for examinations we shall be told to reduce the original to about a third of its size. If we have exceeded the number of words required we must prune our rough draft. At the same time we must make sure that the summary is written in good English.

The final version

If we are satisfied that our draft reads well and is within the limit of the words allowed we may write out the final version. If we have been requested to do so we should state the number of words we have used.

A summary for management will require the same care as one for an examination. Often, however, the final draft will consist of several paragraphs, because tabulation, headings, and paragraph treatment are favoured by many managements.

TENSE

Choice of tense

The authors have discussed the question of tense with several examiners and have found some difference of opinion. However, the examiners of the Institute of Transport instruct the candidate to begin with "The writer said that. . . ." This advice is given in many textbooks, and it appears to be a safe plan to follow, because passages sometimes contain direct speech.

Direct speech must be converted into indirect speech for summaries, and the candidate is already prepared to deal with this problem if he has begun with "The writer (speaker) said that . . . ." Although, therefore, the English examiners of the Associated Examining Board do not *insist* that summaries shall be written in the past tense, it does seem that a candidate will never actually be *wrong* if he selects the past tense. Moreover, summaries for management are usually needed for reports of events in the past, and it is reasonable to write about these events in the past tense. This is, of course, the practice followed by newspapers in their summaries of speeches.

Direct and indirect (reported) speech

Converting direct to indirect or reported speech does require the observance of certain rules which will now be outlined.

It is necessary to change all the pronouns to the third person, use the past tense, and replace all the words which suggest nearness by words which indicate remoteness of time and place. Sometimes it is desirable to use nouns rather than pronouns to give the full meaning. Thus:

DIRECT SPEECH

> The personnel manager said, "I cannot grant you day release to attend a technical college, unless the departmental manager gives his approval."

INDIRECT SPEECH

> The personnel manager said that he could not grant the apprentice day release to attend a technical college unless the departmental manager gives his approval.

In changing verbs to the past tense we should remember that even the future can be stated in the past. Thus:

TENSE IN THE ORIGINAL PASSAGE	TENSE IN THE SUMMARY
they are	they were
they are meeting	they were meeting
they will agree	they would agree
they may arrange	they might arrange

We may find that the original is already in the past tense. We should convert the past tense into the past perfect tense, but this rule need not strictly be observed, provided we begin our summary with past perfect verbs.

ORIGINAL IN PAST TENSE

> The Home Secretary said, "The Prime Minister asked the public to join a new corps—the Local Defence Volunteers."

PAST PERFECT TENSE

> The Home Secretary said that the Prime Minister *had* asked the public to join a new corps—the Local Defence Volunteers.

Although some rules of guidance for summarising have been given, readers will understand that there can be no formula for solving the most difficult part of summary-writing—the selection of

VII. SUMMARISING INFORMATION

essential points. With practice we can learn to discriminate between significant and trivial matter.

A SPECIMEN PRÉCIS

Readers can compare their own attempts at summarising the following passage with the summary offered by the authors.

Original text

> We all hear a great deal these days about the object of business. Especially is this the case now that we have a mixed economy with private business existing side by side with public corporations and other forms of publicly owned undertakings.
>
> Who can doubt that the main purpose of the company must be to make a profit? Unless there is the profit motive it is not possible to decide whether the private enterprise is being conducted efficiently or not.
>
> I am strongly of the view, however, that we have in addition important obligations to certain sections of the community, obligations which could well be termed the social responsibilities of management. First of all, there are those obligations which the management has towards its shareholders. Without the shareholders no company could have come into being; neither could it continue to exist. Some of these responsibilities are covered by legislation, of which the Companies Act is the latest measure. Other obligations, on the other hand, are not covered by such statutory provisions.
>
> It is not only to the shareholders that the management has obligations. The days have passed when the employees were regarded as mere numbers having no rights at all. Most of us have given a great deal of thought to the problems of personnel management over the past few years and have formed certain conclusions.
>
> Workers these days require security and they should be given the opportunity of having as long a period of employment as the company can grant them under the prevailing circumstances which will, of course, vary from time to time. Another factor, here, is that management will find it advantageous to provide good working conditions. The Factories Acts have brought the law into line with modern practice, but I have always taken the view that we should, where possible, try to improve even on these standards.
>
> Are there any other responsibilities to our employees? I consider that it is essential that there should be adequate machinery for joint consultation, which should not only be practised but should be seen to be practised.
>
> Moreover, the management has obligations to the community as a whole. First of all, I feel bound to mention research, which I regard as consisting of three main categories—industrial research, market research and management research. Research is an important factor because we must pursue it relentlessly if we are to continue to be efficient. This, I must stress, applies whether we provide goods or whether we provide services to the public at large. Furthermore, these days firms have factories in many parts of the country, not to say the world. We have some duties towards the people who are living in these places and I take the view that we have a positive role to play in making the local amenities better.

Under today's conditions it is very important that all members of the company should be aware of what we are trying to do. A good system of communications should be available so that employees at all levels and at all times should be completely apprised of the social obligations of the management. (541 words)

Précis

The Social Responsibilities of Management

The primary aim of business must be to earn a profit, since this serves as a measure of efficiency. But there are other essential responsibilities of management. For example, there are important legal and other obligations to the shareholders without whom the company would not continue in existence. Management also has responsibilities to employees. These responsibilities comprise the provision of secure employment, good working conditions, and joint consultation. The responsibilities of management to the community at large include industrial, market, and management research, vital if the enterprise is to continue to provide its goods and services efficiently. Moreover, a company should contribute towards the advancement of the amenities in the area in which it is situated. A good communications system will then ensure that the employees have a clear understanding of the social obligations of the management. (141 words)

SUMMARIES OF CORRESPONDENCE

Sometimes we shall deal with correspondence which is required by senior management for a decision. Our superiors will ask us to prepare a summary of the correspondence if it runs to several letters. The method we should adopt is similar to that outlined for general summary work.

For professional examinations we shall have to regard ourselves as *impartial observers*. Thus our heading might be:

A summary of the correspondence between Mr W.H. Brown of 175 Cross Street, Middleditch, Loamshire, and the Fount Motor Company Limited of West Bromlake, Lakeshire, about the purchase of a second-hand 1½-litre Fount Ajax car.

A summary of this correspondence by the secretary of the Fount Motor Company might be headed as follows:

A summary of the correspondence between Mr W.H. Brown of 175 Cross Street, Middleditch, Loamshire, and the company about the purchase of a second-hand 1½-litre Ajax car (Rg. No. XYZ 1234).

We should remember that both managers and examiners will expect us to select the essential points of the correspondence. Some letters may be merely acknowledgments and may not need to be mentioned at all. When we have read the correspondence carefully and prepared notes under the letter dates we should write a draft which should read as a continuous narrative. We shall succeed in

VII. SUMMARISING INFORMATION

this task if we have understood the theme of the correspondence. In our final draft we should, in our own words, set out the points, so that the emphasis given in the summary corresponds with that in the letters. For examinations we should note the number of words we have used.

The method which has been adopted for working an example is suitable for examination purposes. Readers may find that their managements prefer tabulated summaries.

The correspondence

> 25 West Lane,
> Noelwit,
> Loamshire, NO4 6AA
> 25th March 19 . .

The Manager,
Leyworth Garage,
Lay Street,
Noelwit, Loamshire, NO4 6AA

Dear Sir,

You will recall that on Thursday 23rd March I placed a deposit of £135 on a second-hand Type A Fount Ajax car. I shall not require hire purchase facilities as I have arranged for the balance to be covered by a personal loan through my bank.

I intend to collect the car on Saturday 1st April, but I should like you to attend to several items before I take delivery. First, I require inertia reel safety belts to be fitted to the front seats and diagonal straps to be fitted to the rear seat. Secondly, I wish to have a fog lamp fitted. Lastly, I consider that the battery should be replaced.

I realise that I will have to meet the cost of these additional items.

Yours faithfully,

A.B. Chatlin

> Leyworth Garage,
> Lay Street,
> Noelwit,
> Loamshire, NO4 6AA
> 27th March 19 . .

Mr A.B. Chatlin,
25 West Lane,
Noelwit, Loamshire, NO4 6AA

Dear Sir,

Type A Fount Ajax Car (XYZ 1234)

Thank you for your letter of 25th March. As I stated over the telephone yesterday, I have ordered the additional equipment for your car, but I may have some difficulty in obtaining before 1st April, the diagonal straps for the rear seat. If these straps cannot be fitted before you take delivery I can arrange for this work to be carried out at a later date.

Please let me know if you would like me to arrange for the car to be insured. The premium on a sum of £1,455 would be £90. The premium would increase the total charge to £1,656, and with the deduction of the deposit of £135, the balance to be paid would be £1,521.

Yours faithfully,
J.D. Stone
MANAGER

25 West Lane,
Noelwit,
Loamshire, NO4 6AA
28th March 19 . .

The Manager,
Leyworth Garage,
Lay Street,
Noelwit, Loamshire, NO4 6AA

Dear Sir,

Type A Fount Ajax Car (XYZ 1234)

Thank you for your letter of 27th March. Do not worry about the diagonal straps for 1st April, as I shall not be taking any passengers, apart from the driving instructor, during the period I am learning to drive. I think the fitting of these straps could be left until I bring the car to the garage for the first service.

Please insure the car for £1,455.

Yours faithfully,
A.B. Chatlin

Summary

A summary of the correspondence between Mr A.B. Chatlin of 25 West Lane, Noelwit, Loamshire, and the manager of the Leyworth Garage, Lay Street, Noelwit, Loamshire, about the purchase of a second-hand Type A Fount Ajax car.

On 25th March Mr Chatlin referred to the deposit of £135 and stated that he did not require hire purchase terms. He would collect the car on 1st April but required it to be fitted with a new battery, diagonal straps, and a fog lamp. The manager replied that the work, except possibly the diagonal straps, would be completed by 1st April, and that the insurance premium on £1,455 would be £90. The balance would then be £1,521. Mr Chatlin accepted the insurance quotation and stated that the diagonal straps could be fitted at the first service.

VII. SUMMARISING INFORMATION

QUESTIONS

1. Write a précis, in about 180 words, of the following passage which contains 560 words.

In a property conscious society, vandalism, which is deliberate destruction or defacement of other people's property, arouses much public anger, for vandalism represents not just financial loss but a direct inversion of the idea of possession. In 1965 one British city suffered damage from this cause at the rate of about £1,000 a week. Personal violence can sometimes be understood, and theft is also explicable because the offender's gain is obvious; but the adjectives used to describe vandalism reflect our perplexity. We call it "sheer", "wanton", "malicious", "senseless" destruction and in the face of such incomprehension our reaction is obviously punitive.

Criminologists have conducted almost no research on the topic, yet like other forms of violent behaviour, vandalism must somehow be meaningful to the perpetrator and understandable in terms of his environment. Attempts at understanding are thwarted almost at once, since vandalism is a particularly safe and anonymous kind of offence. Rarely can clues be found as to the identity of the offender. Some organisations simply write off a certain amount of damage to their property, and offences are not even reported. Hence the detection rate for vandalism is among the lowest for all offences.

One American study distinguished three variations: predatory, vindictive and wanton. Predatory vandalism, as its name implies, covers damage done for gain, such as the smashing and looting of parking meters or gas meters. At least half the damage to public telephone booths is caused by attempts to extract money from the coinboxes. In vindictive vandalism the motive is to express antagonism or hatred towards particular individuals or groups. This might involve, for example, damage to a youth club by a person or gang excluded from joining. The same kind of hostile disagreement is exhibited by people who damage symbolic property such as memorials, gravestones and places of worship. One wonders whether the deliberate breaking of signposts in the country is a variation of this same antagonism expressed against the motorist.

By far the largest category is the third, or wanton vandalism, for which reasons seem obscure. Yet even here a vague pattern seems traceable. On the whole, targets are publicly owned; schools, bus-shelters, park trees, street lamps, statues. Again, one notes that while damage to accommodation in cinemas was not very important when the cinemas were in their heyday of popularity, vandalism grew as soon as television forced a crisis.

Patterns of motivation could be uncovered by looking at the background of the vandals. What sort of people are they? Unfortunately, for the reason already stated, only a tiny proportion are dealt with in the courts. We see the results but not the culprits. From those who are caught, it seems that gangs do not often engage in "crazy" acts of destruction. If they destroy any property it is likely to be for a definite purpose. One disturbing feature is to be observed. Vandalism tends to occur in epidemics or waves which are sometimes set in motion by the initial reporting by television or press publicity. There is an amplification or snowballing effect whereby the behaviour

increases in response to the way it is reported. This phenomenon is all the more reason for trying to understand behaviour such as vandalism, and for being cautious about public comment.   (Stanley Cohen in *The Times*)
(Harrow College of Higher Education—internal)

2. Write a précis of not more than 150 words of the following passage:

No one who writes only for business purposes need worry about the graces of literature. He has a straightforward job to do, and the written word is his instrument. He wants to use that instrument efficiently.

Let us take for granted that he has learnt, or can learn, enough about grammar and syntax to write correct English. What he should concentrate upon is clear conveyance of his meaning—the meaning, the whole meaning, and nothing but the meaning.

Humpty-Dumpty, in Lewis Carroll's *Through the Looking-Glass*, said, "when I use a word it means just what I choose it to mean—neither more nor less." We suffer from too many Humpty-Dumpties today—too many writers who believe that no one could think that their words mean more or less than the writers choose them to mean. The first rule every business writer must remember is "These words of mine will be given effect according to what the reader thinks they mean, no matter what I intend them to mean."

Unlike the words we speak, our written words have to do the whole job of conveying meaning by themselves. We are not present at the reader's elbow to explain or enlarge upon them. Not only will the reader make up in his mind his own version of our message, but he will also make up a mental picture of us. The written word is a plenipotentiary—the whole of the reader's mind-picture is based on his reaction to the words alone. Writing, therefore, has a more serious influence on relationships than speaking. As the writer is absent, his personality cannot come into direct contact with the reader. The writer must try, therefore, to make sure that the reader gains from the words not only an accurate impression of what they are intended to say, but as fair an idea as possible of the writer himself.

There is another point to remember, too. Business communications seldom complete their task in the hands of a single reader or group of readers. They usually have to be acted on, and this gives rise to problems of interpretation. If the first reader misinterprets the message, all that follows will be misconceived. Yet, even if the first reader understands it all right, the risks are by no means over. The instruction issued at the top may be short, clear, general and simple, but it has to be expanded as it goes down. The application in greater detail to each set of circumstances will be elaborated, department by department and level by level, till the actions of the ultimate operatives carry it out. It is all too easy for this interpretative process to distort the original message. It may be interpreted differently in different departments, or differently by individuals in the same department. The intention of the originator may be modified in the process; anomalies and inconsistencies may creep in; in extreme cases the policy may even be frustrated entirely. This type of occurrence is a fruitful source of administrative troubles.

There is no one factor which is responsible for misunderstandings. Nor is there any one formula which will safeguard us against them. The price of

VII. SUMMARISING INFORMATION

clarity is the same as the price of liberty—eternal vigilance. The special object of our vigilance should be the state of our reader's mind—his potential interpretations of and reactions to our words.

3. Make a précis (in indirect speech) of the following passage, using about 150 words. Begin with the words: "The writer stated that . . ." Indicate at the end of your précis the number of words you have used.

> By the skin of our teeth we have been spared an electric railway system which would have been obsolete before it could have been finished. When the modernisation plan was announced just over a year ago it looked as if those parts of the railways which were to be turned over to electric locomotives would be supplied with direct current. This, after all, had been the practice in all previous electrification schemes, except that from Lancaster to Heysham, and people seemed to be happy enough with it. But in the last twelve months there has been much heart-searching. Perhaps the most powerful source of uneasiness has been the outstanding success of the several hundreds of miles of railway track in France which have been operated with alternating current (the kind of electricity that comes straight from the power stations) for the last four years. But just to clinch the argument that direct current was not the right electricity to use for driving electric locomotives, engineers have been able to develop rectifiers which are sufficiently compact to fit into locomotives, so that they can take electricity more or less direct from the power station and use it to drive the motors mounted on the axles. So it is that new electrification schemes will be designed for alternating current. Trains and equipment will be cheaper to make than they would otherwise have been, their running will cost less and their control will be simple. In the south of England there will still be a pocket of track committed to the old ways, but this is sufficiently self-contained not to be a nuisance to the rest of British Railways. In any case it would have cost too much to rip up the third rails and start again. The trouble with enormously complicated railway systems like ours is that one wrong move at the beginning of a development may commit generations to the consequent frustration and annoyance. Who now would have chosen the rail gauge that Stephenson decided upon? Yet who would have had the courage to say it should be changed? Luckily not all the inadequacies of our railways are set as hard and as fast as that. Soon we shall have modern locomotives of the types which British manufacturers have been sending overseas for years. Soon we shall have goods wagons with vacuum brakes so that goods trains will be able to travel more quickly and take up less room on crowded routes. We ought to have had them decades ago. (Inst. of Trans. Grad.)

4. The following passage is taken from an article by the Professor of Literature, the Open University, which appeared in *The Times Literary Supplement*. It contains about 600 words. Using reported speech, write a précis in no more than 220 words. At the end of the précis state the number of words you have used.

> It is still reasonable to assume that more students mean more books. Certain possible and indeed probable developments may modify such a picture without changing it fundamentally. A reduction, in real terms, of student grants or their replacement by loans would obviously lead to a decrease in book

buying, however educationally undesirable. Alternative means of communication—more use of television in particular—might in certain contexts have something of the same tendency: but really we know very little about this.

It is hard to conceive of any remotely recognisable system of higher education in which books of some kind did not play the major part, and I don't think there is any evidence that either educationalists or publishers seriously anticipate such a possibility. Whether any development even as far-reaching as the paperback revolution is to be expected in the near future seems doubtful, though certainly in the storing of material in libraries and in the whole area of photocopying and reprographic machinery new developments are likely. Video-tapes are already being used quite extensively, and research involving film archives requires new techniques and kit.

But such devices (I am thinking, of course, of arts and social sciences) supplement rather than replace books, except in special areas of research. The postgraduate student who now spends a large part of his time manipulating various forms of mechanical and electrical apparatus in a library does not yet see these as an overall alternative to books and it seems doubtful whether he ever will. In the Open University, where we shall be using radio, television and tapes on a scale not previously envisaged in this country, our aim is to encourage students to read more books fruitfully, not to provide something better than books. It is not our intention that the media should become the message. The extent to which they modify the message is of course an open question.

On the other hand, it is clear that the *status* of books, the sorts produced, the way they are used, the actual part they play in our educational processes—these have changed considerably, and it would be surprising if there were not further, and perhaps more radical changes.

So much discussion of the higher education "explosion" takes place simply in terms of the universities that it is as well to remind ourselves that not more than half of the students in Britain in fact go to universities. I do not make this point in order to play down the importance either of the universities or the arts and social science faculties. It is obviously a highly significant fact in what is often referred to as a technological age that a very large section, if not the majority of self-conscious, young intellectuals—the schoolboys and girls as well as university students—who are most interested in ideas, most adventurous and critical in their thinking, should be attracted to the arts and social science faculties rather than to those of science and technology. It is they who to a large extent set the intellectual tone and trends—including the political activity—of the universities and, in certain respects, of students as a whole. I do not want to write them off as in any sense an atypical minority—let alone a lunatic fringe. Often they articulate the thoughts and emotions of very, very large sections of their generation. But I do not think one is likely to see the higher education explosion objectively or get its significance right, if one thinks of it primarily in terms of Oxbridge or LSE—important as those institutions are. (ICSA)

5. The following passage from *The Listener* contains about 600 words. Using reported speech, write a précis in no more than 220 words. At the end of the précis state the number of words you have used.

There's no established institution which now feels adequate to the challenges

VII. SUMMARISING INFORMATION

which confront it. Institutions which were developed in the late years of the 19th and the early years of the 20th century find themselves threatened by complex changes that are now under way.

The Church in its various denominational guises experiences pressures for ecumenism, and at the same time pressures for local automony. It has its real estate in the city and its parishioners in the suburbs. There's an urgent demand for moral wisdom which the Church often feels unable to provide. Parochial sects have tended to dissolve in the face of the technologically-induced inroads of secular society, while more cosmopolitan sects seem diluted to the point of having little to offer. Many churchmen feel impelled to engage in battles about poverty and race in the cities, but to the extent that they do so they tend to estrange themselves from the Church.

Universities, too, have found themselves caught among conflicting pressures. Government presses them to adopt new roles, national and regional, for planning, for development, which they're ill-prepared for and which conflict with the traditional ideals of scholarship and liberal education. Students press for a redistribution of power, for education that is more relevant to the world outside the university.

The inventory of threatened institutions caught in the grip of an imperfectly understood instability could be extended in breadth and depth, but enough has been said, perhaps, to show that we're experiencing a general rather than an isolated or peripheral phenomenon.

There are a variety of responses to loss of the stable state. Some of the responses are anti-responses, versions of a refusal to recognise it, and they are destructive in character. One of them takes the form of a return. The idea is: let us return to the last stable state, to the way it used to be. Goldwater in the United States was the political incarnation of that view. Another is the idea of revolt. There is a form of revolutionary response whose war-cry is total rejection of the past, but in such a fashion that the past is permitted to creep in by the back door: where the content of the revolutionary response takes its structure from what it reacts against, with nothing to put in its place, where it takes its direction from established institutions themselves. There is a third kind of response, which is mindlessness. I remember once standing in Little Rock, Arkansas, and watching at night in the square what they did for enjoyment. The kids on motor-cycles would drive round and round the square, the noise was absolutely deafening, and that was amusement in Little Rock. And the message seemed to be: the machine is winning, so why not join it?

Constructive responses to the loss of the stable state must confront the phenomenon directly. They have to do it at the level both of the person and of the institution. If our institutions are threatened with disruption, how can we invent or modify them in such a way that they are capable of transforming themselves without flying apart at the seams. If we are losing stable values and anchors for identity, how do we preserve self-respect while in the process of change?

There is also the assumption that the stable state means that our society, and all institutions, are in a continuing process of transformation. We cannot expect stable states that will endure even for our lifetimes. We must learn to understand and manage these transformations. We must make the capacity for understanding this integral to ourselves and our institutions.   (ICSA)

VII. SUMMARISING INFORMATION

6. The following passage from *The Times* contains about 600 words. Using reported speech, write a précis in no more than 200 words. At the end of the précis state the number of words you have used.

The diffused belief that it is industry that should be called upon to answer for the rapid degradation of the human environment must stand correction. Undoubtedly, foul concentrations of pollution are found in industrial areas or in large conurbations built around industry or industry supported activities, and they contaminate the air and soil and the running and shoreline waters more than anything else. Litter is found even on the high seas because of the huge volume of minerals and fuels industry moves around the world to keep going.

It is equally true that the industrial establishment claims ever more space for itself and the artifacts it pours out in endless streams, contending for precious land with our other needs, limiting us to small living quarters, and doing irreparable damage to the earth's green mantles and the other forms of life on which, finally, our own depends.

But industry is nothing more than the secular, productive arm of society, whose objectives it must serve. Hence the indictment increasingly uttered against it everywhere is substantially misplaced, and should instead be squarely addressed to society as a whole. This observation does not, of course, imply that industry is without fault. More than often from its dominant position it exploits the defencelessness or credulity of consumers, or excites their collective caprices and weaknesses, paying little heed to the community's real welfare or its health. But these are excesses, and better law enforcement or ombudsman intervention should be enough to curb them.

The point we must understand and analyse resides, however, in the underlying, determining factors of industrial activity—in other words, the motivations and orientations of society. The tragedy is that these motivations and orientations are dissonant with new realities of the world—in the field of environment, and generally.

The prime moving force of modern society, derived in both its capitalistic and socialistic incarnations from the Judaic-Christian tradition, seems to be its basic reliance upon its own scientific, technological and industrial capabilities and achievements, and their further development in the future. This intoxicating self-assurance originates in the belief that man is not part and parcel of nature, but master of the earth, a kingdom that he can exploit at will.

All peoples are thus lured into the mirage of unending economic expansion. The symptoms of this growth syndrome are the glorification and pursuit, above all other values, of the material ones symbolised by gross national products and per capita consumption levels. And its most fearsome consequences—exposed in the recent Massachusetts Institute of Technology report for the Club of Rome—are the steady erosion of the life-supporting capacity of our finite, small, overcrowded and probably already sick planet.

The ecological wisdom and sanity, and hence the capacity of survival, of this human system must be most seriously questioned. After a period of

VII. SUMMARISING INFORMATION 131

phenomenal population and production increase, it is still single-mindedly geared to growth, whereas its vital problems have become problems of equilibrium.

Equilibrium is not stagnation. Just look around. Everywhere in the cycles and systems of life, in our own body, in the forests and the oceans, in the struggle among the species and within them, nothing grows endlessly. When something grows something else decreases, and then some forces or events make it decrease as well and other things emerge, in continual adaptation, reciprocally and with the environment. This dynamic, ever-adjusting equilibrium is the secret and reason of all evolution. Outside it there is only decay and the stillness of death.
(ICSA)

7. Write a précis in not more than 200 words of the following passage from *Systems Analysis for Business and Industrial Problem Solving*, S.L. Optner (Prentice Hall, 1965).

Systems may be categorised through their similarities and dissimilarities. Physical systems deal with hardware, equipment, machinery and, in general, real objects or artifacts. These systems may be contrasted with abstract systems. In the latter, symbols represent attributes of objects that may not be known to exist, except in the mind of the investigator. Concepts, plans, hypotheses, and ideas under investigation may be described as abstract systems.

Within the categories of physical and abstract systems, the on-going process may be seen at many levels. The component processes necessary to the operation of a total system are known as *subsystems*. Subsystems in turn may be further described as more detailed subsystems. The hierarchy of systems or the number of subsystems are dependent only upon the intrinsic complexity of the total system. It is conceivable therefore, that some systems may contain an infinite variety of processes. Conversely, other systems contain a finite, limited number of processes. At each identifiable process the analyst may stimulate a system. Systems may operate simultaneously, in parallel, or in series without any restrictions other than those imposed by design or the real world.

Each system may be said to exist within a specific environment. Systems exist within, and are conditioned by, the environment. The first condition of this environment is the boundary within which the system is said to operate. *Environment* is defined as a set of all objects, within some specific limit, that may conceivably have bearing upon the operation of the system.

The business systems analyst cannot conduct unlimited research in an attempt to understand all conditions that have impact upon system operation. The concept of a *boundary* prescribes a limitation within which the objects, attributes, and their relationships are adequately explained and manageable. Systems and their boundaries may be defined simply if the objects are absolute or finite in nature. Physical systems can be described most conveniently in quantitative, performance terms. Abstract systems, however, may not be as easily defined in finite terms. All systems operate within a given environment and a given boundary.

The study of systems may take one of two basic courses, process analysis, or final outcome analysis. In the first, the system may be studied as a number of intimately related subsystems. This microscopic view of the world generates the process type of analysis. In a process oriented analysis, the analyst defines the intermediate outputs of systems. He then studies the means by which they are introduced into serially-related processes for subsequent processing. In process analysis, there are many alternatives or options that qualify as intermediate solutions. Process analysis is frequently associated with real-world problems and physical systems.

Juxtaposed to process analysis is final-outcome analysis, which provides a macroscopic view. Under this method, the system is treated as a whole. The analyst is more concerned with the overriding, end results than the intermediate results. In outcome-oriented analysis, there is no certain knowledge of all the intermediate outputs. Thus, there may be no means to establish the basis on which all of the processes are united in the total system operation.

The goal of the investigator is to make a model of his system, be it physical or abstract. He further attempts to understand the system as an on-going process, given the objects, attributes, and relationships that are combined in the system operation. The model may be mathematical, if the investigator can apply quantitative properties to his problem. If the problem is both quantitative and qualitative in nature, the model may be less rigorous and be no more complex than a system or data processing flow chart. The model maker seeks to reproduce in some "miniature" or manageable form, the real-world operations of the system under study.

If the model is an accurate replica or representation of the real world, it may be termed special purpose. Special purpose models may be brought to bear upon most problems with some calculable expectation of success. General purpose models approximate the real world with something less than the subjectivity and substantive content of the special purpose model. It follows that solutions derived by general purpose models are general in nature; in the same way, solutions derived by special purpose models are special purpose in nature. Neither are applicable to their opposite category of solutions without carefully stated assumptions.

Systems may be centralised or decentralised. In a centralised system, one element or one major subsystem plays a dominant role that may override the other system components. In this arrangement of systems and subsystems, the major subsystem is central to the operation. The minor subsystems are satellite to the central operation. In a decentralised system, the converse may be true; major subsystems are of approximately equal value. Rather than being arranged around a central subsystem as satellites, the major subsystems are serially arranged. Otherwise they may be arranged in parallel, each providing both unique and isomorphic (superficially similar) outputs. In both centralised and decentralised systems, inputs and outputs may be prescribed. Conceptually, both types of systems may be in existence in the physical and abstract systems categories. (ICSA)

8. Give a clear summary, in about 100 words, of these letters. Supply also a heading in which the names and addresses may be included.

VII. SUMMARISING INFORMATION 133

The All-sure Insurance Company,   23rd November 19 . .
Fenchurch Street,
London, EC3A 7BU

Dear Sirs,

I have been considering taking out some form of life insurance, and it has been suggested to me that an endowment policy would be more advantageous, especially as the the two may be combined.

Would you please send me details of the types of policy you offer and premiums payable?

Yours faithfully,
F.N. Noble

F.N. Noble Esq.,   25th November 19 . .
8 Hitherto Lane,
Smarden,
Kent, SM6 1KE

Dear Sir,

Thank you very much for your enquiry of the 23rd November. For your information we are enclosing a prospectus giving details of the more popular types of life and endowment insurance.

Endowment policies have proved themselves to be an excellent form of saving and of provision in the event of early decease. As you will see, they fall into two main groups—those with bonus and those without.

The premiums payable are dependent upon the age of the insured person on the birthday following the date on which the policy is signed and (in the case of those over the age of forty) upon the result of a medical examination made by a doctor appointed by the Company.

If you require further information please complete and post the enclosed stamped and addressed postcard. Our local agent, to whom it is addressed, will then call upon you and give you any assistance you may require.

Yours faithfully
THE ALL-SURE INSURANCE COMPANY
L. Beeson

The All-sure Insurance Company,   29th November 19 . .
Fenchurch Street,
London, EC3A 7BU

Dear Sirs,

I have completed and am returning the Proposal Form which was attached to the Prospectus you sent to me on 25th November. As you will see, I have decided to take out an endowment policy, with bonus, to mature when I am sixty-five years of age.

As I shall be forty in January, I assume that it will be necessary for me to have a medical examination. If so, will you please arrange this as soon as possible for, naturally, I wish the policy to be completed before the 25th January, which is the date on which my birthday falls.

Yours faithfully,
F.N. Noble

(RSA Stage II—Intermediate, *modified*)

9. Summarise the following letters as briefly as possible, but omitting nothing of importance. Do not exceed 100 words.

WEEKS AND LANE LTD,
18 Moorgate,
London, EC2B 6BU

Messrs J. & W. Firth,　　　　　　　　　　　　　3rd July 19 . .
The Harbour,
Portsmouth, Hants PO5 6HA

CONFIDENTIAL

Dear Sirs,

Mr Edward J. Bright

We have recently interviewed for a position on our staff Mr Edward J. Bright, who tells us that he was employed by you for a period of three years in the capacity of Assistant Sales Manager, at a salary of £10,250 per annum, and that he left you on 31st May in consequence of finding his prospects of advancement blocked in your organisation.

This young man appears to us to possess the qualities which we are seeking, and we are considering appointing him as Sales Manager of a new subsidiary company which we are inaugurating shortly.

We should therefore appreciate it if you would give us in confidence your views on his suitability for such a post, and would at the same time tell us how far you consider he was justified in the attitude which led to his resignation from your firm.

Your comments on his honesty, general reliability, and punctuality would also be greatly valued, and we shall be pleased if at any time we can offer you a similar service in return.

Yours faithfully,
WEEKS AND LANE LTD

VII. SUMMARISING INFORMATION

J. & W. FIRTH,
The Harbour,
Portsmouth, Hants PO5 6HA

Weeks and Lane Ltd,   6th July 19 . .
18 Moorgate,
London, EC2B 6BU

CONFIDENTIAL

Dear Sirs,

Mr Edward J. Bright

We thank you for your letter of 3rd July and have pleasure in giving you the information for which you ask.

Mr Bright was employed by us as Assistant Sales Manager throughout the period which he has stated, and his work was consistently competent and thorough. He came to us with excellent references from his previous employer, and he justified them in every way during the whole of his service with us. His reason for leaving was exactly as he has told you and, while we were very sorry to lose him, we quite understood that, unless we could offer him a better business future, we could not expect to retain him much longer. This is a family firm, and the position of Sales Manager, for which he is by now well qualified by experience as well as by ability, will shortly be in the hands of a member of the family.

You may, therefore, appoint him to the position you suggest with every confidence that he will do all that you require of him. We feel sure that you will find him punctual, loyal, and completely honest, as we have always done, and we wish him every success for the future.

Yours faithfully,
J. & W. FIRTH

WEEKS AND LANE LTD,
18 Moorgate,
London, EC2B 6BU

Messrs J. & W. Firth,   12th July 19 . .
The Harbour,
Portsmouth, Hants PO5 6HA

Dear Sirs,

We are very grateful for your letter of 6th July, and for the valuable information which it contains.

We have interviewed Mr Bright a second time and have decided to appoint him in the light of your remarks. We are asking him to begin work on Monday 16th July.

Yours faithfully,
WEEKS AND LANE LTD

(RSA (STC)—Stage III—Advanced, *modified*)

VII. SUMMARISING INFORMATION

10. Summarise the following letters as briefly as possible, but omitting nothing of importance.

> The Glade,
> Ravens Lane,
> Coptley, Bucks CO8 6BA
> 9th May 19. .

The Manager,
The Queen's Nurseries,
Basildon, Essex, BA7 1ES

Dear Sir,

I have bought plants and seeds from you for several years but, although I have been pleased with the bright colours and large blooms of many of the flowers, none of them in recent months seems to have had any fragrance.

At the back of my present house I have a balcony overlooking the garden about twelve feet above ground level, with approximately forty feet of oak trellis below it. Up this trellis I grow a number of roses, chosen from your last year's catalogue especially for their scent, but there was no fragrance at all.

I wonder whether, in the search for large and colourful blooms, the scent of many of our garden flowers has been lost.

Perhaps you would let me know if there is anything that I can order which you can guarantee will have a rich perfume. I did not receive a catalogue from you this year.

Yours faithfully,
B.A. Brooke

> The Queen's Nurseries,
> Basildon,
> Essex, BA7 1ES
> 12th May 19 . .

Dear Sir,

I am sorry you have had cause to complain about some of the plants bought from our nurseries.

Though it is true that certain flowers have lost the fragrance they once had, many recent introductions have just as much scent as their predecessors and I am quite certain that if you are really searching for subtle or rich perfumes there is no lack of choice.

There are some plants, of course, which are grown for their scent alone and not for their beauty. Notable among these is the half-hardy nicotiana. In my opinion it is an untidy plant and its flowers are not graceful or beautiful, but the scent on a summer's evening especially after rain is really delightful. Even the dwarf varieties have a delicious scent, though it may not be quite so strong. A few of these planted near the house in some remote corner would give you a most fragrant scent.

VII. SUMMARISING INFORMATION 137

Perhaps you would like to try to grow next year under glass a few sweet peas which have more scent than the outdoor ones, and the Clucana lily is one of the most beautiful and fragrant.

I am enclosing my new *Seed Guide* and illustrated *Plant Catalogue*, which you should have received last January. It may be that you did not receive them owing to your change of address, but I shall be pleased to send you any late planting flowers if you will let me know immediately.

Yours faithfully,
B.S. Gold,
The Queen's Nurseries

(RSA (STC)—Stage III Advanced, *modified*)

11. The following passage is taken from "West German Industrial Relations in Action", an article by R.T. Chappell which appeared in *Professional Administration*. It contains about 1,050 words. Write a summary using not more than 300 words.

An extremely important feature of the industrial relations system in West Germany is the existence of a separate legal machine concerned exclusively with employment disputes. The Labour Courts have been operating in Germany since the 1920s and under the present legislation (Labour Courts Act 1953) a three-tier system of local and regional Labour Courts and a Federal Labour Court has been established. The courts consist of a stipendiary magistrate and two or four assessors selected from both sides of industry.

Labour Courts decide on disputes arising from contracts of employment, collective agreements and the operation of the Works Constitution Act; they also have jurisdiction in disputes between individual workers if the disputes have a direct connection with their employment. Ninety per cent of all legal actions concern claims by individual workers against their employers. German workers seem to be much more ready to use the courts to seek redress for their grievances—for one thing they don't share the suspicion of solicitors and others who implement the law that British workers have. The legal procedure is simple in a Labour Court and the fees are lower than those operating in the civil courts.

A worker may represent himself or have the services of his union; if one side uses a lawyer, the other side may automatically be given a lawyer and often no charge will be made.

In the German industrial relations system there is no formal government conciliation service but a valuable element exists in the courts. Judges always seek to bring the parties together to make a settlement—preferably out of court. If no formal judgment is required the parties to the dispute do not incur legal fees and the judge is spared the task of writing a report. Thus in 1971, a total of 31,000 cases were settled in North Rhine Westphalia by 32 local labour courts but fewer than 4,000 cases required a formal judgment.

The Labour Courts are an essential corollary to the German system of legally binding contracts. First, it must be stressed that the German constitution guarantees to every individual and to all trades and professions the right to form associations to safeguard and improve working and economic conditions. This means that everyone has the right to join a trade union or an employers' organisation; conversely everyone has the right not to join an employee or employer association. Thus there is no acceptance of the principle of the closed shop in Germany although there are examples of high membership figures in some branches of industry.

Under the Collective Agreements Act 1949 all agreements made by employers and trade unions are binding on all members of the association on whose behalf their respective organisations have signed the contract. Moreover, on application by either side of the industry the Federal Minister of Labour may extend the legal validity of a collective agreement to cover all employers and employees in one particular industry. When this action is taken the collective agreement has the same force as a law passed by the German parliament.

West Germany has a dual system of collective bargaining: trade union and works council bargaining. Collective agreements between unions and employers are normally negotiated on a local, regional or federal basis for all workers and employers in one particular industry and the bargaining is undertaken by the officers of individual unions. The German equivalent of the TUC, the DGB, has no power to supersede the authority of the separate unions although it does attempt to coordinate bargaining policies.

Union agreements usually lay down minimum wages and working conditions which are often supplemented by plant agreements. These agreements are, however, not negotiated by union officials or by lay representatives as is common in Britain: instead they are made by works councils elected in a secret ballot by all employees of a firm. German unions can of course still be extremely influential in plant negotiations and they usually have little difficulty in securing the election of union members. A union agreement always takes preference over a plant agreement and if the union wishes to do so it can write into the collective agreement all those items normally left to the local plant agreement.

The Federal Constitution guarantees trade unions the right to strike, but they accept the principle that the strike is a last resort and accordingly union rule books are very strict about strike procedure. For example, the secret ballot, one of the controversial elements of the 1971 Industrial Relations Act in Britain, is the essential prerequisite for a German strike. The executive of a union may formally approve a strike only if 75 per cent of the members concerned have voted for industrial action. Moreover, the union must take account of the state of the industry and the economic condition of the country as a whole. In addition, full consideration of the public interest must be given so that hospitals and similar institutions will be excluded from strike action. It should perhaps also be pointed out that a railway strike is virtually unthinkable, because there is an acceptance by the unions that public services should not be disrupted.

Sympathetic or political strikes are not allowed. Industrial action must be directed against the particular employer concerned and may not be extended to other companies. Intimidation by pickets and threats against third parties, as happened during the last miner's strike in Britain, render an otherwise lawful strike illegal.

The stringent rules on strike action imposed by both the Government and the unions are not the distinguishing features of German industrial relations—similar arrangements exist in most industrial countries. Co-determination is the controversial aspect of the German system. The intention to give workers a share in making industrial decisions has its origins in the Weimar Republic Works Council Act of 1920, but the present extensive scheme was set up in 1952 by the Works Constitution Act and has been revised this year.

Works councils must be established for all companies employing more than five workers. Each works council is elected by the workers as a whole and reports to them quarterly. The purpose of works councils is to promote industrial harmony and cooperation and they are given wide powers including the right of approval to the appointment, dismissal and promotion of employees. Disputes are settled by arbitration or reference to Labour Courts.

CHAPTER VIII

REPORT WRITING

In a useful booklet *Report Writing* issued by the British Association for Commercial and Industrial Education, the term "a report" is defined as "a document in which a given problem is examined for the purpose of conveying information, reporting findings, putting forward ideas and, sometimes, making recommendations". The authors think that this definition could be improved by the addition of the words "as the basis for action".

There seems little point in submitting information to management unless it is required. *The Times* once carried a leader on the weight of paper on official and business desks: there can be no doubt that there should be fewer and shorter reports. Our report should not be written unless we have a purpose; if we have a purpose every word and diagram must be chosen so that they help to attain the desired end.

It is customary to classify reports into: *(a)* short reports, and *(b)* formal reports. Perhaps "informal" and "formal" would be better terms of contrast, because the trainee report writer might fall into the error of assuming that formal reports should, like the Bullock Report, exceed two hundred pages. All reports should be kept short.

Another classification distinguishes memoranda from reports. Memoranda are reports initiated by the writer. True reports are those requested by superiors. The layout of reports is similar whether they are requested or as the result of the supervisor's enterprise.

THE INFORMAL REPORT

Structure

The structure of informal reports is simple, and the following sequence is suggested.

1. A statement of the objective of the report.
2. A statement of the facts about the subject being investigated.

3. A presentation of possible solutions, with the advantages and disadvantages of each course clearly indicated.
4. The recommended solution with reasons.
5. The supplementary evidence in appendixes so that the body of the report is not obscured by detail.

This form should be adequate for most reports. For some reports to management we shall not be required to submit recommendations, but merely to provide the evidence. Thus, we may wish to inform our superiors of a conference we have attended or of the significance of a learned paper. It should be remembered that the report may still form the basis of action, because management may decide, for example, after reading a report on a course, not to send supervisors on that course in future.

For the fact-finding report the sequence would be:

1. the purpose;
2. the facts;
3. the conclusions;
4. the appendixes.

Layout

However short the report, it should be broken down into the divisions stated above, so that the reader may easily grasp the meaning of the information given. Reports should not challenge the reader to understand them; they should rather provide a challenge to the writer to write briefly, simply, and clearly.

Headings and sub-headings should be used to give the report an appearance of not being overcrowded. Short paragraphs will at once aid comprehension and make the report look attractive.

Some report writers omit to give a suitable title. A title is most important, because it enables the reader to decide immediately whether the communication deserves prompt attention or whether it may be left until other more urgent correspondence has been considered.

As the informal report is usually submitted as a memorandum, it may be set out in the following manner:

CONFIDENTIAL   1st January 19 . .

From: Mr D. Smith, Personnel Manager.
To: Mr J. Brown, General Manager.
        (Copies to: Mr S. Lee, Chief Accountant
                    Mr W. Long, Office Manager)
        Reference CZ/15/16.

Review of General Office Establishment

Paragraph 1. The terms of reference, viz. the instructions from the General Manager to review the establishment.

Paragraph 2. The increase in departmental work and the overtime worked over, say, the past two years.

Paragraph 3. The choice of continuing with overtime, employing new staff, changing the qualifications of entry to attract better staff, or changing the pattern of work to allow machinery to be used with fewer workers. (This paragraph could extend over perhaps two paragraphs: reference would be made here to the statistics given in the appendixes.)

Paragraph 4. The recommended plan with reasons.

Reports which carry a recommendation for action often result in a change in the company's expenditure. Management must then, always, be given the cost of any proposal. Our superiors will be pleased to learn of any suggestion leading to cost reduction.

Examination questions on report writing usually require an answer of three to five hundred words. The aim of the question is to determine the candidate's ability to present technical information in clear, simple English.

In some examination questions the report is required by the board of directors. The memorandum may then be replaced by the letter, so that the board will be addressed "Gentlemen" and the writer (commonly the secretary) will sign under the complimentary close, "Yours faithfully". Sometimes the question will ask the candidate to prepare a report of a committee. This type of report could begin:

To the members of the Loamshire Education Committee.

Report of the special sub-committee on organisation and methods.

As instructed by Minute No. 256 of 31st December, your committee have examined the report of the preliminary survey by the consultants Jones, Brown and Partners and report as follows:

1. The survey revealed that although during the past four years the work of the authority had increased in two sections (Works and Establishment) the work in the remaining departments had remained steady (Appendix "A" contains a detailed examination of the work of each section).

2. The number of clerical assistants has increased in all sections. During the period surveyed the council reduced the hours of working from 38 to 36, so that a slight general increase in numbers was to be expected in the absence of a reorganisation of clerical work (Appendix "B" gives the establishment of each section for the past five years).

The general report would end with the committee's recommendations, which could be introduced as follows.

Your committee recommend:

1. That the typing pool be combined with that of the health department to provide a typing establishment of 25.

2. That the vacancy for an assistant education officer should not be filled, but that the senior administrative assistant on the further education section

should have a deputy on Grade Scale 6 whose duties would include those of the assistant supplies officer.

That the welfare and supplies section should each have its establishment reduced by two clerical assistants.

4. That the establishment and works sections should each have an additional clerical assistant, and that initially the posts should be filled by the transfer of staff from the welfare and supplies sections.

5. That the two remaining assistants no longer needed in the welfare and supplies sections be allocated to other sections as soon as suitable vacancies arise.

THE FORMAL REPORT

Structure

Formal reports based on a detailed examination of a problem usually require more divisions that the informal report. Formal reports are sometimes so long that the writer provides a summary of recommendations before the evidence. Another method of overcoming the problem of the long report is to produce an abridged version. This solution is appropriate if the report is intended for both the specialist and the layman. Readers will recall that that the Beveridge Report on social insurance was issued in abridged form, so that the evidence and recommendations could be considered by a wide readership. However, the authors wish to reiterate their plea for brevity: brief reports are the ones most likely to succeed as the basis for action.

The usual pattern for the formal report is:

1. title-page;
2. contents page;
3. summary of report or of recommendations;
4. introduction;
5. main part of report;
6. conclusions;
7. recommendations;
8. appendixes;
9. references.

Managements sometimes require reports to follow a different pattern from the one outlined above. For example, some managements may insist that reports have the conclusions and recommendations at the beginning. Others like the conclusions and recommendations to appear at the end of the report, but prefer them to be shown together. In an official report the references are often given as footnotes, rather than in a special section at the end of the report.

VIII. REPORT WRITING

In the absence of any guidance from management, we should follow the usual pattern. We should, however, remember two important points: firstly, the design should enable the report to be presented in the most suitable manner; secondly, the form is not more important than the contents. A well-set-out report with a logically developed argument is useless, unless the facts are provided to support the argument.

Layout

We now examine in greater detail the structure of the formal report.

THE TITLE PAGE

The title page gives the name of the author, the subject of the report, the date of the report, and in most business reports the reference number. In an official report by committees the names of the people responsible for the report may be included in the subject heading, thus:

COMMISSION ON INDUSTRIAL RELATIONS

Report No. 33

Industrial relations training

The title of the report often requires considerable thought, because the title should summarise the report. If the title is too general it may not perform this function. A long title may sometimes be needed; it should be followed by an explanatory sub-title.

Rapid Reading Courses for Business Executives:
Their Scope, Use, and Value

THE CONTENTS PAGE

The contents page is necessary for a long report and will be prepared after the report has been completed. It should refer to the section headings (paragraph headings in a short report) and indicate their importance by indentation or by different types of size of print.

The following page is taken by permission of the Controller, Her Majesty's Stationery Office, from *Report No. 33 of the Commission of Industrial Relations,* 1972:

CONTENTS

		paragraph	page
	The reference		viii
	Preface		viii
	PART A: THE COMMISSION'S APPROACH		
CHAPTER 1.	**The need for industrial relations training**	1	1

	VIII. REPORT WRITING	145	
CHAPTER 2.	The scope and conduct of the reference	12	4
	PART B: THE PROVISION OF TRAINING		
CHAPTER 3.	The current provision		
	the extent of industrial relations training	29	9
	the content of industrial relations training	39	13
	the providers of industrial relations training	44	15
CHAPTER 4.	The recipients of training		
	management generally	57	19
	personnel managers and staff	75	23
	supervisors	81	24
	trade union full-time officers	92	26
	shop stewards	100	28
	joint management/union training	123	33
	employers' association staff	126	34
	other employees	129	35
	young employees	134	36
	conclusion	136	36
	PART C: PROBLEM AREAS IN INDUSTRIAL RELATIONS TRAINING		
CHAPTER 5.	The training programme		
	the identification of training needs	140	38
	the content of training	149	40
	co-ordination between the providers and sponsors of training	158	41
	the evaluation of training	160	42
CHAPTER 6.	Tutors, teaching methods and materials		
	tutors	163	44
	tutor training	171	46
	teaching methods and materials	176	47
CHAPTER 7.	The finance of training	185	49
	PART D: RECOMMENDATIONS		
CHAPTER 8.	Recommendations		
	employers and trade unions	203	52
	employers	218	56
	trade unions	222	57
	employers' associations	226	58
	CBI	228	58
	TUC	229	59
	TUC and CBI	232	59

VIII. REPORT WRITING

ITBs	233	60
the public education service	237	60
examination boards and professional associations	247	62
the education departments of the broadcasting authorities	249	63
Government	250	63
Conclusion	257	64

APPENDICES

1. MINIMUM STANDARDS FOR INDUSTRIAL RELATIONS TRAINING

Senior managers	66
Line managers	67
Supervisors	67
Personnel and industrial relations specialists	67
Shop stewards	68
Employees generally	68

2. TRAINING FOR CHANGE IN INDUSTRIAL RELATIONS

Introduction	69
Step 1: Review the operation of industrial relations	70
Step 2: Agree what changes are needed	72
Step 3: Establish priorities for action and plan the programme of change	73
Step 4: Agree what contribution training can make to the programme of change	73
Step 5: Determine who needs training and what their training needs are	75

3. TRAINING METHODS FOR INDUSTRIAL RELATIONS TRAINING

Deciding training priorities	78
Training methods	78
Teaching methods and materials	80
The provider of training	80
Evaluating industrial relations training	81
Selected bibliography	82

4. DETAILS OF SIX COURSES ORGANISED UNDER THE AUSPICES OF NATIONAL BODIES

TUC basic training course for shop stewards	83
NEBSS certificate in supervisory studies	84
Training Within Industry: job relations course for supervisors	86
Examinations for IPM Membership	87

VIII. REPORT WRITING

	Diploma in Management Studies	89
	Graduate examination for IWSP Membership	90
5.	Survey of places of employment	91
6.	Organisations seen during the inquiry	93

LIST OF TABLES

TABLE 1.	Industrial relations training received in 1970—by category of employee	10
TABLE 2.	The percentage of establishments where some employees received industrial relations training in 1970—by size of establishment	12
TABLE 3.	The content of industrial relations training provided in 1970—by category of recipient	14
TABLE 4.	Organisations providing industrial relations training in 1970—by category of recipient	16

THE SUMMARY OF THE REPORT OR OF THE RECOMMENDATIONS

A summary is useful because some of the people who receive the report are interested in the conclusions or recommendations only. Others may have their interest stimulated by the importance of the conclusions and decide to read the whole report.

A summary of recommendations should contain paragraph references in the main report and the procedure is illustrated by an extract from the summary of recommendations of the Urwick Report on management education, 1947.

> 1. The Committee wishes it to be clearly understood that there is no implication in this Report that young men or women can be trained as managers in industry or commerce by following certain courses of study at Technical or Commercial Colleges. Theoretical study alone cannot make a manager. (Paras. (2)(*c*), 6.)
>
> 2. That action is necessary if multiplication of courses in management is not to dissipate national facilities which are already inadequate. So long as each professional institution requires its own syllabus in this field, this must create difficulties for the teaching institutions. (Paras. 19-23.)
>
> 3. That the professional institutions should accept the obligation to include in their syllabuses as large a common management content as possible and confine specialised demands in this field to the essential minimum. (Para. 27.)
>
> 4. That courses leading to qualifications in management should be limited to two stages, namely, "Intermediate" and "Final". (Paras. 29-35.)
>
> (Reproduced by permission of the Controller, HMSO)

VIII. REPORT WRITING

THE INTRODUCTION

The introduction will say why the report has been written and will indicate the problems examined. In particular, the introduction will give the terms of reference and explain the methods used to obtain information.

The following are the reference, preface and paragraph 21 from Report No. 33 of the Commission on Industrial Relations, 1972, and are reproduced with the permission of the Controller of Her Majesty's Stationery Office.

THE REFERENCE

The Secretary of State for Employment refers to the Commission on Industrial Relations for inquiry and report the facilities for training in industrial relations available to the members and staff of employers' associations and trade unions and to employees generally, including those engaged in management.

NOTE:

The reference was originally received on 29 May 1970, at which time the Commission was established by Royal Warrant. The Commission became a statutory body on 1 November 1971 when Section 120 of the Industrial Relations Act came into force. The Secretary of State for Employment then re-referred the above reference to us on 4 November 1971, under Section 121(1) of the Industrial Relations Act 1971.

PREFACE

This report describes the industrial relations training we found provided in 1970 and 1971. It discusses the need for such training and the various aspects of and providing it. It makes recommendations for improving both the quantity and quality of industrial relations training.

Detailed information and statistics on the amount and nature of industrial relations training being provided is to be given in a separately bound supplement to this report.

A practical guide for unions and employers on planning industrial relations training is published separately. The guide covers the recommendations on planning industrial relations training for the workplace found in Chapter 8 and in Appendices 1, 2 and 3 of this report.

21. Our detailed fieldwork inquiries were mainly carried out in the first half of 1971. One of the notable features of the subject was the paucity of information on the extent and type of industrial relations training being provided. Even in the area of shop steward training, where most research had been undertaken, the extent of industrial relations training provided other than through the TUC scheme was largely unknown. For this reason we felt it necessary to embark on an extensive programme of inquiries. An important part was a postal survey sent to over 6,000 places of employment randomly selected from all establishments (excluding local authorities) in the United Kingdom each employing 100 or more people, representative of approximately 10 million employees in full-time employment. (A similar survey was sent to a sample of local authorities, representative of a further

VIII. REPORT WRITING

1¼ million full-time employees.) With over 60 per cent of the questionnaires returned, the surveys proved to be invaluable sources of information. We were assisted in carrying out the surveys by Social and Community Planning Research. Appendix 5 gives further information on the scope of the surveys, and briefly outlines the methodology used. Full details, and over 80 tables from the surveys, are to be published in the supplement to this report.

The purpose of the introduction is to give a background information. But the reader is interested in the foreground. For this reason introductions should always be brief.

THE BODY OF THE REPORT

The text gives the facts *relevant* to the problem. The writer discusses the facts and comes to certain conclusions. In this part of the report he examines the advantages and disadvantages of following different courses of action. Some writers prefer to make recommendations as they discuss each part of the problem and to summarise the recommendations at the conclusion (or beginning) of the report.

The reader will be helped to follow the development of the thesis if this section of the report is provided with apt headings and subheadings. He will also be helped if the supporting material is not allowed to obscure the solutions presented. For example, in any report the cost of a solution must be given. Cost calculations may be involved, and the writer may wish to include tables of prices. Data of this sort may safely be placed in an appendix, but the writer must ensure that a reference is given in the text.

THE CONCLUSIONS

These are reached from the facts presented in the report. If the conclusions have been given in each sub-section it is useful to provide a summary of conclusions. The summary will be appreciated by those readers who do not wish to read the whole report.

THE RECOMMENDATIONS

Recommendations are made by the author on the basis of the facts and the conclusions drawn from the facts. Recommendations unrelated to the evidence are invalid.

Some report writers provide a separate section headed *Summary of Recommendations* (*see above*) if they have given recommendations in each sub-section. Others give a combined *Summary of Recommendations and Conclusions.* The arguments for and against these practices are less important than the need for the report to be clear and informative.

THE APPENDIXES

The appendixes contain the supporting evidence for the points made in the body of the report. Sometimes the appendixes are used to elaborate on recommendations. Thus the Urwick Report on management education contained four appendixes, two of which set out in detail the proposed syllabuses for intermediate and final examinations in management.

The test to apply on what to put in the appendix is: What will help the reader? Detail tends to obscure the purpose of the report, and the writer who uses an appendix hopes to simplify the body of the report. The use of the appendix, however, causes some inconvenience to the reader. He is required to refer to the back of the report each time he wants further information. For this reason appendixes should not be used for simple statistics and sketches. Moreover, the appendix should always be numbered or lettered, and its reference number or letter should be included in the appropriate sub-section of the report.

THE REFERENCES

These should be given at the end of the report and should include all the books, papers, and reports consulted in compiling the report. Help from other sources should be quoted in the introduction or in footnotes to the page on which the sentence is used.

Writing the report

THE FIRST PAGE

We have now to consider how we should produce our report. We should arrange our material in the order in which we wish to present it in the report. This will enable us to plan the section headings and sub-headings so that our report has a logical development. Our plan will represent a rough draft of the contents page.

Some writers prefer to write the report in the order of the contents page. Others prefer to write the conclusions first and then arrange the body in such a way that the conclusions are supported. The authors think that, although it is not necessary to write the report in the order of the contents, the main part should be written before the conclusions. Moreover, it is useful to draft the introduction so that the report does not afterwards stray from its intended path.

The report should be written with plenty of space for amendment. For this reason, we shall find it a good plan to use one side of the paper only and to have double spacing. A wide margin is helpful for the insertion of correction notes.

CHECKING THE REPORT

Some writers recommend that the first draft should be left for a few days before the correction is made. They argue that this practice enables the author of the report to make a fresh approach to his task. We may not be able to afford the time if our report is required urgently, but we can reduce errors by reading our draft to an assistant who should be given the original copy. We should always have the drafts checked in this way.

Mr W.L.G. Nash has further advice to offer in an informative article entitled "The Presentation of Technical Information", which appeared in the then *Glamorgan College of Technology Mining Society Magazine*. He suggests that we make a deliberate mistake occasionally to keep our assistant awake.

When the draft has been retyped and checked once more it is useful to hand our report to a colleague for his observations. Any comments which he may make can now be embodied in the final draft. Alternatively, we may wish to ask our superior to look at the report critically before it goes to top management. Before the final draft is typed we should ensure that we are sound on three important points. Firstly, we should check that page, paragraph, and section numbers are correct, and that the cross-references are accurate. Secondly, we should satisfy ourselves that we have made no grammatical or spelling errors. Finally, we should be able to affirm that our report does not contain words foreign to the reader.

ILLUSTRATIONS

Illustrations and tables may save several paragraphs of writing, and will therefore help to keep our report short. The problem of where to place these aids to comprehension may be solved in this way: small diagrams which refer to one particular section may be included in the body of the report; large diagrams and tables or diagrams to which reference is made in more than one section may be placed in an appendix. Diagrams and tables should be numbered.

NUMBERING THE REPORT

Government reports adopt the simple system of having the main sections in roman numerals and the paragraphs in arabic numerals. The paragraph numbering is a continuous sequence as follows:

SECTION I
  (1)
  (2)
  (3)
  (4)
SECTION II
  (5)
  (6)
  (7)
SECTION III
  (8)
  (9)
  (10)

Appendixes are numbered alphabetically, and each appendix has its own sequence of numbers, thus:

APPENDIX A
TITLE
   (1)
   (2)
   (3)
   (4)

APPENDIX B
TITLE
   (1)
   (2)
   (3)

Further subdivision within government reports is given by small roman numerals or by letters, thus:

(1) (i)
    (ii)
    (iii)
    (iv)

or

(1)
   (a)
   (b)
   (c)

Reports for business may follow this plan or give a separate sequence for paragraphs within each section. If the second method is adopted we obtain a sequence as follows:

1. THE PRESENT SCHEMES

A. *Salaried Staff Scheme*
   (i)
   (ii)
   (iii)
B. *Manual Staff Scheme*
   (i)
   (ii)

A third method is the decimal system. This system shows the main sections with arabic numerals and the subsections with serial decimal numbers. Further subdivision is shown with another series of decimals, thus:

5 (Main Section)
5.1 (First sub-section of Main Section)
5.1.1 (First subdivision of the first sub-section of Main Section 5)

VIII. REPORT WRITING

Abbreviations

We shall need to use abbreviations in our reports, and our problem will be to ensure that our readers understand our shortened version. Firstly, we must be consistent in our use of abbreviations; otherwise we shall confuse our readers. Secondly, we should always use the full word if the abbreviation is likely to give rise to ambiguity. An illustration of the problem of abbreviation is provided in the letters NUS. The NUS can be the National Union of Seamen or the National Union of Students.

The National Coal Board's *Report Writing Manual* has recommended the adoption of the abbreviations stated in British Standard 1991:(1961-75). The following general principles are taken, with permission, from the board's useful manual.

1. Figures should be grouped in threes, but commas should not be used to separate groups of figures; instead a space should be left in the following manner:

78 293
not 78, 293

2. When writing decimal numbers a "0" should always precede the decimal point

0·239
not ·239

3. The full stop should not be used after an abbreviation unless its omission is likely to cause ambiguity. For example, the abbreviation for litre is l (not l.); but where, in typewritten copy, the "l" is the same as figure one, a full stop can be used to distinguish the abbreviation from the number. Likewise, the abbreviation for inch (or inches) is "in", but a full stop is sometimes necessary for clarity; for example "a gradient of 6 in. in the yard".

4. The solidus (/) should be used in abbreviations for derived units, hence:

feet per second	ft/sec
feet per second per second is	ft/sec^2
	(not ft/sec/sec)

5. The use of the letter "p" denoting per should be discontinued, thus:

Revolution per minute is	rev/min, not r.p.m.
Mile per hour is	mile/h, not m.p.h.
Kilometre per hour	km/h, not k.p.h

6. Abbreviations should not be written in the plural. Thus:

one yard should be written	1 yd
five yards should be written	5 yd, not 5 yds
one pound should be written	1 lb
five pounds should be written	5 lb, not 5 lbs
five litres should be written	5 l, not 5 ls

(The use of "tons" is permissible, since this is not a contraction.)

STYLE

This book has considered in the chapters on the written word, punctuation, and business correspondence the style suitable for business communication. Literary style is unnecessary for reports: simplicity of presentation is vital. Short, simple sentences grouped in short paragraphs which have been properly headed will help the reader to grasp the meaning of our argument. We shall succeed if we develop our argument logically and keep to a minimum the number of words necessary for the presentation of our report. By practising report writing and by studying the reports of other writers we shall develop a satisfactory style.

Finally, we should remember that our report is going to be read by a person, not a calculating machine. To be understood, the report must be written in sentences. The following quotation from *The Times Educational Supplement* illustrates what happens when a report is written in non-sentences.

> **Secondary Modern:** Eight per cent of mathematics teachers are graduates, of 12 per cent having honours degrees; 31 whom two per cent have honours degrees; seven per cent of science teachers are graduates, with none having an honours degree.
>
> **Comprehensive** (two): 35 per cent of mathematics teachers are graduates, with per cent of science teachers are graduates, of whom eight per cent have honours degrees.
>
> (From a report on "Science Teaching Contrasts" in the *Guardian*.)

A NOTE ON QUICKER READING

Quicker reading courses are becoming increasingly popular, and it is necessary to mention them in this book. On both sides of the Atlantic politicians and administrators have taken quicker reading courses in an attempt to keep up with the mounting volume of official reading matter. It was said that President Kennedy could read at the speed of 1,000 words a minute. This speed is four times the average reader's speed, but 500 words a minute is within the reach of most people.

There is another way of tackling the volume of reading matter—to reduce it. Many executives have an excellent rule that reports should not exceed one sheet of foolscap. This principle can be carried further. Managements can provide questionnaires to ensure that subordinates provide them with the information they require. Unfortunately, not all managements review their communications system often enough to discontinue unwanted report forms.

Some managements prefer their supervisors to write reports rather than complete forms. This practice does offer scope for a supervisor's initiative; it may also provide a supervisor with a chance to ramble at length. It is certainly a mistake for management to offer a large sheet of paper for "further comment". The sheet will always be filled.

Although the authors think that stemming the flow of correspondence is more important than trying to read more, they consider that quicker reading techniques can help the manager to be more efficient in his job. The manager must, however, be discriminating in his choice of material.

Extravagant claims have been made for quicker reading. Some American students have asserted their ability to read classical works in twenty minutes. Novels are written to be enjoyed; reports are not. Quicker reading is largely irrelevant to the works of literature: it is highly relevant to business communication.

Basically, quicker reading courses try to cure the faults in reading habits which most people develop in childhood and retain all their lives. These faults are:

1. VOCALISING

The reader says each word in his head. Thus, the speed of reading never goes beyond the speed at which the reader reads aloud. Yet the mind can work at a much faster speed than the mouth.

2. NARROW EYE SPAN

Many of the readers who say each word in the head also read word by word. These readers can with practice take in four or five words with each separate look at the line of the words.

3. LOOKING BACK

Some readers look back at previous phrases although they have perfectly understood the meaning. Probably this habit arises because the mind is not fully occupied and is associated with the next fault of looking for too long.

4. LONG LOOKING TIME

Many readers spend too long looking at each phrase. With practice, this time can be drastically reduced.

Because the mind is capable of accepting information at a fast rate, it is probably distracted by other activities when we read by saying the words. Hence the experts argue that comprehension increases with an increase in reading speed.

Films are often used to present courses designed to improve reading skills, and one of the best known is that produced by Harvard University. The speed of the presentation of phrases prevents vocalising, and the reader cannot look back once the phrase has been shown. Moreover, the reader cannot spend much time on each phrase, as it quickly makes way for the phrase which is to follow.

Lastly, the reader is forced to widen his eye span, because the groups of words are made progressively longer as the film progresses. The set of films gradually builds up to a reading speed of about 500 words a minute. This is double the average reading speed.

For their short courses the authors have successfully used film strips in a projector fitted with a shutter.

Both the film and the film-strip methods are supplemented by reading-speed and comprehension tests on set passages.

It is important that the faster speeds attained in a classroom should be maintained in the office. Managers who attend quicker reading courses should daily practise on office memoranda, newspapers, and technical journals the techniques learnt. If this practice is conscientiously carried out the reading speed will be permanently improved. It is usual for reading speeds to be doubled with little, if any, loss of comprehension.

QUESTIONS

1. Describe in detail what procedure you would follow and what points you would remember when writing a report.

2. As the training officer of a large industrial undertaking you have recently visited the United States and Europe to investigate the training methods used by foreign rival organisations. Write a short report on your findings and recommendations to the general manager.

3. Write a memorandum to your personnel manager advocating the formation of a supervisors' association in your own company. Reference should be made to the objects of the association, its proposed constitution and activities.

4. Write a short memorandum (about 100/150 words) on modern co-operation between employers and employees. It is expected that topical events during the last (say) twelve months will be given consideration. (ICSA)

5. The chairman of your company requires a report for circulation to the board of directors, analysing a recent decline in the company's sales in some directions and also suggesting both reasons for the decline and methods of countering it. As secretary, make the required report. (ICSA)

6. Draft a memorandum to your superior suggesting additions to the employee services. State your reasons and the expected advantages to be obtained.

7. As secretary of the staff social club, you have been asked to arrange a continental holiday. Submit a short report to the social committee giving details of possible holidays which could be arranged at an approximate cost of £250 to each member of the holiday party.

8. As the supervisor of the despatch department of a medium-size firm manufacturing electronic equipment submit a report to your superior on the recent losses from theft. Indicate the action which you have taken to prevent further losses.

VIII. REPORT WRITING

9. The staff manager of a building society has asked you, as local branch manager, to give details of one of your clerks who is being considered for promotion. In about 200 words make your report under the paragraph headings of personal qualifications, previous experience, branch experience, education—including special short courses and qualifications.

10. Write a report to an appropriate person on one of the following.

(a) An accident you have witnessed.

(b) The performance of an apprentice in your department.

(c) The performance of a newly installed piece of machinery or plant with which you are familiar.

11. Write a formal report on the course which you have just completed, bringing out those aspects which have been of particular value. (NEBSS)

CHAPTER IX

COMMITTEES—THEIR VALUE AND GENERAL STRUCTURE

DEVELOPMENT OF THE USE OF COMMITTEES

Many of us find these days that more of our time is spent in attending meetings of various types than in the past. For it would be true to say that organisations everywhere are making increased use of committees to help deal with the problems of management which they encounter. This technique has been adopted for many reasons in recent years. The fundamental cause is that it is very difficult to direct effectively the activities of a large organisation.

In this country, as in most of the industrialised nations of the world, the number of large units has tended to increase. We must not consider that this is entirely a new development, since it originated towards the end of the last century.

Experience in the study of economics as a science in its own right showed that there were many gains to be made as the scale of production increased. A typical example is economy in materials where, say, the cost of patterns can be spread over a larger output. Industry seized advantage of economies such as these, and we have witnessed in this period a growth of large-scale business by amalgamations which have been either by horizontal or vertical integration.

By horizontal integration is meant a combination of separate undertakings operating the same process or closely related processes. The firms in a vertical combine are at different stages of production.

Not unnaturally there has been a similar movement in the field of government. Since the end of the last century we have witnessed an increase in the number of government departments and also in the size of them. Wars and the conditions which existed after them have been major factors in this development. Today most people recognise that the government has a positive part to play in maintaining and improving the country's welfare. The promotion of exports is a notable example at the present time. Moreover, it is widely agreed

IX. COMMITTEES—VALUE AND STRUCTURE

that the government should also do all in its power to promote the growth of industrial and agricultural production.

Those industries which are nationalised contain many, if not all, of the features of other large-scale organisations. Moreover, organisations as diverse as building societies and trade unions are continuing the process of merger. Yet there is a contrary movement to smaller cost-centred units within the enlarged entities, and this reverse process is likely to be accelerated by the increasing use of micro computers which allow more important operating decisions to be made by middle and lower management.

To some extent the problems of the management of the large organisation have tended to become similar in character. Dealing particularly with the subject-matter of this chapter we may say that government departments, nationalised industries, local authorities, and the many large companies have come to use committees to help cope with their management problems to a much greater extent than ever before. The safety regulations under the Health and Safety at Work, etc. Act 1974 allow for the appointment of an estimated 150,000 union-nominated safety officers throughout the private and public sectors. These regulations will also enable unions and employers to agree on arrangements for setting up safety committees at places of work.

Thus, as organisations of many different types have become increasingly complex and people have been employed in a specialist capacity, committees have become necessary. Committees are a method by which the many specialist activities which we find in organisations today can be co-ordinated so that excessive departmentalism can be avoided. All branches of a business can then come to work together as a team with a sense of common purpose.

It has been said that the problem of co-ordination is largely one of communication. For without really effective communication co-ordination is very difficult indeed, if not impossible. It is preferable if co-ordination of the various activities takes place at the earliest possible stage. This ensures that from the very beginning agreement on courses of action is obtained and that development proceeds on the right lines in accordance with the plan. Committees based on sound committee practice have proved to be an effective method of securing this early co-ordination.

Strictly interpreted, a committee is a person or persons to whom limited powers are committed by a parent body. An example of this with which many of us are familiar is the executive committee. This is elected from members at an annual general meeting to deal with its affairs. An account must then be given of its activities at regular intervals.

It is customary today to give the word "committee" a much wider meaning than this. The expression is commonly used in organisations of all types to cover the activities of any group of people who deliberate about certain matters with a view to action.

Yet even if we are prepared to use the word in this sense, there are groups of people who cannot even so be considered as committees. An example here is the staff conference, which is extensively used to ensure effective co-ordination. The conference acts in an advisory or consultative capacity only; the members do not possess any voting power.

Sometimes it is necessary to consider whether or not to set up a committee to deal with a certain matter. Mention may be made of the use of committees in various aspects of personnel management. These committees are becoming more widely used in the selection of staff. In this way every aspect of the applicant's suitability for the post can be reviewed. This is particularly valuable in present-day conditions, where mobility within the organisation is essential.

MODERN COMMITTEE USES

The more recently evolved uses of committees, however, have been associated with the problems of growth. Thus, in very large undertakings the questions of co-ordination and control may be met by setting up management committees usually under the chief executive to deal with the many and diverse matters which arise. A typical example would be a finance committee, the functions of which might well include, in addition to the general control, such items as the provision of liquid capital and the control and investment of reserves. It is generally agreed that the two main functions of management committees are training for management succession—a necessity in these days of rapid technical change—and co-ordination. For example, in the case mentioned above finance would particularly need to be co-ordinated with production and sales if the business were to be successful.

Committees are also used today when a system of budgetary control exists, by means of which all aspects of the business are budgeted for. One of the elements is the setting up of a budgeting committee on which all departments are represented, often by their chief officers. In some of these committees the budgeting officer of the finance department is chairman; in other firms the chief executive is the chairman, the budget officer acting as secretary to the committee. The committee will be responsible for the reconciliation of the budgets submitted by the various departments of the business and also for the smooth operation and control of the budget.

In personnel administration, committees may be used in a variety of ways. Many undertakings have realised the wisdom of preparing a written policy document which would, of course, contain details of the communications policy. Several of these firms have been successful in bringing foremen and shop stewards into their discussions on the document. When this has occurred the companies have appointed a policy drafting committee to consider the details.

Committees are also useful for training purposes in the smaller firms. Here, it is not always possible to adopt the policy of job rotation whereby staff are given the opportunity of working successively in a number of different departments. Committees are used to enable young executives to obtain a broad view of the work of the organisation as a whole and to gain valuable experience of the activities of other departments.

It is, however, not everybody who has the chance in his work to acquire committee experience. But there are fortunately clubs, religious organisations, political groups and professional bodies who are often only too pleased to welcome members who are prepared to spend some of their spare time assisting in the management of their association's affairs.

Readers who lack committee experience are advised to volunteer for service on one of these committees, which from time to time need officers. There is a great deal of useful work waiting to be done on many of these committees. The experience will serve as a practical training for management.

For the purposes of joint consultation committees are, of course, essential. Joint consultation has been considered earlier in the book (*see* Chapter II), and we do not intend at this point to do much more than underline the vital role which these committees play in communications. Some writers go so far as to maintain that joint consultation is the only means by which information can be transmitted effectively today. The joint consultation machinery may well consist of, for example, joint industrial councils, works councils, joint productivity committees, committees for suggestion schemes, works rules committees, disciplinary committee, absentee committee, theft committee, appeal committee, safety committee.

Much more attention should be given to accident prevention. Few people can be aware that in most years Britain, which enjoys a position at the top of the European accident-prevention league table, loses more days in industrial output from industrial accident absences than from strikes. Boys and girls under the age of eighteen years of age are particularly likely to be victims of factory accidents. In factories in this and in other countries where management is alive to the problem special training has taken place.

The British Safety Council is playing a very important part in drawing attention to these industrial hazards. Even so, good communication at all levels is needed to reinforce the measures adopted to minimise the dangers which exist in industry. A safety committee at once provides an effective means of ensuring that the organisation's safety policy is understood and places a measure of responsibility on the representatives of the employees. Moreover, supervisors and employees gain valuable experience in the practice of communication in an atmosphere free from the rancour which often mars other consultative committees.

The following text illustrates the constitution of a typical factory production committee, while Fig. 17 shows its organisation. (Text and illustration by courtesy of Joseph Lucas Limited.)

Specimen constitution for a factory production committee

Objects

The committee will operate in an advisory and consultative capacity and will provide for the following functions:

A direct means of communication between management and all employees.

A basis for constructive co-operation in obtaining—
  (a) The best possible shop efficiency.
  (b) The best possible shop conditions.
  (c) The well-being of all employed in the works.

A channel for discussion and consideration of any other matters concerning employees except those covered in the agreements between the company and the trade unions, such as wage rates and hours of work.

Membership

1. The committee will be known as the Factory Production Committee.
2. Management will be represented on the committee by the chairman, secretary, and up to four other members.
3. Employees will be represented on the committee by ten or more employees' representatives, covering all departments.
4. Election of employees' representatives will take place in January of each year and will be by ballot. Management representatives will be appointed by the management.

Duties

The committee will consider and make recommendations on any matter referred to it, provided such matters come within the scope of the objects.

Sub-committees

The committee may set up temporary or permanent sub-committees to which it may co-opt additional members to enable them to operate effectively.

The committee will elect employees' representatives on the following sub-committees and on any other committees that are from time to time set up.

  Materials sub-committee
    (a) Economy of raw materials
    (b) Economy of maintenance materials

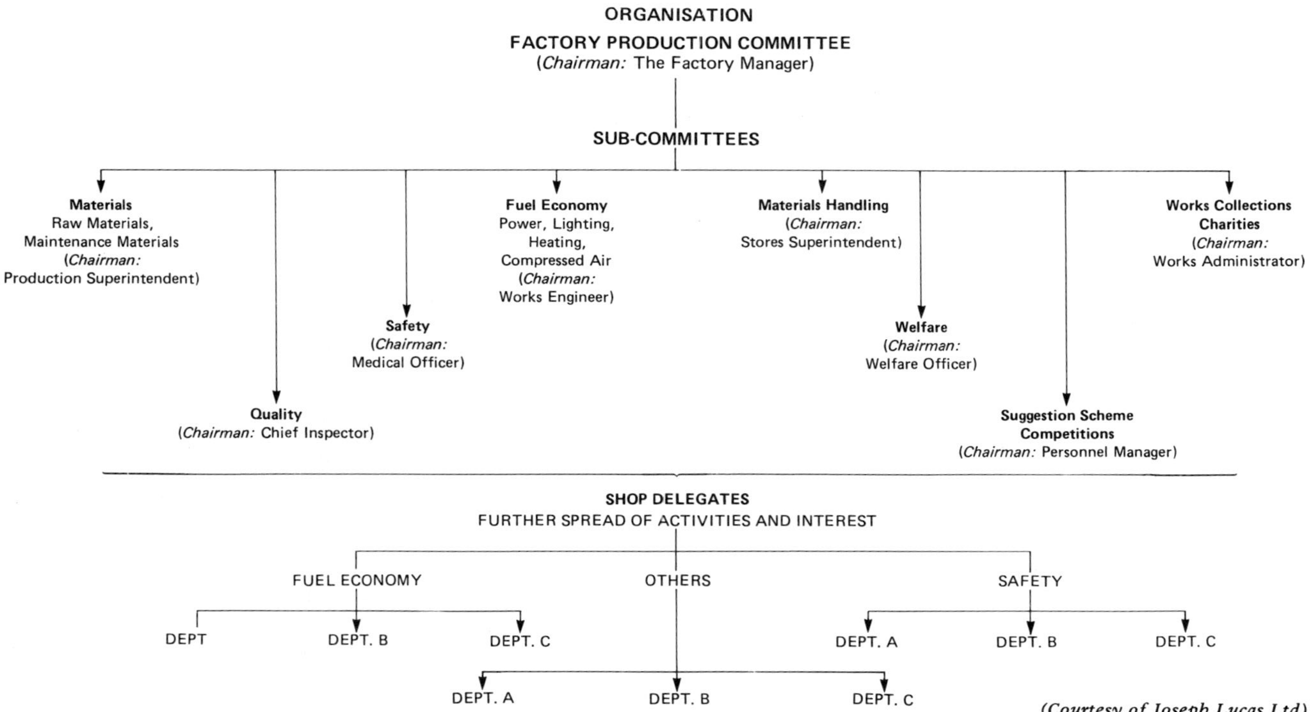

ORGANISATION
FACTORY PRODUCTION COMMITTEE
(*Chairman*: The Factory Manager)

SUB-COMMITTEES

Materials
Raw Materials, Maintenance Materials
(*Chairman*: Production Superintendent)

Quality
(*Chairman*: Chief Inspector)

Safety
(*Chairman*: Medical Officer)

Fuel Economy
Power, Lighting, Heating, Compressed Air
(*Chairman*: Works Engineer)

Materials Handling
(*Chairman*: Stores Superintendent)

Welfare
(*Chairman*: Welfare Officer)

Works Collections Charities
(*Chairman*: Works Administrator)

Suggestion Scheme Competitions
(*Chairman*: Personnel Manager)

SHOP DELEGATES
FURTHER SPREAD OF ACTIVITIES AND INTEREST

FUEL ECONOMY — DEPT, DEPT. B, DEPT. C, DEPT. A

OTHERS — DEPT. B, DEPT. A, DEPT. C

SAFETY — DEPT. B, DEPT. C

Fig. 17. *Organisation of factory production committee.*

(*Courtesy of Joseph Lucas Ltd*)

Quality Sub-committee
Safety Sub-committee
Fuel Economy Sub-committee
　Power, lighting, heating, compressed air, etc.
Materials Handling Sub-committee
Welfare Advisory Sub-committee
Suggestions Scheme Sub-committee
Competitions Sub-committee
Works Collections and Charities Sub-committee

The use of committees by Marconi-Elliot Avionic Systems Ltd

In Chapter II we dealt with joint consultation, and examples were given of the present-day use of committees in several different organisations. The pattern of joint consultation committees adopted by the Marconi-Elliot Avionic Systems Company at Basildon, Essex, was discussed at that point.

There are other meetings held by the company to pass on management decisions. Managers of the two divisions (Aeronautical and Electro Optical Systems) regularly meet production, sales and technical managers and other executives are also in attendance for the senior management financial and project meetings.

Supervisors' discussion groups

Some companies have supervisors' discussion groups. Often the initiative for their formulation comes from the supervisors. Other groups we have known have been formed as the result of the initiative of the management. In the main we have found their function to be educational. Discussions take place about management problems.

Visits are, in addition, arranged to discover how other firms deal with their problems. Some of these visits are confined to a tour of the plant, but many supervisors have found that more useful are those visits which include a discussion of common supervisory problems between the visitors and the supervisors of the host-firm.

Welfare committees

In addition, committees are widely used for the administration of employee services. Under this heading are included such items as the canteen, recreational facilities, and a whole range of welfare services. There are then many opportunities for employees to make their views known. Moreover, managements can use committees to obtain the workers' agreement to new schemes before their introduction.

Committees and horizontal communication

Committees are, however, one of the ways employed by organisations of all types these days in an attempt to prevent a communications breakdown which can have the most serious consequences.

IX. COMMITTEES—VALUE AND STRUCTURE

In some ways the problems raised by the relationships created by line management, that is the "downward" aspect of communications, are less complex than those which arise in horizontal relationships, i.e. between people of comparable status. Here a failure of communications is more easily brought about. A number of ways have been evolved to overcome this difficulty. It may be said, however, that committees generally represent the best solution of maintaining good communications at this level.

THE ADVANTAGES AND DISADVANTAGES OF COMMITTEES

It is useful at this stage to detail the points in favour and also those against the use of committees for the purposes of communications.

Advantages

There are considerable advantages in using committees including the following.

1. People can become expert in certain matters and can in this way sometimes devote a great deal of their attention to affairs for which they have a particular aptitude.

2. Members of committees can bring to bear on the problems discussed a much greater variety of experience than could possibly be possessed by one man. Much useful information can thus be pooled.

3. In the course of the discussions ideas may occur spontaneously to the members which would probably have never arisen but for the meeting. New methods of dealing with a work problem, for example, can be brought forward in this way. Such ideas can have considerable repercussions on the future activities of the organisation. For instance, possible lines of expansion may be suggested.

4. Committees are a way in which men and women, too, are given a chance to make a really worthwhile contribution to the many facets of the organisation in modern conditions. In this way, personnel are brought face to face with the problems involved in such matters as the administration of such employee services as sports facilities. The more enlightened employers give every encouragement to their employees to take part in these affairs.

5. Committees enable managements to find out the reactions of their employees to policies or to proposed policies. The grievances of individuals and groups of individuals can be made known, so that possible causes of friction can be dealt with amicably at an early stage. In this manner, a two-way flow of ideas can be continuously maintained, and joint consultation take place with employees at a formative stage.

6. The interests of the employee can be safeguarded, because he has a representative body to put his case.

Disadvantages

There has been an unfortunate tendency on the part of some managers to assume that when a new communications problem arises the first action to be taken is to form a committee to deal with it. It is vital to recognise, therefore, that there are several serious disadvantages in the use of committees for this purpose, among them the following.

1. Delay in dealing with the issues with which the committee is charged is a common source of criticism. There is at present in all of us the desire to put off making decisions if at all possible. Particularly is this so with committees.

2. It is necessary to give notice of meetings to ensure attendance of a representative selection of members. At times this means that the decisions which have to be made at the meeting cannot be arrived at for some time.

3. At meetings much time can be wasted in irrelevant discussion. The effect of this on the attendance at meetings which are optional is plain for all to see.

4. A final criticism which is frequently put forward is that an extremely knowledgeable or dominant chairman or secretary can, at times, exercise almost dictatorial powers.

Various organisations have used committees to a certain extent in the past. Boards of directors have used them to deal with problems which confront them where such a power is permitted by the articles of association, namely, the rules governing the internal management of a joint-stock company. The functions of the committees so formed are laid down by the parent body. These functions should be determined when the directors appoint the committee.

SIZE OF COMMITTEES AND SUB-COMMITTEES

We have dealt with suggestion schemes in Chapter II, when attention was drawn to the booklet entitled *A Study on Suggestion Schemes* produced by the Nottingham and District Productivity Association. Readers will remember that this sub-committee considered that the number of voting members on a suggestions committee should not be less than three and that it should always be an odd number. In respect of all committees and sub-committees the size is an important factor. The number of members should be sufficient to enable the various points of view to be represented. On the other hand, there should not be so many serving on the committee that discussion on the items drags on indefinitely.

As with committees which are appointed to administer suggestion schemes, it is sometimes desirable for there to be an odd number of members to prevent deadlock. Our legal system contains a

IX. COMMITTEES—VALUE AND STRUCTURE

number of examples of this doctrine. On the side of both civil and criminal law, appeals from lower courts to the Criminal and Civil divisions of the Court of Appeal are usually heard by three judges.

OFFICERS OF COMMITTEES

The officers of a committee usually include a president, vice-president(s), a chairman, an honorary secretary, and an honorary treasurer. Sometimes the president and vice-president do not take an active part in the work of the committee. The officers and members of the committee commonly serve for a fixed time, for example, a year, or for some other period in accordance with the constitution. As we mentioned earlier, it is a very helpful experience to have served on a committee as one of the officers.

An officer is usually aware of many of the difficulties which can be expected to arise at any particular meeting. Preparations can often be made in advance and any necessary information obtained, so that the most effective use can be made of the committee's time. Sometimes the dilemmas which we think will happen are procedural.

Fortunately, a number of very good guides exist to help us with the detailed problems which arise from time to time in the conduct of committee business. It is a sound idea for those of us who are connected with any activities which require a knowledge of committee procedure to possess a copy of one of these books. In this respect *The Law of Meetings* (the Hon. Sir Sebag Shaw, LL.B, and His Honour Judge E. Dennis Smith, LL.M, *The Law of Meetings— Their Conduct and Procedure*, 5th edition, Macdonald & Evans, 1979) can be confidently recommended.

The growing importance of committees as a means of communication makes it imperative that we should deal in this book with the main points which are likely to arise in committee work. Although it is quite often the practice for such meetings to be conducted in a very informal way, unless there is some measure of discipline, fruitful discussion becomes out of the question. Demands on the time of managerial staff are so great these days that it is vital that every minute should be used as profitably as possible.

It thus becomes necessary to have some idea of the rules which are normally applied to the conduct of meetings. Even if not all of us serve as chairmen, secretaries, or one of the officers, we can, as ordinary members, assist greatly in the smooth running of the work of the committee. Should the time come, as well it may, when we find ourselves involved in more responsible duties, the background knowledge and experience will be invaluable. Although the precise procedures adopted will clearly vary over the very wide range of committees which will be used for the purposes of communications, the fundamental conduct which is employed is more or less similar.

QUESTIONS

1. What are the main reasons why committees are now more widely used than in the past?

2. Discuss the types of committees which are used in the organisation in which you work.

3. What are the main advantages and disadvantages of using committees for communication purposes?

4. Discuss the view that the committees are a complete waste of time and that only individuals are able to achieve anything.

CHAPTER X

COMMITTEES—THEIR ORGANISATION AND PROCEDURE

ESSENTIALS OF A VALID MEETING

Occasions will arise in communications work where committees are conducted in a formal way. For a meeting to be validly held in such circumstances three essential conditions must be fulfilled. In the first place the meeting must be properly convened. This means that a proper notice must be issued by persons authorised to do so. They may well be the committee's officers. The proper authority for this purpose will be contained in the rules of the committee.

Secondly, the meeting must be properly constituted. There must be a properly appointed person in the chair and a quorum of members present. The final requisite of a valid meeting is that it must be held in accordance with the rules, governing regulations, or standing orders.

Each of these three conditions will be considered in more detail in the pages which follow, under the general headings of *Notices, The chairman,* and *Procedure.*

NOTICES

It is customary to give notice of the meeting to every person entitled to be present in accordance with the rules for the regulation of the business. This procedure should be followed even when meetings are held on fixed dates, for example, the first Friday in every month, or when members are issued with a year book or schedule of meetings. Unless the practice is made of sending a notice on each occasion, there is always a danger that a change in arrangements, caused, for example, by the absence of the chairman, will not be notified to members.

The notice should be signed by the secretary and should specify the date, time and place of the meeting. Since all of the items may well change from time to time, care must be exercised to ensure that none is omitted from the notice. It is also vital to make sure that the accommodation proposed is in fact available when required, and that it is not being used for some other purpose. Furthermore, the secretary should be at the place of meeting well before the appointed time, so that he can make certain that the seating and other physical arrangements are satisfactory.

Where special business is to be transacted a clear indication should be given in the notice. Where the regulations, as is usually the case, require so many "clear days' notice", the day of service and the day of the meeting are excluded. For example, if the rules specify seven clear days' notice and the notices are issued on 10th November, it is not normally possible to hold the meeting before 19th November. Notice may be waived if all members who are entitled to be present are, in fact, present and agree. Should there be no provision in the rules, seven clear day's notice would be considered to be reasonable.

There is nevertheless an exception which should be mentioned at this point. The regulations may require that certain matters, details of which they will contain, may be considered at meetings of a special type only, or that special notice must be given of the intention to deal with these matters. Where the normal notice is seven days the rules may specify that fourteen days' notice is required for a special meeting or the consideration of special business.

THE CHAIRMAN

HIS ELECTION

Where no person has been selected to act as chairman, the first business of the meeting is to decide who shall occupy the chair. The secretary will usually take the chair briefly while the election of the person to fill that office is taking place. The chairman occupies the central seat, with the secretary usually on his left.

HIS DUTIES

It is customary to say that the chairman has certain duties and powers. The duties of the chairman are as follows:

1. to ensure that his own appointment is in order;
2. to make certain that the meeting is properly constituted and that the quorum is present;
3. to preserve order;
4. to take business in the correct order;
5. to prevent irrelevant discussion;
6. to see that the standing orders (i.e. the rules made to ensure the proper conduct of the business) are observed;

X. COMMITTEES—ORGANISATION AND PROCEDURE

7. to give adequate opportunity to those who wish to speak, subject to condition 5 above;
8. for formal meetings, to allow no discussion unless there is a motion before the meeting;
9. to ascertain the sense of the meeting, and to put motions and amendments in proper order. (*See* the section on motions.)

HIS POWERS

The chairman's powers are usually given as:

1. to maintain order;
2. to order the removal of disorderly persons;
3. to give rulings on points of procedure;
4. to decide points of order;
5. to adjourn the meeting if it is impossible to maintain order;
6. to conduct the business of the meeting, so that the results are made known.

One problem which sometimes arises is whether the chairman has a casting vote. The answer is that only if it is conferred by standing orders has the chairman an additional vote, which he can use in the event of the voting being equal. At common law the chairman has no casting vote.

The chairman is expected to control the debate, and for the sake of emphasis we set out the rules which he should observe. Firstly, he should determine the order of speaking. In general, supporters and opposers of the issue should be given equal opportunity to put their views. Secondly, he should try as far as possible to prevent interruptions to the business of the meeting. Thirdly, points or order, that is, questions raised without notice, drawing attention to any departure from prescribed procedure in debate, should be dealt with promptly. Fourthly, the chairman should see that discussion is relevant to the motion.

The chairman can, of course, help to prevent irrelevance by summing up at various stages the agreement which has been reached. He can also reiterate the arguments for and against the motion. Lastly, where proceedings are formal, members should be allowed to speak only once on each motion. The mover has, however, the right to reply.

The chairman of a committee if he carries out his duties and exercises his powers effectively has no easy task. Chairmanship can be a rewarding function, because in communications work the committee chairman has a vital role to play.

We have discussed elsewhere (*see* Chapter II) the problem of passing information to shop-floor workers. There is often a similar problem confronting committee chairmen. Committee members often do not read their agenda. If the business is to be concluded the chairman must study the agenda carefully *before* the meeting (preferably with the secretary). He will often find it useful to have some ready-made motions drafted, otherwise time will be wasted by the committee on the wording to be used.

PROCEDURE

Preparation and record-keeping

AGENDAS

An agenda has been defined as "a document sent out to all members of a particular body setting out the business proposed to be transacted at a meeting". It is advisable to circulate the agenda with the notice calling the meeting wherever possible.

At one time it was not considered correct to use the word "agenda" for the paper on which was listed the items to be transacted at a meeting. This used to be called an agenda paper. Strictly speaking, too, the word agenda is the plural of the Latin word *agendum*. Present-day English usage, however, permits us to speak of "agendas" and also to use the word "agenda" for the document listing things to be done at the meeting.

There are many advantages of having an agenda for committees. For example, if notice is given to members of the business to be transacted they will have an opportunity of considering the matters, so that they will be prepared for the discussion at the meeting. Moreover, the wording of the items on the agenda will aid the preparation of the minutes. Often the alteration of a few words to change them to the past tense is all that is necessary to prepare the minutes. A further advantage of an agenda is that it ensures that no item is overlooked.

Even when it is not convenient for some reason or another to circulate the agenda to members before the meeting, a copy should be prepared for the chairman to facilitate the business to be considered.

Secretaries with experience seem to acquire their own systems for collecting items to appear on the agenda, which should, of course, be drawn up in full consultation with the chairman. A good plan for the preparation of an agenda is to keep a box file for each committee, in which to keep papers or notes of matters to be dealt with.

The agenda will set out the order of the business to be transacted. Items which are included cover the following:

1. appointment of chairman (unless there is a regular chairman);
2. approval of minutes of previous meeting;
3. correspondence (if any);

X. COMMITTEES—ORGANISATION AND PROCEDURE

4. reports of committees, sub-committees, and officers;
5. finance business;
6. any special business to be considered (details should be given);
7. motions of which notice has been given;
8. general business;
9. date of next meeting;
10. any other business.

Some authorities recommend that it is unwise to include more than one item on the agenda on which there is likely to be a great deal of discussion. It will not, of course, always be possible to adopt this principle, but we consider that it is sound advice, for there will always be matters which will benefit from a full and frank exchange of view. Hasty and ill-considered decisions, which are the bane of any committee's existence, can in this way be kept at the minimum.

It is often the practice for other documents to be sent with the agenda, for example, statistical summaries of various types. The precise nature of this information will depend usually on the wishes of members as expressed at previous meetings. There is a tendency for members to call for reports and information to be prepared, and then to give them scant attention at a later meeting. Much valuable time is also spent on preparing regular reports, often of a statistical kind, which could be presented more effectively in other ways, for example, chart form. Since the question of the usual visual methods adopted to present information is dealt with in Chapter I, we do not intend covering this aspect of communications again here.

NOTE TAKING AT COMMITTEES

It is also necessary for the secretary to evolve a plan for recording his notes, for it will not only be necessary to refer to them when the minutes are being prepared but also at some later stage if any question arises about the business which was transacted at the meeting.

Some secretaries of committees like to have single-sided copies of the agenda and other documents sent to the members pasted into a stiff-backed A4 notebook. The right-handed pages should be left blank so that notes can be made of the proceedings at the meetings. This method has several advantages. For example, a fairly full note can be taken on a particularly contentious matter. An alternative way is for the secretary to make his notes on the agenda paper itself.

The notes taken at the meeting will be of the briefest type commensurate with accuracy. The secretary also usually keeps a folder which contains his agendas over a period of time and a copy of the minutes of the meeting. One of the present writers was secretary to a committee at one time where one of the members was himself in the habit of preserving agendas and minutes in this way. Moreover, the member used to bring them with him to meetings in case a query was raised. Needless to say, this had the effect of keeping the secretary on his toes at all times.

Motions

Strictly speaking, a motion is a proposal moved at a meeting, that is, one that is for discussion and later decision. If the motion is voted upon and agreed it becomes a resolution. We find, however, that the words "motion" and "resolution" are used by many people to mean the same thing. In fact, the Companies Acts use the word "resolution" in both senses.

It is desirable that all business should be introduced to the committee by way of a "motion". In formal procedure a motion should be proposed and seconded (where necessary to conform to the orders, rules, etc.). Nevertheless, it is quite permissible in committee work for the chairman to put a proposal to the meeting without proposer or seconder. At meetings of shareholders, for instance, it is not essential that motions should be seconded unless so provided by the articles of association, the regulations of the internal management of the company.

Rules frequently lay down that motions should be in writing signed by the mover, and be handed to the chairman or secretary (or clerk). It is essential that motions should be within the powers of the meeting, and also relevant to the purpose for which the meeting was called. Due notice as provided by the orders, rules, etc., must be given of the proposal to consider the motion. The consent of the meeting is normally necessary before a motion is dropped. At the end of the mover's speech the motion is normally put to the gathering commencing with the word "That . . ."

Sometimes members of a committee, because of other legitimate demands on their time, are unable to be present throughout the whole of the meeting, much as they would like to be able so to do. In such circumstances, they time their attendance, in the light of their previous experience of the committee's work, so that they can take part in the discussion of the items about which they hold particularly strong views. It is for this reason that motions should be considered in the order in which they are set out on the agenda, unless the meeting decides otherwise.

As the result of the discussion the meeting may decide to accept or reject the motion it has had under consideration. But the deliberations of the meeting may be interrupted by raising a point of order, an amendment, or moving what is called a formal motion, for example, the closure. A point of order may be raised without notice with the object of calling attention to any departure from the prescribed procedure in debate.

X. COMMITTEES—ORGANISATION AND PROCEDURE

AMENDMENTS

An amendment is a proposed alteration to a motion. The regulations normally provide that it is open to any member other than the proposer and seconder of the motion to move or second an amendment to it. The effect of an amendment may be either:

1. to omit or insert or add certain words to the motion; or
2. to omit certain words and to insert other words.

Amendments to motions have a habit of reducing meetings to chaos, and a few principles may be of assistance at this point in the chapter.

Amendments should be as brief as possible, and no amendment should be accepted which is irrelevant or inconsistent with an amendment which has been previously adopted. An amendment should also not be a mere negative, since the mover of the amendment could secure the result he wishes to obtain by voting against the original motion.

An amendment which has been moved (and seconded if necessary) should not be withdrawn without the consent of the meeting. A single motion may be the subject of a number of amendments. In this case, the amendments should be put to the meeting in the order in which they affect the main motion. Should an amendment be carried, the original motion is altered accordingly and put as what is called the substantive motion. The substantive motion may be further amended. It is the usual practice that the mover of an amendment has no right of reply and that no person is permitted to move or second more than one amendment to any one motion.

If amendments are allowed to be moved to amendments the result can be very confusing. Should the chairman consider that the amendment is generally acceptable, the mover of the amendment should be invited to vary it. Alternatively, if the particular amendment is rejected it is possible for a further amendment to be moved in its stead.

After the final amendment has been put to the vote the chairman should dispose of the substantive motion. Should the substantive motion not be passed, the original motion is not revived.

RECISSION OF RESOLUTIONS

A resolution cannot be rescinded at the meeting at which it is adopted or at any other adjournment of that meeting.

It may be possible for a resolution at a meeting to be passed rescinding matters transacted at a previous meeting. Whether such a rescission can be validly effected or not depends upon the circumstances.

We must be guided by the regulations which govern the proceedings. If specific provision is made for the rescission of resolutions, the prescribed procedure must be stringently observed or the purported rescission will be ineffective.

FORMAL MOTIONS

We intend including a few remarks about formal motions, since these are sometimes raised even when the rules of debate are not strictly applied. Formal motions concern the conduct of business of the committee. They need not be in writing, nor is notice required of the intention to move such a motion. The chairman has discretion to accept or reject the previous question, closure, or "that the meeting do consider the next business". There is also a fourth formal motion "that the meeting be adjourned".

The form of the previous question is "that the question be not now put". It may be moved only when the main motion is under consideration and by a person who has not spoken on the main question. If carried the main question cannot be put again at that meeting, although it may be brought forward at a future meeting. If the previous question is lost the main question must be put to the committee at once.

The form of the closure which is sometimes confused with the previous question is "that the question be now put". This formal motion, which may be moved upon a main question or an amendment, has the object of curtailing discussion. If the closure is carried the question is put to the vote at once; if it is lost, discussion on the original motion or amendment continues. As indicated earlier, the chairman has power to refuse such a proposition.

A motion "that committee proceed to the next business" can also be raised against a main question or an amendment. As a rule, no discussion is permitted on such a motion. Should the "next business" be carried, the committee proceeds to consider the next item on its agenda. On the other hand, if the committee decides not to proceed to the next business the rules usually lay down that a similar motion may not be raised until a fixed time has elapsed.

Methods of voting

Often it will be possible to reach agreement without the necessity of taking a vote. Clearly there is a great advantage in being able to do this. Too great an emphasis upon the different points of view should be avoided in communication. Indeed, we consider that the feeling of there being "two sides" in industry whose views and interests are diametrically opposite is outmoded. Other bodies, too, have realised the danger of stressing differences in opinion. Readers will, for example, be aware that at the meetings of the British cabinet votes are seldom taken.

On occasion, however, it will be necessary to ascertain the feeling

X. COMMITTEES—ORGANISATION AND PROCEDURE

of a meeting on a matter before it. There are seven main methods of voting.

1. *By acquiescence.* Members present agree with the suggestion by clapping.
2. *By voice.* Supporters say "aye" and opponents "nay" and the chairman declares the result. This is, of course, not a very precise way of finding out the views of the meeting. The method is used only when there can be no doubt of the decision.
3. *By show of hands.* Members present have usually one vote each under most regulations.
4. *By division.* Members divide themselves and file into different rooms or lobbies. They are then counted by tellers, one or two being appointed for each side of the motion. This method is followed in the Houses of Parliament.
5. *By poll.* The demand for this, which is a common law right, must be made immediately the decision on a show of hands is given. It is up to the chairman to decide whether the poll is taken immediately or at a later date. The result of the voting by show of hands is abandoned. The normal method of voting by poll is for every member entitled to vote to sign a paper headed "For" and "Against" the motion. The rules or regulations lay down the number of votes to which members are entitled.
6. *By ballot.* Each member drops a paper into a ballot box indicating his choice. Bodies with widespread membership often have provision in their rules for postal ballots.
7. *By proxy.* Where voting is allowed by proxy a member may appoint another person to attend meetings and vote on his behalf. The term "proxy" is also used to mean the proxy paper itself by which the person is appointed.

It is necessary for the regulations of the body to contain provision for the appointment of proxies if this right is to exist, since there is no common law right for members to appoint others to act and vote for them at meetings.

Any other business

The item "any other business" should not be taken as the opportunity to raise matters for which proper notice should have been given. Typical items which are permitted under this heading are urgent important questions which have suddenly arisen and minor items which are not mentioned on the agenda. It is at this stage of the agenda that the chairman can indicate his worth, for he should be careful what business he accepts for discussion. Consideration of items which are important but not urgent must be left until the next regular meeting of the committee. Some items raised under "any other business" will need to be considered by other agencies, for example, sub-committees or special (or *ad hoc*) committees of the parent body.

A sub-committee is appointed by an ordinary committee to deal with some special aspect of the business on its behalf. The recommendations of the sub-committee require to be ratified by the committee in question. A special (or *ad hoc*) committee, on the other hand, is one which is appointed for a particular purpose. In some cases it will be constituted of all the members of the parent body with power to act, whereas a sub-committee usually consists of part only of the members of the committee.

Adjournment

Some experts on the question of committees consider that, if possible, a meeting should never be adjourned, but should continue its deliberations until the whole of its business has been completed. The reason for this is that there is always present among the most efficiently conducted committees a tendency to avoid coming to grips with the problem. At times we all defer making decisions, hoping that in the meantime the circumstances will change and that the difficulty will resolve itself. Readers will remember that we have already referred to this point in dealing with the disadvantages of committees.

Occasions will, however, arise when it becomes necessary to adopt such a procedure. The chairman has no power to do this against the wishes of the majority of the meeting. If the meeting consents, the chairman may adjourn under special powers if they are given to him by the rules. When the meeting is so disorderly that business cannot be transacted the chairman may also adjourn the proceedings. A final possibility of adjournment occurs when there is a failure to make or keep a quorum, i.e. the minimum number of members whose presence is necessary for the valid transaction of business.

Although the adjourned meeting is merely part of the original one, notice of the adjournment should be sent to all members entitled to attend.

Unless due notice has been given, no fresh business may be brought up. The usual procedure for the purpose of minuting is that only one set of minutes is prepared for both the original and adjourned meeting.

In practice, occasions will arise where, even at the start of the adjourned meeting despite all the most determined efforts of the officers in the meantime, a quorum is not present. Sometimes the best plan is to explain the difficulty to the members and suggest that routine business should be dealt with in the hope that enough members will eventually arrive so that the proceedings can be regularised.

It may be necessary for important and urgent business to be transacted when a quorum is not present. There is no difficulty if the next meeting of the committee confirms the action taken, as is invariably the case when the chairman and vice-chairman are experienced and aware of the views of the members on the issues of the day. One method often adopted when day-to-day decisions have to be made on behalf of committees which meet infrequently is for the chairman to consult the more influential members when necessary. In this way when there is any doubt in the minds of the chairman and vice-chairman about the probable reaction of members a few minutes' discussion with their colleagues will confirm or modify their first reactions.

MINUTES

Minutes are a concise record of the decisions reached at a meeting and of the business transacted.

From this definition it follows that the set of minutes which is normally prepared after each meeting is not a report of a meeting. Therefore, the writing up of the minutes will not normally record summaries of the views of the various members of the committee who took part in the debate.

It is usual when taking over the position of minuting secretary to follow the procedure which it has been customary to adopt in the past, and to improve upon it in the light of the experience gained. For instance, quite often it will be found that the minute of each resolution contains the name of the proposer and seconder (if any). Generally, there is not great advantage in conforming to this procedure except where business is done by formal resolution.

In matters like these, any standing orders there may be serve as a guide. For example, it may be essential for the voting strength of the two parties to be recorded in the minutes by virtue of the regulations governing the procedure. Occasionally, the situation will arise where a member asks for his name to be recorded as having voted for or against a particular matter. This request will, of course, be accepted.

Minutes should be headed with the name of the committee and indicate where and when the meeting was held. The minutes should, as far as possible, be concise, impartial, precise, and free from any ambiguity.

They should state only the names of those present, the business done, and decisions made. Particular care should be taken to ensure that credit is given for attendance, as this is the first (and sometimes the only!) item at which members glance when they receive their copies of the minutes.

X. COMMITTEES—ORGANISATION AND PROCEDURE

It is sometimes difficult to decide upon the amount of detail to be included. The two main factors which determine this are the normal practice of the body in question and the prevailing circumstances. Sufficient information should be contained in the minutes so that they are of real use for reference purposes. The exact matter which was considered should be clearly stated. If, for example, the plan of an intended new building was under discussion full information of the proposed site, plan number (in case there are subsequent revisions), estimated cost, and materials to be used would probably be relevant, and also details of any modifications to the plan which the committee considered necessary. Similarly, where contracts and appointments are being dealt with, sufficient details must be given to identify the subject-matter precisely.

Most regulations covering the conduct of procedure provide that the minutes signed by the chairman of the meeting, or of the next succeeding meeting, are prima facie but not conclusive evidence of what happened at the meeting. Minutes are usually read at the next meeting, unless they have previously been circulated to members. If the meeting approves the minutes as being an accurate record of the proceedings they are signed by the chairman.

Any correction should be initialled by the chairman or referred to in the minute recording the signing, as below.

> The minutes of the last meeting were confirmed and signed by the chairman, subject to the inclusion of the name of Mr R.W. Brown in the list of members appointed as a special sub-committee to consider the plans of the proposed new sports pavilion (see Minute 182.)

It is not possible to alter the minutes after they have been signed by the chairman. Should it be desired to alter a decision, a new resolution should be passed. Mention should nevertheless be made of the fact that it is usual to have a rule that no resolution which has been rejected shall be brought up again for a certain period from the date of its earlier rejection. Sometimes it is possible for previous resolutions to be cancelled or varied. If it becomes apparent that an unwise decision has been made, the sooner it is reversed the better.

As indicated earlier, the minutes should be a complete and accurate record of the business done at the meeting to which they refer. Great care should always be taken to check that no item is omitted. It is advisable where minutes pass through a number of hands before they are finally approved for a complete check to be made at the final stage.

Apart from the more obvious errors of grammar, spelling and punctuation, which should be guarded against rigorously, the numbering of minutes themselves and any subdivisions within the minutes

X. COMMITTEES—ORGANISATION AND PROCEDURE

merit careful attention. It is too easy for a typist or a printer to omit a minute completely, and a final check of the numbering is a worthwhile safeguard.

It is essential for the minutes to be indexed and for the index to be kept up to date. Much time will be saved if this work is carried out systematically. It will then be possible to trace any decision with the least possible delay. Readers who encounter any problems about indexing are advised to consult a suitable reference work, for example, G. Norman Knight, *Indexing, The Art of: A Guide to the Indexing of Books and Periodicals*. There are a number of methods of indexing minutes. We consider that the balance of advantage lies with numbering them consecutively throughout the minute book. The items are then indexed under the subject headings referring to the minute numbers. Where necessary, cross-references should be made.

CONCLUSION

In this book we have devoted two chapters to committees as a method of communications, their uses, and the procedure which it is customary to follow so that they can function effectively. It is necessary to deal with these matters because the use of committees in communications work has increased a great deal. Moreover, in the constant search for methods of promoting better industrial understanding, committees will be formed to an even greater extent in the future.

It is necessary, however, to end this section of the book with a word of warning. We ourselves have been required to attend over the years far too many meetings, most of which have lasted far too long. Committee meetings should not be called immediately a fresh problem presents itself.

Their usefulness is limited, and many assume the air of social gatherings. But, having said this, we must admit that in communications work the committee can, by pooling the knowledge possessed by a number of people with varied experience, help to secure face-to-face agreement. Committees can also be of considerable assistance in bringing about a sense of common purpose throughout an organisation.

Few of the more complicated devices, which are being gradually introduced into organisations today to achieve a similar object, are as successful in attaining the desired ends.

QUESTIONS

1. Outline the duties of the secretary of a committee.
2. You are a member of a committee which is conducted on fairly informal

lines. You consider that it would be an advantage for members to have notice of the detailed matters which come up for consideration. At the moment few of the members agree with your view. Prepare a written memorandum in which your arguments are presented.

3. Consider the advantages and disadvantages of supporting the appointment of the person who is a good chairman, but has no very decided views of his own, to the chairmanship of an important committee.

4. Draft the agenda for a meeting of any committee of which you are a member.

5. Prepare the minutes of the meeting mentioned in Question 4.

CHAPTER XI

ASPECTS OF EXTERNAL COMMUNICATIONS

INTRODUCTION

Some writers think that communication in organisations of all types is exclusively an internal matter; that the function of communication is to control. Control in a management sense usually means to ensure that the instruction issued, or the plan of operation, has been carried into effect.

Control of an organisation thus becomes a major way in which co-ordination is brought about. This applies whether budgetary control, that is, the system by which all aspects of the business of an organisation are budgeted in advance, is used or not. Control thus comprises the unification and co-ordination of the various units in an enterprise. This is not merely through a vertical chain of command from superior to subordinate; it also includes horizontal co-ordination, i.e. the linking together of people of comparable status in the different branches of an organisation.

We consider, however, that to argue that communication is only a matter of control is to take far too narrow a view of this subject. To our way of thinking the external aspect of communication is at least of equal importance. By the external aspect of communication we mean all matters affecting the firm's or company's reputation in the outside world. We have covered elsewhere in the book several ways in which the organisation's reputation can be enhanced, but in this chapter we would like to deal in a little detail with one or two other important methods of external communication, including the use of the telephone and public relations.

USE OF TELEPHONES

The telephone is widely used in organisations today to enable business to be carried out without the necessity of a personal meeting. Most of us find it a great advantage to be able to communicate in this way, especially where speed is important. We should, however, bear in mind at all times that the telephone conveys rapidly an impression of the efficiency or otherwise of any person or undertaking. Letters do, of course, have a similar effect.

Yet despite its widespread adoption as a means of communication, there is very little written about the subject of the use of the telephone for business purposes. We are glad, therefore, to have this chance of mentioning an inexpensive booklet called *A Guide to the Use of the Telephone in Business,* published by the British Association for Commercial and Industrial Education.

The reason for the increased use of the telephone by undertakings of all kinds is not difficult to discover. Business letters are costly to write and take a certain amount of time. There is therefore a tendency for many of us to prefer to use the telephone. It does not always follow, however, that telephone conversations save time. Often it is not possible to make contact with the person desired; numbers may be engaged. A call may well take longer than dictating a letter, and this point should constantly be borne in mind by executives.

Greater attention is now paid than previously to the various aspects of business management. Yet oddly enough there is a widespread disregard of the damage to an otherwise efficient organisation that bad telephone habits can cause. Any member of an organisation who makes or receives a telephone call at any time has an opportunity of influencing the attitude of the caller, and no one more so that the telephone operator.

Telephone operators should be carefully selected and trained. It is a very poor organisation indeed which puts its least-able employee on its switchboard. The telephone operator is usually regarded by callers as the representative of the entire organisation and is able easily to create an incorrect impression of its efficiency.

The booklet mentioned earlier in this chapter wisely draws attention to the fact that the essential qualities of the telephone operator, in addition to verbal intelligibility, are speed, courtesy, accuracy, discretion and resourcefulness. These points should be taken into account when we are selecting operators.

It is, of course, possible for potential operators to attend a training school for telephonists. Training for telephone operators can also be given within the company. This should be the rule rather than the exception.

In business time is money. Frequently a great deal of time can well be wasted and confusion caused because people taking calls do not at the outset make clear to the caller who is answering the telephone. If we are operating a switchboard or otherwise answering incoming calls we should announce the name of the business or its

XI. EXTERNAL COMMUNICATIONS

telephone number. If we are receiving calls through an extension line we should similarly let the caller know our name or the name of our department or section.

We are all guilty of bad telephone habits at times, and we should do our best to avoid them. For example, members of staff, even senior ones, should be encouraged to think before lifting the telephone and to make those calls that are essential at off-period rates. A good system is to list on a piece of paper beforehand the points to be raised and to have at hand any documents or files to which reference may have to be made in the course of the conversation. Otherwise the discussion may drift on and no agreement on all essential points be made before the telephone conversation comes to an end. It is useful to request information to be telephoned back, as much time and money is wasted while people wait for details to be found in central filing systems.

Telephone conversations should be brief, consistent with making ourselves clearly understood. We should try to cultivate this habit. It does not mean that we need to be abrupt and discourteous. Business telephone conversations are always made for some purpose. It is therefore useful at the end of a telephone conversation to summarise the points on which agreement has been reached.

We do not apologise for stressing the fact that courtesy is very important in all forms of communication. This is especially important when using the telephone, because it is often difficult to correct an initial bad impression, however innocently this may have been created. With personal interviews it is frequently possible to make amends if we have inadvertently said the wrong thing, but with other forms of communication we must be constantly on our guard. Good telephone manners are imperative!

Sometimes telephone queries arise as the result of a letter. On other occasions the reply, being needed urgently, may be by a telephone call. We have found it extremely helpful to ensure that all outgoing correspondence carries the writer's telephone extension. For large organisations this is essential, but even the medium or small-sized company can benefit considerably by adopting this practice.

Not only is caution necessary in the selection of telephone operators; other employees who use the telephone constantly should be carefully chosen. In some departments and sections the most junior member is given the task of answering all incoming calls. This is not a sound practice. The inexperience of the newcomer, however willing he or she may be to help, usually creates a very poor impression of the company. The more junior members should gain their experience first by answering calls on the internal telephone system before they have an opportunity of taking calls from people outside the organisation. Even so, sectional heads should give instructions on how to take a call and also test from time to time the performance of all the members of their staff.

Many aspects of the use of the telephone are a potential cause of trouble. A frequent source of harm and loss of goodwill is the transferring of incoming telephone calls from one extension to another. We are all familiar with the frustration which is caused to us when, on telephoning a large organisation, nobody seems to know who, exactly, is dealing with the matter. Often we get so annoyed that we slam the receiver down and write a letter. Frequently, however, we take this lack of efficiency as being typical of the company and place our order elsewhere. The golden rule is never to transfer an incoming call unless this is absolutely necessary. Often it is possible to deal with the query or to take a note of the caller's name and address and telephone number. As with many other management matters, staff training is fundamental. Where communication is good within a company the necessity of transferring incoming calls to other departments or sections should not be frequent.

Another difficulty which often arises stems from the use of the telephone for personal calls. It is important that the policy of the organisation about private external calls should be made clear. We have known organisations where the switchboard was sometimes jammed with private calls; we have also known others where, even when it was essential to get in touch with a member urgently on a private matter, it was very difficult for contact to be made. Probably the best system to follow is that the use of the company's lines for private calls should not be allowed except in an emergency. We do not wish to be dogmatic about this point, however, since other solutions have been found to be more practical in some companies.

The use of the telephone as a means of communication both internally and externally is bound to increase greatly in the years ahead. In fact, some technical colleges have run part-time courses on the use of the telephone for those who are shy or nervous when confronted by the instrument. Students of all ages have come forward to make use of the facilities provided, and the Post Office and British Telecom officials have co-operated in this important work.

Many people lack confidence when speaking on the telephone, and confidence does not always come with continued practice. Experience has shown that, probably because of this lack of confidence, many people talk too much when they are telephoning. The Post Office and British Telecom have undoubtedly helped the cause of communication in a management sense by the maintenance of lower rates of charges for brief telephone calls.

It will be essential at times when using the telephone to identify a letter, and it is desirable for all members of the organisation to use

XI. EXTERNAL COMMUNICATIONS

the Post Office alphabetical code which is reproduced below.

A for Alfred	J for Jack	S for Samuel
B for Benjamin	K for King	T for Tommy
C for Charlie	L for London	U for Uncle
D for David	M for Mary	V for Victor
E for Edward	N for Nellie	W for William
F for Frederick	O for Oliver	X for X-ray
G for George	P for Peter	Y for Yellow
H for Harry	Q for Queen	Z for Zebra
I for Isaac	R for Robert	

PUBLIC RELATIONS

The Institute of Public Relations has defined public relations as the deliberate, planned and sustained effort to establish and maintain mutual understanding between an organisation and its public. Textbooks dealing with this subject in depth offer a range of definitions, and interested readers can consult a readable work by Herbert Lloyd entitled *Public Relations*.

Relationships with customers and prospective customers can be improved by the use of good public relations. All those who have these contacts, either directly, for example, salesmen, or indirectly, for example, correspondents, have the responsibility of promoting the goodwill of the undertaking. Most companies these days insist that their employees should conduct themselves in all their dealings with the public as if they were rendering a service. It is a shortsighted policy to carry on a business with the sole object of making as much money as quickly as possible. The smaller customer should be treated with as much courtesy as those who submit large orders.

We should remember that to be able to provide an efficient service to customers implies a complete knowledge of the products which the company makes or the services which it provides. All employees should be trained on this principle.

Relationships should also be sound with the suppliers, who will inevitably give the company better service than they will give to those firms who are not so concerned with public relations.

An organisation, too, makes an impact on the market it serves. This impact can result from the advertising material, the quality of its products, its after-sales service, the concern for the amenities of the areas in which its buildings are sited, and the conduct of its employees. We do not exclude international markets. Many of our companies have a profound influence abroad.

The relationships with employees have been covered elsewhere in this book, in particular in Chapter I. We have argued that modern workers, educated to a higher standard than their predecessors, would wish to know far more about the policies and balance sheets of their organisations.

Public-relations work is therefore as necessary for government departments, nationalised industries, and local authorities as it is for businesses large and small. Trade associations and trade unions, too, devote some of their resources to the public-relations aspects of their activities. Most organisations will upon request supply details of their products or services.

We cannot list in this book the many sources of information. Telephone directories (especially those for the London area) are, of course, a useful means of finding the addresses and telephone numbers of likely sources of facts.

In teaching and writing we have on many occasions been extremely thankful for the help which has been given to us in our quest for up-to-date information. We are able to cite a useful example of good public relations work undertaken by the Dunlop organisation. A well-produced booklet published by Dunlop is readily available for educational purposes, and among the items covered in this publication are the history of the company, its capital structure, the products manufactured, home factories, raw materials, selling, research, and personnel.

Some large companies charge specialist officers with a great deal of the work of external communications. For example, there may be a public relations or information officer through whom the information about the enterprise's work is co-ordinated. It is obviously wise that all material given to the press should, where possible, be handled in this way. On the other hand, it is as well to remember that each individual employee is an ambassador of his company. Glossy brochures are not the only or necessarily the best form of external communication.

Complaints

Customers with complaints should be treated with the utmost care and courtesy. Customer satisfaction must be the aim at all times: we should avoid adopting an aggressive attitude. On the other hand, we must not be too timid.

The first step is to secure all the necessary information about the complaint. For instance, the customer's name and address, the date of purchase, the exact nature of the complaint and what the customer wants done regarding the complaint. Thus, depending upon the circumstances, the customer may require a replacement, redelivery, credit, refund of cash or he may wish only to register the complaint.

Each organisation should have its own rules regarding the handling of complaints. If the complaint is justified, we should admit it. Customers, as a rule, do not wish to create too much fuss. We should not attack manufacturers, wholesalers or other organisations even if they may be in the wrong. Above all, we should show the customer that we are interested and wish to help.

We can expect that complaints will not be limited to the late or wrong delivery of goods. Customers may also complain of lack of service, poor service, or incivility on the part of the staff and may wish to inform the management. If complaints are not handled efficiently, loss of trade may be a direct result and the tone and standing of the organisation may suffer as well.

Some companies have found that an entirely new approach to the reduction of customer dissatisfaction may result from the introduction of a job enrichment programme. Thus a laundry in north-west London has abolished the complaints department and has given the responsibility for customer relations to the work groups undertaking the laundry tasks. Customers are notified of the names of the employees who have laundered the articles and are encouraged to speak directly to members of the group. Originally the job enrichment programme was designed to reduce labour turnover: this it has achieved but a significant by-product has been the improvement in customer relations.

Open days

THE VALUE OF OPEN DAYS

As professional educationalists and parents, too, for that matter, we have frequently been impressed by the value for communications purposes of having "open days" in schools and other educational institutions. On such occasions it is possible for everybody to gain a clear idea of what the school or college is endeavouring to do. All present, including the students and staff it must be confessed, learn a great deal in this way.

It has thus been very interesting for us to see that some firms are now instituting an "open day". In this way it becomes possible for members of the general public, including shareholders of the company, to see something of the developments which have taken place.

Open days combine both internal and external aspects of communication, for the wives and other members of the family of employees can also have the opportunity to see for themselves the conditions in which the employees work. Thus, in the long run it can be of a considerable advantage for there to be an awareness in the *homes* of people who are employed that the job is really worth while and that the company is performing a useful function for society as a whole.

Finally, the employees themselves have a wonderful chance of learning of the valuable work which goes on in other departments of the organisation. After all, one of the difficulties which good communication seeks to overcome is excessive departmentalism. All too often we consider that the work we are doing is of paramount importance and that performed by others in the organisation is of much less value. "Open days" are thus a way of enhancing pride in the job and also in the firm. We often hear reports of such "open days" which have proved extremely popular. In one recent interesting example ticket applications from the employees of one of the divisions of a very large company were so numerous that in the end it became necessary for the premises to be "open" on four separate occasions.

It seems to us that, in attempting to solve their communications problems, managements will want more and more to organise "open days" and small exhibitions of this type. We are not thinking of large shows, which may be handled professionally, but smaller affairs, which have to be staged from time to time and put on by members of the organisation.

Many "open days" and exhibitions which are organised by experienced non-professionals are extremely successful. We think therefore that it may be helpful to set out for readers a few hints which have proved useful to us.

HINTS ON ORGANISING EXHIBITIONS

In planning an exhibition or an "open day" it is essential to know in advance the amount of space which will be available. The type of audience and the purpose of the exhibition should be known to the organiser from the start. It is clearly important to be aware whether the people visiting the exhibition will be technically minded or if they will be members of the general public.

Advertising and publicity should be arranged at an early stage so that intended members of the audience can reserve the date. Early arrangements should also be made with any other companies and organisations who are co-operating, for example, in presenting exhibits. Celebrities who may be speaking or opening the proceedings should also be approached at an early stage to ensure that they will be available. Photographs may need to be taken early so that they can be incorporated in the publicity.

One of the essentials of success for every exhibition or "open day" is that everybody should see as much of the exhibition as possible. Brochures detailing the exhibits should therefore be prepared and made available for every member of the proposed audience. Outside exhibitors, too, should be encouraged to provide handouts and leaflets.

Screens are invaluable for displaying exhibits. They may also be used to separate parts of the exhibition from one another. Moreover, they can indicate the route to be followed by the visitors.

When the general layout has been decided an adequate supply of signs should be prepared. This is very important, and it is advisable

XI. EXTERNAL COMMUNICATIONS

for an independent check to be made just before the exhibition commences to make sure that there is sufficient signposting. Visitors will also appreciate a clear indication of the cloakroom arrangements.

Where possible, effective use can be made of visual aids. For example, enlarged newspaper reproductions, animated diagrams (especially if self-operated), and automatic slide projectors are all tried methods of providing interesting exhibits.

Conferences

In organising a conference we must give personal attention to every detail.

We must be clear about the objectives of the conference we are holding. In deciding on the date for our conference we should check that it does not clash with any other known function to which our potential audience may be invited.

We should then allocate a budget for the conference and fix a venue and time.

At this point we should draw up a guest list and order and send out the invitations.

When the replies have been received, it may be possible to invite additional guests.

We should arrange the catering, check the parking facilities and send out the journey instructions which should normally include a site map and advice on travel routes.

Arrangements must be made for the speeches and we should prepare adequate notes for our speakers (speech preparation is dealt with in Chapter III).

We shall often need to arrange for the press and a photographer to be present although some of our conferences will be organised for our own management and may deal with confidential policy matters. If the conference is open we should ensure that the press representatives are properly briefed and given copies of press releases and speeches.

If we are arranging a large open conference we should check the public address system and acoustics, the toilet and the cloakroom facilities. We must ensure that the staffing is adequate and that staff have name badges.

Most organisers provide a visitors' book and produce a list of acceptances to hand to each guest.

A staff briefing is a final preliminary to a successful conference.

Advertising

Whatever form advertising takes, its main function is communication. We cannot be content to wait for customers to come to us: we must go out of our way to attract custom by constantly advertising our goods and services and by publicising our business.

There are various ways in which we may do this and the following are the main methods.

1. Branding and pre-packing of goods.
2. Cinema advertising.
3. Circulars and catalogues.
4. Door-to-door canvassing.
5. Exhibitions.
6. Free samples and gift vouchers.
7. Mechanical advertisements and electrical signs, etc.
8. Posters, e.g. on walls, in transport vehicles.
9. Press, including periodicals and house magazines.
10. Television and radio programmes.
11. Window dressing and interior display.
12. Point-of-sale announcements made in supermarkets and departmental stores.

When companies advertise in the press they usually provide a key to identify the source of the response and thus to assess the effectiveness of the advertisements placed. The method most commonly used is to insert in any coupon in the advertisement a code letter which identifies the publication together with figures which give either a serial number for the insertion or better still the date, month and year.

When readers are reluctant to cut out and use the coupon, the organisation's address can be prefixed by a room number, a departmental number or a named individual and this can be varied for each advertisement.

We sometimes have to deal with some aspect of the company's recruitment advertising. For example, we may be required to draft a classified or display advertisement for a post. The advertising staff of newspapers and periodicals or advertising agencies may be consulted on these occasions, but there are several principles which should be borne in mind.

The advertisement should do the following.

1. *Communicate.* It is essential that the right audience is being addressed. For example, an advertisement for a specialist like an accountant should be inserted in appropriate professional journals.

2. *Produce sufficient replies.* It is useless receiving hundreds of replies if most of the candidates are unsuitable for the post in question. There has obviously been a failure to communicate properly.

3. *Minimise unsuitable applicants.* The advertisement you draft must set out to minimise the number of wasted replies: these create extra work and cause a large number of disappointed and irritated applicants.

4. *Create a continuing image.* The good advertisement can project

a long-term recruitment image. In this way suitable candidates will make contact with the company without waiting for a specific job advertisement to appear.

Press releases
Press releases are used to bring an item of news, which might otherwise pass unnoticed, to the attention of the various news media. To be read and used, the press release, or handout as it is sometimes called, must conform to certain requirements.

Thus, the information must be of interest to that particular publication. It must have news value and be written and presented in an understandable form. Moreover, the information must not be stale. Finally, it must reach the right person.

Ideally, we should prepare a separate press release for each publication and we should adopt the appropriate house style.

When writing and issuing press releases we should ensure that good quality paper is used. The size of press release paper should be A4 (210 mm × 297 mm). Press releases should be typed and duplicated on one side of the paper only. It is the usual practice to provide double spacing between lines and quadruple between paragraphs.

Paragraphs should be short as they always are in popular newspapers. The first paragraph should contain the basic facts of the story. Later ones should expand the theme and give additional information.

If we have a press release which runs to more than one page, we should ensure that we do not divide a paragraph between two pages.

Unless the information is given on the top of the first page of the release, it is usual to conclude as follows:

> For further information
> please contact:
> (name and telephone number).

Every release must carry the date of issue and should indicate when the information may be made public.

Works magazines
As with exhibitions, works magazines provide both an internal and an external channel of communication. They are one of the best ways in which current information about an organisation and its people can be freely and frankly made available. We have studied carefully many different kinds of publications of this type. Some are very simple magazines of a few pages, usually duplicated: other works magazines are much more elaborate and printed and published in a professional manner on good paper.

A very popular type of staff journal is the one produced along the lines of a newspaper. We are great readers of newspapers, and there are therefore sound reasons for adopting this format. Many of the newspapers appear weekly, and this enables management to give up-to-date information to the employees.

Most employees find these magazines not only interesting but also instructive. Where an organisation consists of many groups, departments, or sections, works magazines can prove very helpful for communications purposes. Descriptions are given of the contributions made by the various parts of the organisation, and news is given of the staff working in them. For example, personal news items are always of great interest, and some employees are keen to supply material which may be used.

We do not propose to minimise the detailed work which is inevitable in producing a magazine even of the most simple type. Sometimes it is necessary to decide whether to sell these publications to employees or to give them away. The issue is that people value goods for which they pay. However, if the aim of the journal is to communicate and to help improve labour relations the journal should reach every member of the organisation. By charging for the journal the organisation may exclude from readership those with whom it particularly needs to communicate.

The National Coal Board, with the object of improving its internal communications, has published *Management News*. This is a bulletin for circulation exclusively to managerial staff. Its object is to fill in the background to policy decisions, the reasons behind them, progress in achieving objectives and problems encountered. In this way it is intended that the National Coal Board executives should be able to defend the board against uninformed criticism. This bulletin appears about six times a year and is issued to all managerial staff, including colliery under-managers.

Some magazines are made available to the general public and are usually inexpensive. Some, indeed, like the Halifax Building Society's *Home Owner*, are free and are full of interesting general articles. Another group of magazines caters for industrial customers, and for this type of magazine there may be a nominal charge, although some are free.

Modern industrialisation has created many social problems, one of which is the loss of the sense of belonging among most of the workers. Thus, works magazines have a very worthwhile function to perform in making the employee feel a member of a team and also in giving him back his sense of belonging.

ADVERTISEMENTS FOR COMPANY MEETINGS

A further aspect of external communication is advertisements for company meetings. Most readers will probably be aware that every

XI. EXTERNAL COMMUNICATIONS

company registered under the Companies Acts must hold a general meeting of its members at least once in every calendar year. At the general meeting the directors must lay before the company a profit and loss account and balance sheet. To the balance sheet there must be attached a report by the directors on the state of the company's affairs and the amount, if any, recommended for dividend. It is at the annual general meeting that the election or re-election of the retiring directors and auditors takes place.

It has been the practice for many years for the proceedings at annual company meetings to be reported by the press. More recently, companies have paid for their own reports to be inserted in newspapers. The reports submitted by companies in this way have in the past often been indistinguishable from editorial matter. It is now normal practice for newspapers to print the word "advertisement" above the title "company meeting report" for any company report which could otherwise be confused with editorial matter.

An additional development has been the circulation to shareholders with their notice of the meeting of a printed booklet or folder containing the statement of accounts and director's report.

The principles of good communication which have been discussed elsewhere in this book are in evidence in the design of company meeting advertisements.

Up to a few years ago almost all advertisements of this type were published in a style very similar to editorial matter. Lately, however, much thought has been given to the design of the advertisement. Designed display of company meeting announcements is a relatively new form of advertising. Photographs, diagrams, charts, and a greatly improved layout have all helped to make absent shareholders and the general public aware of a company's achievements.

One danger is that this form of publicity is very costly. Great care must be taken therefore to ensure that the advertisements and booklets are read by the people for whom they are intended.

CONSUMER AND CONSULTATIVE COUNCILS

We have been very surprised to see that recent books have been written about communications without referring to the work of the consumer and consultative councils which have been set up in several of the nationalised industries.

We welcome the opportunity of mentioning the scope of these councils, especially as they have been the subject of criticism. For example, they have been attacked as being unrepresentative of the body of the consumers.

In their plans for the nationalised industries the government in 1945 recognised that the producer and consumer interests covered two separate fields. On the producer side the workers were given full scope through their unions for consultation, details of which are given elsewhere in this book. The consumer's viewpoint was to be safeguarded through the consumer and consultative councils specially established for that purpose.

There is a broad distinction between the *consumer* councils of the coal industry and the consultative councils of electricity, gas, and transport, although the staff of the gas consultative councils style their organisations gas consumer councils.

The functions of the consultative councils are wider than those of the consumer councils. They do not merely provide channels for complaint or for defending the consumers' interest, and it is because of this that their title is *consultative* council rather than consumers' council. They act in a two-way capacity as a channel of communication, first to explain the boards' attitudes and policies to consumers and, in reverse, to convey the consumers' needs and points of view to the boards.

The government had in mind that the councils should provide a democratic machinery in close touch with the requirements of each area, which would enable the consumer to know what is going on and to make his requirements known.

QUESTIONS

1. "External communication is far more important than the internal aspects of communication because it influences turnover." Comment on this statement.

2. Write a short report on how you would select and train a telephone operator.

3. "Public relations should be the responsibility of the public relations department. Everybody else should devote himself to the job for which he is paid." Discuss this view.

4. To what extent do you consider that public relations officers have social responsibilities?

5. "The consumer today is being crushed by big business on the one hand and trade unions on the other. It is true that consumers' consultative councils exist in the nationalised industries, but they are both unknown and ineffective. The consumer needs a new deal and a chance to have his views heard not only by the nationalised industries but also by all companies and businesses." Discuss this point of view and explain how you think that it could best be put into practice.

6. As the managing director of a small company manufacturing consumer goods how would you deal with the various aspects of public relations?

7. The chairman and managing director of a small private company employing about 500 people is considering what special arrangements, if any, should be made to provide adequately for the public relations of the company. Prepare a memorandum which he could put before the other members of the board, outlining the problem, and suggesting how it should be dealt with.

CHAPTER XII

THE TEACHING OF COMMUNICATIONS

We have decided to include in this book a chapter on teaching communications, because this topic forms part of many courses arranged at the present time.

Some of these courses prepare students for formal examinations, such as the Certificate of the National Examinations Board in Supervisory Studies. The bias on these courses is towards the written word, because the examination consists of written papers.

The less-formal courses usually place greater emphasis on the spoken word, because many supervisors and managers who can cope with their piles of paper do not like facing an audience. Courses of this type always arrange practical sessions devoted to public speaking, group leadership, and committee procedure.

At Burton Manor, Wirral, Cheshire, residential short courses are available for supervisors and managers on general aspects of management, but special attention is given to the problems of communications: The course members are allocated to discussion groups, each one of which is given a project. This project gives the group an opportunity of working as a team and affords practice in the art of collecting material and presenting an argument. Moreover, at the end of the course the group secretary has to prepare and submit a report.

The project method is also used at the Electricity Council's residential training college at Horsley Towers, Effingham, Surrey. The value of this method of instruction is that the consideration of a topic can be conducted in depth. Projects are particularly suited to residential courses where the trainers aim to stimulate thought and understanding, but have been widely adopted by companies and colleges offering other types of management courses.

The larger industrial companies have their own residential centres for management training, and we may expect increasing attention to be given to problems of teaching communications.

Much of industry is still organised in small units, and for the smaller firms the courses will probably have to be arranged on their own premises. They may be able to use the services of a few communication specialists, but most of the work will be done by their own managerial staff.

For this reason we shall now discuss the principles of teaching applied to communication.

THE PLACE OF THE FORMAL LECTURE

The lecture is the standard method of teaching all subjects at most universities and many technical colleges. This method is widely criticised by educationalists because there is little contact between lecturer and student.

In its extreme form the lecture method is inappropriate even for academic purposes, and much of the teaching in the newer universities and in the polytechnics takes place in small tutorial groups.

The purpose in teaching communication is to improve the way in which thoughts are communicated, and therefore the formal lecture has little place in the teaching of this subject.

The value of the formal lecture is that we are enabled to convey our message quickly. Informal methods increase both student participation and the time taken to deal with the subject.

There is no reason why the lecture method should not be modified and some informality introduced. Firstly, the lecturer should not try to deal with too many points. Even if the lecturer assumes that the audience have some knowledge of the subject, he should restrict the number of headings to about half a dozen. This principle of the limit of the span of comprehension is also discussed in Chapter III.

Secondly, the lecturer should not devote the whole of the session to his lecture. In a period of an hour the lecture should not exceed forty minutes. The remainder of the time may be spent:

1. questioning the students to find out how much they have learnt from the lecture;
2. inviting questions from the students to clear up any points of difficulty and to enable them to participate;
3. posing several questions for group discussion;
4. requiring the group to do written work based on the lecture.

It is useful to conclude with about five minutes devoted to a summing up of the theme of the session.

Another way in which informality may be introduced into the formal lecture is by the use of teaching aids. Teaching aids are discussed in detail later in this chapter.

In the formal lecture the student should be encouraged to take notes. Time should preferably be set aside for this purpose. Psychologists tell us that we forget half of what we learn within half an hour of hearing it. At the end of a month we are lucky to retain a fifth of the information we are given. The student must therefore keep a record for future reference.

Notes serve other purposes. Firstly, they help to focus attention on the salient points of the lecture. Secondly, they help to consolidate what the student has learnt. Finally, they aid the student to express himself in writing.

The student should always be encouraged to supplement his notes from sources outside the lecture room. He will find it useful to have a loose-leaf notebook, because he will easily be able to relate his own material to the lecturer's.

INFORMAL TEACHING TECHNIQUES

Because the lecture has limitations as a teaching method, informal techniques are widely used. The aim of all informal methods is to involve the student in the activity.

Case studies

The case study may be used for teaching communication. It provides the group with a management problem in which they gain practice in decision making, and oral and written expression. Case studies are designed to bring out management principles.

The Industrial Society have a number of useful film-strip case studies in their catalogue, including one specially devoted to communication problems. Other case studies may be obtained from Cranfield Institute of Technology, Cranfield, Bedfordshire, and the Institution of Industrial Managers, 45 Cardiff Road, Luton, Bedfordshire, LU1 1RQ.

Most firms will have their own case histories which could form the basis of problems for all discussion.

Syndicate work

Case studies are usually conducted by the syndicate method. For this method, the class is divided into groups which provide a variety of experience. Each group has a chairman who is expected to report the finding of his group on the problem they have discussed.

Because the syndicate method enables all members of the class to participate in solving the problem, the method may also be used for other purposes.

Discussions

The function of discussion sessions in communication training is to give practice in oral expression. It is useful for the course supervisor to lead the group in discussion on the first occasion so that the group members may learn the elements of chairmanship. The chairman should prepare a short dissertation on the problem to be discussed and should be careful not to present a biased outline.

He should have a list of headings and questions so that the discussion does not lose direction. Each member of the group should be encouraged to make a contribution, and the chairman should ensure that the ready talkers do not monopolise the discussion.

At the end the chairman should summarise the discussion. The students should take notes of the points made by other speakers. In this way members of the group can make a more effective contribution.

If a series of group discussions is to take place, the course supervisor should arrange for the chairmen and topics to be settled at the first meeting. Talk for its own sake is of little value. The aim should be to encourage informed discussion.

In-tray method

By the in-tray method the students are required to give decisions on communications which appear on their desks. The communication could be a letter of complaint from a dissatisfied customer. The student would draft the terms of the reply to the letter and indicate any other action which he thought necessary to deal with the complaint.

This method may be used to test the group's reaction to a single problem, or it may be used to give each student a different problem to solve.

Opportunities should be given for discussion so that the experience of the group may be pooled.

Lecturettes

In Chapter III we discussed the principles of public speaking. The lecturette is an integral part of any comprehensive communications course.

Course supervisors may have some difficulty in assessing the contributions of members of the group. The best method of criticising lecturettes is to make comments under the following headings:

1. voice;
2. manner;
3. pattern of lecturette;
4. verbal illustration;
5. awareness of audience;
6. any other points e.g. consulting notes, suitability of visual aids.

CRITICISM OF REPORTS

Communications lecturers may find useful the following check list, reproduced, with permission, from the National Coal Board's *Report Writing Manual*:

Structure and layout
(a) Is the title page complete and well laid out?
(b) Is the layout clear and easy to follow?
(c) Are any essential parts of the structure missing?
(d) Are the main parts of the structure in the most suitable order for this report?
(e) Do headings stand out?
(f) Is the numbering of paragraphs uniform?
(g) Are the appendices clear and helpful?

Content
(a) Is the summary or abstract (if included) confined to essentials and a fair statement?
(b) Does the introduction state clearly:
  (i) The subject and purpose of the report?
  (ii) The date of the investigation?
  (iii) By whom the report was written?
  (iv) For whom the report was written?
  (v) The scope of the report.
(c) Does the main part of the report contain all the necessary facts and no unnecessary information?
(d) Is the order of the main part of the report right? Is the problem clearly stated? Does detail obscure the main issue?
(e) Are the sources of facts clear?
(f) Do conclusions follow logically from the facts and their interpretation?
(g) Are possible solutions abandoned without reason?
(h) Are terms used, e.g. abbreviations and symbols, suitable and consistent?
(i) Are there any statements whose meaning is not quite clear?
(j) Are facts, figures, and calculations accurate?

General
(a) Is the report objective?
(b) Are there criticisms which can be made of the report's recommendations?
(c) Is the report efficient and businesslike and likely to create a good impression?
(d) Could a non-technical man directly or indirectly concerned with the report understand it?
(e) Could anyone reasonably take offence at anything in the report?
(f) Is the report positive and constructive?
(g) Does it make clear what decision, if any, is required and by whom?

TEACHING AIDS

Unrelieved lectures do not hold the attention of an audience for long. Teaching aids bring variety to the learning process. In the teaching of communication aids are essential.

XII. TEACHING OF COMMUNICATIONS

We shall deal in this chapter with aids not discussed elsewhere in the book.

Blackboards

The advantage of the blackboard is that arguments and discussion can be summarised. By the use of capital letters and coloured chalks main headings can be emphasised.

Simple diagrams may be drawn to illustrate the talk. More complicated charts and tables can be attached to the blackboard.

The blackboard is a flexible teaching aid, because our argument can be developed step by step and be related to the experience of our students. Moreover, additional information may be added to the existing framework.

If, however, all the blackboard space is filled the student may be confused.

Duplicated notes

To summarise the lesson and to give additional information, lecturers sometimes provide students with duplicated notes. This device is useful when students have limited time for study.

There are serious disadvantages. Firstly, if the student is given the notes at the beginning of the lesson he may pay scant attention to the teacher. The student assumes there is nothing further to learn about the topic.

Secondly, the student will probably not value the notes, since he has not written them himself. Moreover, he may not understand ready-made material so well as his own notes.

The use of cassette-recorders

Cassette-recorders which are now available in many homes are of considerable help in obtaining full value from the spoken word. Many educational institutions, too, are now making a great deal of use of them in their work. The greatest value comes when somebody else is criticising the content and manner in which we have spoken. On the other hand, the benefits to be gained from self-criticism should not be ignored. We are all, fortunately, becoming increasingly aware of good speaking and are able to make self-appraisals.

Often people are unable to recognise their own voices when played back to them for the first time. When we have an opportunity of listening critically to the sound of our own voices we should ask ourselves the following questions.

1. Is the voice pleasant to listen to?
2. Has the pitch been varied to avoid monotony?
3. Are the words pronounced clearly?
4. Is what is said grammatical?

5. Are the vowels given their full value?
6. Are the consonants sounded, especially the final ones?
7. Has the material been put over well?
8. Is the content and delivery good enough to hold the attention of an audience?

The course supervisor, too, will find this list valuable for assessing the contributions.

Often the effectiveness of oral communication can be enhanced considerably by practice. The cassette-recorder is a sound and up-to-date method of improving our oral communication.

Teachers of oral communication should remember that their purpose is to encourage managers to speak effectively. Their aim should not be to turn foremen into BBC announcers. It is important that supervisors should give instructions clearly, and the cassette-recorder will reveal speech faults. These faults should be remedied, but without an attempt to introduce full-scale elocution lessons.

Overhead projector

One of the principles of public speaking requires that the speaker shall maintain contact with his audience. The speaker maintains this contact by looking at his listeners. However, if the speaker decides to use a film or a film strip to support his argument he retires to the back of the room. In this way he destroys the relationship he has established with the audience.

The overhead projector is an attempt to overcome the disadvantage, because the speaker can, throughout his talk, face the audience. Teachers who are good artists will be able to draw useful sketches as the lesson proceeds; others will be able to use prepared diagrams. The overhead projector enables information to be added or erased to suit the development of the lecture. Although many lecturers use the overhead projector as a substitute for the blackboard, the best use for this projector is in large display images of transparencies which can be easily prepared on both wet and dry copying machines. The Thermo-Fax overhead projector is intended for use with the Thermo-Fax copying machine, which produces, in a few seconds, a transparency for the projector.

Students on a communications course should be encouraged to prepare their own diagrams and transparencies for the talks they intend to give. The best encouragement will be the example of the lecturer.

Closed circuit television (CCTV)

Among the more recent teaching aids this has proved to be of unique value in that it enables people to be objective about situations in which they have been deeply involved. The interview, the case-study group, the lecturette, and so on can be recorded and played back either at once or later for constructive comment by a tutor. It is surprising how quickly that people engaged in some activity will forget the presence of the camera. A portable CCTV system may be bought at a modest price. For projects, the discipline of making a simple instructional programme forces the students to be precise and to identify the telling points in a presentation.

Video cassette-recorders and video discs

CCTV equipment has become an invaluable aid in the teaching of communications and in promoting the acquisition of the skills of interviewing, negotiating, and marketing. However, where a trainer wishes to use a television programme to be the basis of a discussion as part of a communications skills programme he may well find the use of a video recorder extremely helpful. Many serious programmes are televised outside normal business hours and the video recorder can be set so that the accompanying cassette records the programme for playing back to the group during the daytime training sessions. The VCR is, of course, helpful not only to groups but to individuals following Open University courses whose associated transmissions often take place very early in the morning.

Video discs and their playback machines, which are increasingly becoming available, offer the means whereby companies can provide material for use by trainers to ensure more uniform standards of accuracy in the transmission of general information, instructions and training programmes. The consensus view seems to be that video discs tend to provide a better quality picture than that given by cassettes but without the advantage of a recording facility. It is asserted too that video discs can be produced at very low cost. Indeed the arguments put forward against the use of video discs and VCRs are similar to those made by the protagonists of audio cassette-recorders and record players.

It will be clear from the discussion of the methods which may be used in teaching communication that the subject is essentially practical. Teachers in the departments of education never tire of telling their students that we learn by doing. The adage certainly applies to the subject of this book. A communications lecturer should set aside ample time for practical periods on report writing, business correspondence, and public speaking.

APPENDIX I

EXAMINATION PAPERS

This appendix gives, with permission of the Institute of Chartered Secretaries and Administrators and the London Chamber of Commerce and Industry, modified question papers which we trust will be found useful by teachers and students alike.

THE INSTITUTE OF CHARTERED SECRETARIES AND ADMINISTRATORS

COMMUNICATION

Six questions only to be attempted. Answer Questions 1 to 4 inclusive and ONLY TWO from Questions 5, 6 and 7.

Time allowed—3 hours

You are advised to spend about 45 minutes on Question 1.

1. Using your own words as far as possible, write a summary of the following passage of about 500 words from Fourth Rivers Lecture given by Lord Hailsham to the Institute and printed in the journal *Professional Administration*. Use not more than 150 words. Supply a title and state the number of words you have used.

> Autonomy is essential to professional status and it is essential as a safeguard to the public which requires in such matters to be protected against shoddy standards and political interference. This autonomy does not limit itself to qualification for entry. It is essential that a profession should be in control of its own special disciplines and professional ethics. Each profession has rules of conduct which are binding on its members. It is of course important that these, too, should not conflict with the generally accepted ethical code to which all are expected to conform, and that all the codes involved should be aimed at the public advantage and not merely the advantage of the profession itself. But the idea that a profession can exist whithout a special code of conduct binding upon its members is not, I think, acceptable. The rule that chartered accountants, barristers, solicitors and doctors in private practice should not advertise, and the various regulations which are made from time to time varying, relaxing, or extending this general prohibition are aimed as much at the

protection of the public against the quack as the protection of the practitioner against unfair competition. The rule that the barrister or the medical consultant does not accept instructions direct from members of the public is to protect the specialised character of the service he provides, and not simply to provide jobs for solicitors or GPs.

If a profession is to be autonomous in respect of its ethical rules, it must be equally autonomous as to its means of enforcement. This is not to say that I necessarily criticise the co-option of lay members on to the Solicitors Disciplinary Committee, or the particular, and publicly promulgated, constitution of that or the General Medical Council. It is important that members of the public should have confidence in the tribunal and that both the profession and the public should be protected. But the general rule should be that the profession itself should declare and police its own rules subject only to overriding considerations of public interest and public policy. In this respect the professions differ from the requirements of industry and commerce where quality control of the product is best assured by competition and advertising and the danger of the quack and charlatan is in general less acute, and where present, should be the subject of legislation.

A third, but essential, ingredient in the continued existence of a profession as such is that the professional should remain independent in his judgment and in the integrity of his advice whether he remains in private practice as a freelance, or whether he operates under a contract of service as part of an industrial or public concern. I imagine that the overwhelming number of chartered secretaries and administrators are so employed. So is an increasing number of solicitors and barristers and so are the doctors employed in hospitals or by the NHS. Chartered engineers and chartered accountants are not characteristically one or the other. Nor are architects. But no employer has the right to ask a salaried professional to prostitute his professional judgment, and his professional association ought always to be prepared to fight for his interest if it is threatened in this respect. *(30 marks)*

2. As secretary of your firm's sports club write *(a)* a formal letter of resignation to the chairman of the club *(b)* an informal and private letter to the chairman, a friend of yours, explaining in more detail why you wish to resign. *(15 marks)*

3. The chairman has asked for a review of the committees operating within your organisation. Write a report on the advantages and drawbacks of these committees and make suggestions for changes you would like to introduce.
(15 marks)

4. Describe the various ways in which the press can be of help to a business or industrial organisation. *(15 marks)*

5. "What matters at an interview is not what is said, but how it is heard." How far do you think that this is true? *(15 marks)*

6. Draft a short talk which, as personnel officer, you would give to a small group of new junior employees on time-keeping. *(15 marks)*

7. What sort of diagrams, charts or tables would you suggest for inclusion in the annual report of an organisation of your choice? *(15 marks)*

APPENDIX I 207

THE INSTITUTE OF CHARTERED SECRETARIES AND ADMINISTRATORS

COMMUNICATION

Six questions only to be attempted. Answer Questions 1 to 4 inclusive and ONLY TWO from Questions 5, 6 and 7.

Time allowed—3 hours

You are advised to spend about 45 minutes on Question 1.

1. Using your own words as far as is possible, write a summary of the following passage of about 500 words from *The Times*. Use not more than 150 words. Supply a title and state the number of words you have used.

The growing awareness of consumer protection issues has focused fresh attention on advertisements and what can and cannot be said in them. It is argued that the consumer buys products on the basis of information contained in advertisements and that the information should be accurate and fairly presented. All sides of the industry are acutely aware that this has not always been the case. The history of advertising is littered with examples of false and misleading statements made in an (often successful) attempt to make people part with their money.

In most developed countries there is legislation to prevent outright dishonesty, and media proprietors, and others on whom some of the stigma inevitably rubs off, see it as in their own best interest to make sure that this is observed. There is however a wide area where advertisements which although not unlawful may be said to harm the consumer in some way, or may be considered undesirable on other grounds such as decency, taste or morals. It is that area which is coming under new scrutiny, especially in Britain. In the past year an existing code of practice agreed by advertisers and advertising agencies as well as by media proprietors has been strengthened. Starting in January a scheme to raise funds by a self-imposed 1 per cent levy on all advertisements except television and radio has come into operation to finance the new measures. Special voluntary regulations for alcoholic drink products have been introduced and a separate tobacco code is expected shortly. In Britain the scheme is administered by the Advertising Standards Authority, which is concerned to see that all advertising should be "legal, decent, honest and truthful". The voluntary regulations operate against a background of legal controls. There are more than 60 laws affecting either advertising in general or specialised areas of it in Britain.

Among the most important is the Trade Description Act 1968, which prohibits false and misleading statements about goods and services, including their cost.

False and misleading statements are also a specific offence under French law whether published copy, visual or spoken word. The officials responsible for verifying infringements are empowered to require advertisers to substantiate their statements. If they cannot, the law makes provision for corrective advertising at the discretion of the judge. It is also forbidden under French law to make any comparisons with competitors' products, since that is seen as an infringement of article 1382 of the civil code which prohibits unfair competition. Neither of these requirements exist in the British controls. In Italy there is a voluntary code of advertising practice approved by the national Federation of Italian Advertisers and modelled on similar lines to that in use in Britain. The German laws on advertising are much more specific and restrictive. It is a legal requirement that advertising statements must be true. In addition advertisements must not refer to competitors either directly or indirectly, in a way that might interfere with the latter's competitive chances.

(30 marks)

2. As personnel officer write a letter of 200 words to the principal of your local college to tell him about a post that will become vacant in your office at the end of the term. Explain the type of work, the conditions of employment, and the qualifications and personal qualities you require. *(15 marks)*

3. Owing to a decline in trading results you find you are unable to give members of your office staff a rise in salary, which they expect to receive. As managing director write a tactful circular letter to explain the firm's position and to mollify the disappointment members of the staff will feel. Indicate in the letter what you think might happen if the increase in salaries were granted. *(15 marks)*

4. You have a friend who has a nervous temperament, is often badly dressed and talks too much. He is both conscientious and hardworking, but lacks self-confidence. He is shortly to go for interview before a selection board. What advice would you give him? *(10 marks)*

5. What is meant by "efficient reading"? What steps should one take to improve one's reading efficiency. *(15 marks)*

6. What is the meaning of *(a)* a bar chart, *(b)* a pie chart, *(c)* a line graph? Illustrate your answers by diagrams and a brief explanation of each example. *(15 marks)*

7. Explain the meaning of the following terms often used at meetings:
   Ad hoc; addendum; casting vote; *ex-officio;* lie on the table; *nem. con.; quorum; sine die; ultra vires;* unanimous. *(15 marks)*

THE INSTITUTE OF CHARTERED SECRETARIES AND ADMINISTRATORS

COMMUNICATION

Six questions only to be attempted. Answer Questions 1 to 4 inclusive and ONLY TWO from Questions 5, 6 and 7.

Time allowed—3 hours

You are advised to spend about 45 minutes on Question 1.

1. Using your own words write a brief report of 150 words based on the following passage of about 500 words from *The Times*. Supply a title and state the number of words you have used.

It was not so long ago that wall to wall carpeting was considered the height of luxury in homes and unheard of in offices. Today, carpets are commonplace in airports, public houses, cinemas, offices and a wide variety of industrial premises. The carpet marketing department of the International Wool Secretariat estimates that over half the floor-coverings sold annually are carpets whereas in 1960 only about a quarter were. About a third of carpet sales today are to industrial users who 20 years ago would not have dreamt of laying carpets outside the boardroom. There are many reasons for industry's growing preference for carpets to smooth linoleum or vinyl floor-coverings. Its sound absorption qualities are appreciated in open-plan offices and typing pools. There are tangible savings in its superior heat insulating properties, to offset the initial cost which is typically double that of its smooth surfaced rivals. Probably the consideration which exerts the biggest influence is that cleaning and maintenance are easier and cheaper. Most smooth floor coverings need four separate treatments—washing, mopping, drying and polishing. A single action, with a vacuum cleaner, suffices for carpet cleaning. The time involved and consequently the all-important wages bill is cut to a fraction. Carpets do have some formidable disadvantages. Good maintenance is probably more important than for any other floor-covering. Embedded grit can drastically shorten the life of a carpet by cutting into the pile and breaking fibres. As a result carpets must be cleaned regularly for economic as well as aesthetic reasons. Carpets also stain more easily than smooth floor surfaces. Oil and grease, if left, may in addition to discolouring the carpet affect the life of the fibres. Different types of carpet fibres react differently from dirt. A recent report examined eight carpet fibres extending from acrylics and modacrylics to wool, testing them for soil and stain resistance and ease of cleaning. Each showed different characteristics but although most had stain resistance, no carpet was stain proof. Periodically (how often depends on how they are used) all carpets need more intensive cleaning treatment than can be given by a vacuum cleaner. A number of cleaning organisations specialise in these treatments. One process uses steam to penetrate deeply into the carpet pile, loosen and extract packed dirt, oil, grease and other substances. The more usual method is a shampoo treatment. There is a variety of special foam-based carpet cleaners that avoid wetting the carpet. To do so can cause the colours to run. The principle is that, once dried, the foam and dirt can be removed from the carpet together.

It is impossible to remove some stains such as cigarette burns or other substances which damage the fibres themselves. In such situations carpet tiles—which can be removed and replaced piecemeal—come into their own. Carpet tiles are fairly new in Britain. Introduced in the 1960s, they are, as their name suggests, squares loosely but firmly fitted. The first carpet tiles had a tough hairy consistency. Since then the ranges have been extended to printed and tufted varieties. *(25 marks)*

2. Write a profile of some 400 words, real or imaginary, of a company secretary or senior administrator. Explain what qualities he possesses and the handicaps he has had to overcome in the course of his career. *(15 marks)*

3. As a safety officer write a report to your chief executive of an accident

that has occurred in your firm because of a breach of safety regulations. Make recommendations which should prevent the recurrence of such an accident. *(15 marks)*

4. You receive a telephone call from a colleague in another office two miles away asking you to direct him to your office through a town. Imagine he wishes to visit you *(a)* at once, *(b)* in two day's time.

You are required:
   (i) for *(a)* above, to set out your immediate telephone instructions in writing;
   (ii) for *(b)* above, to draw a sketch map showing the route, which you will send him by post;
   (iii) explain the advantages and disadvantages of these two methods of communication. *(15 marks)*

5. Give two main aims of a firm's suggestion scheme. Give the main points you would incorporate in a scheme you were asked to devise. *(15 marks)*

6. Explain how you would use a tape recorder in a training session for telephone operators. Which aspects of the job would you emphasise as important? *(15 marks)*

7. What are the main channels of communication that can be used in a large organisation to give information to employees? *(15 marks)*

THE LONDON CHAMBER OF COMMERCE AND INDUSTRY

PRIVATE SECRETARY'S DIPLOMA EXAMINATION

PRIVATE SECRETARIAL PRACTICE
PART I—COMMUNICATIONS

INSTRUCTIONS TO CANDIDATES

Answer all questions.

1. Your company is proposing to move to new office premises in another part of town where transport facilities may be less attractive. This may cause problems for some of the staff. Arrangements are being considered, but meanwhile various rumours have been circulating amongst the staff.

Draft a circular letter from the managing director to all staff which will prevent unnecessary alarm without committing the company to any specific course of action. *(25 marks)*

2. Summarise the following passage in about 120 words:

The swing away from pass-fail school exams began with CSE. From the beginning, this has been a graded exam. Grades range from 1 (equivalent to an O level pass) to 4 (supposed to be the level of the average 16 year-old) and 5 (worse than that, but showing some achievement) with an "unclassified" certificate for rock-bottom entries (which has meant under 10 per cent of the total). In 1974, it similarly became impossible to "fail" O level, which became a graded exam too. Grade 3 is the equivalent of a bare pass, 1 and 2 are above that, 4 and 5 beneath a pass, with an unclassified certificate below that. So the stage would seem set for the kind of merger the Schools Council proposes, into one new Certificate of Education (Foundation) exam, with three grades above the old GCE pass mark, four below (equivalent to the four lowest CSE grades), with an unclassified certificate for the rump.

The trouble is that the ability range to be covered by such an exam system would be enormous. Already, with the school-leaving age raised to 16, the proportion of children taking CSE and O level in English and maths goes well beyond the top 60 per cent of the ability range for which those exams are supposed to cater, and the new exam is to be no more restrictive. Examining boards have been experimenting with different ways of making the exam all things to all pupils of all abilities, stretching the able without daunting the below-average, but the problems are clearly formidable. And there is another complication. The schools Council is busy designing a completely new exam, for which the CSE boards have reported great demand, for "new" (which means less academic) sixth-formers: the Certificate of Extended Education, for which trial papers were taken this Summer.

The CEE is designed for 17 year-olds for whom A levels are an improbable target and O level unsuitable. But CEE is also to be a graded exam. Its grade 3 was also planned to equal CSE grade 1 (i.e. the old O level pass mark and grade 3 of the new Foundation exam. The CEE, unlike the O level, but like the proposed Foundation exam, will have the flexibility of CSE, in that schools would be able either (mode II) to design their own syllabuses for external examination, or even (mode III) to assess their own pupils (monitored by external moderators), as well as (mode I) to follow the traditional externally decreed, externally examined type of syllabus.

The Economist (436 words) (*35 marks*)

3. Answer both parts A and B.

3A. Inflation Accounting is becoming more widespread. Show your ability to understand the subject by answering the questions printed below:

Accounts generally record actual historical market transactions rather than estimated current values. They do not try to reflect the "true worth" of a company. Although accounts have traditionally been prepared on an historical cost basis there is now an increasing desire to allow for the falling value of money over time. A generally conservative approach is a feature of accounting treatment, although companies are increasingly inclined to become more realistic.

(a) Why are the market transactions called "historical"?
(b) In what way do conventional accounts not reflect "true worth"?
(c) Why should there be any need to allow for the falling value of money?
(d) What is the implication of the word "realistic"? (*20 marks*)

3B. Wage statistics have become part of everyday conversation. Show your understanding of the following passage by answering the questions printed below:

Wage rate figures for August 1975, and total wage and salary earnings figures for July 1975 were released by the Department of Employment on Wednesday. The rate of increase of total earnings (which include overtime and shift bonuses) had been running significantly below that of hourly wage rates for some time, due to reductions in overtime working and to increases in rates which simply consolidate earlier gains in bonuses. In the year to July, total wage and salary earnings rose by 27½ per cent— up from a year-on-year rate of 25½ per cent in June, but down from a 28½ per cent rate in May.

(a) Name two factors in total earnings which do not affect hourly wage rates.
(b) Why did the consolidation of bonuses affect the two sets of figures?
(c) In what way did early gains in bonuses affect more recent increases in hourly rates?
(d) In your own words—what happened to wage inflation during the period discussed in this passage? (20 *marks*)

APPENDIX II

SELECT BIBLIOGRAPHY

CHAPTER I
Pitfield, R.R., *Business Organisation*, 2nd edition, Macdonald & Evans, 1982.

CHAPTER II
Whitehead, K., *Industrial Relations*, Teach Yourself Books, 1977.
Bank, John and Jones, Ken, *Worker Directors Speak*, Gower Press, 1977.
Report of the Commission of Enquiry on Industrial Democracy, HMSO, 1977.
Trade Union and Labour Relations Act 1974, HMSO.
Stewart, Margaret, *Employment Conditions in Europe*, Gower Press, 1972.
Drucker, P.F., *The Practice of Management*, Pan Books, 1968.
Morrisey, George L., *Management by Objectives and Results for Business and Industry*, Addison-Wesley, 1977.
Employee Communications Unit, *Communications with People at Work*, Confederation of British Industry, 1978.

CHAPTER III
Shearring, H.A. and Christian, B.C., *Talks and How to Give Them*, Allen & Unwin, 1970.
Tips on Talking, 2nd edition, British Association for Commercial and Industrial Education, 1977.
Roget, *Thesaurus of English Words and Phrases*, Longmans, 1982.

CHAPTER IV
Fowler, H.W., *A Dictionary of Modern English Usage*, 2nd edition, Oxford University Press, 1968.
Moor, Christopher, *Answer the Question*, National Extension College, 1980.
Gowers, Sir Ernest, *The Complete Plain Words*, HMSO, 1973.
Hudson, Kenneth, *The Dictionary of Diseased English*, Macmillan, 1978.
Gardner, John, *People and Communication 3. Students' Book for National Level*, Cassell, 1979.
Wainwright, Gordon R., *People and Communication: A Workbook*, Macdonald & Evans, 1984.

CHAPTER V
Partridge, Eric, *You Have a Point There*, Hamish Hamilton, 1964.

CHAPTER VI
Gartside, L.G., *Modern Business Correspondence*, 4th edition, Macdonald & Evans, 1985.

Dudeney, Charles, A., *A Guide to Executive Re-employment,* Macdonald & Evans, 1980.

A Guide to the Writing of Business Letters, 5th edition, British Association for Commercial and Industrial Education, 1976.

CHAPTER VII

Knight, G. Norman, *Indexing, The Art of: A Guide to the Indexing of Periodicals,* Allen & Unwin, 1979.

CHAPTER VIII

Waldo, Willis H., *Better Report Writing,* 2nd edition, Rheinhold, 1966.

Report Writing, 2nd edition, British Association for Commercial and Industrial Education, 1977.

Report Writing Manual, National Coal Board.

CHAPTERS IX AND X

Perry, P.J.C., *Hours into Minutes,* 4th edition, British Association for Commercial and Industrial Education, 1975.

Shaw, Sir Sebag and Smith, E. Dennis, *The Law of Meetings,* 5th edition, Macdonald & Evans, 1979.

Taylor, H.M. and Mears, A.G., *The Right Way to Conduct Meetings, Conferences and Discussions,* 7th edition, Elliot, 1974.

CHAPTER XI

A Guide to the Use of the Telephone in Business, 9th edition, British Association for Commercial and Industrial Education, 1975.

Lloyd, H., *Teach Yourself Public Relations,* 3rd edition, Hodder & Stoughton, 1978.

Lloyd, Herbert, *Public Relations,* Teach Yourself Books, 1980.

CHAPTER XII

Haney, W.V., *Communication and Organisational Behaviour: Text and Cases,* Irwin, 1967.

Chandler, G., *How to Find Out: A Guide to Sources of Information to All,* Pergamon, 1966.

Parsons, C.J., *Problems in Business Communications,* Edward Arnold, 1977.

INDEX

Abbreviations, 153
Adjournment, 178-9
Advertising, 191
Agenda, 172-3
Any other business, 177-8
Apostrophe, 97-8
Article writing, 81-3
Assignments, 81
Association of Medical Secretaries, 61
Attitude surveys, 18
Authority, principle of, 23

Blackboards, 202
Briefing groups, 38
Bullock Report, 40
Business correspondence, 101-17
   summaries of, 122-4
Business and Technician Education Council (BTEC), 81
Cartograms, 12-13
Case studies, 199
Cassette-recorders, 202-3
Chairman, 170-2
Charts, 9
   bar, 9-10
   compound bar, 9-10
   Gantt, 12
   organisation, 24
   pictograms, 9
   pie, 9
   Z, 10
Closed-circuit television (CCTV), 12, 203-4
Collecting material, 55
Collective bargaining,
   see Joint negotiation
Colon, 92-3
Comma, 89-90
Committees
   advantages and disadvantages of, 165-6
   officers of, 167
   size of, 166-7
Communication
   by silence, 54
   external, 183-96
   full employment and, 6
   horizontal, 48-9, 164-5
   lines of, 18
   methods of, 7-8
   objectives of, 2
   productivity and, 3-4
   scope of, 2-3
   teaching of, 197-204
   training and, 2
   visual methods of, 9-16
Company meeting advertisements, 194-5
Competitions, 45
Complaints, 188-9
Comprehension, 118
Conferences, 191
Consumer and Consultative Councils, 195
Contracts of Employment Act, 6
Curriculum vitae, 116

Dash, 93-4,
Design of forms, 113-14
Dictating machines, 111-12
Diploma for Personal Assistants, 61
Direct speech, 120
Discussion method, 199-200
Drucker, Peter, 18
Duplicated notes, 202

English grammar, 86-9
Essay writing, 75-81
European Economic Community (EEC), 6, 25, 40
Examination technique, 74-5
Exhibitions, 189-90
Extended essays, 80-1

Factory Production Committee, 162-3
Films, 12
Film slides, 12
Film strips, 12, 156, 203
Finding employment, 115
Ford Motor Company, 34-8
Forms, design of, 113-14
Full stop, 91

Glacier Metal Company Ltd., 41-2
Grammatical errors, 86-9
Graphs, 9-11
Grievances, 3, 35-6

Heading of letter, 105-6
Health and Safety at Work, 42

Indexing, 181
Indirect speech, 120
Induction, 2

INDEX

Industrial democracy, 40-2
Industrial Society, 43
Instruction manuals, 115
Instructions, 57-8
Internal communication, 115-16
Interviewing, 58-9
In-tray method, 200
Inverted commas, *see* Quotation marks
Italics, 97

Jargon, 66-7, 110-13
Job applications, 115
Job descriptions, 24-5
Job evaluation, 25-6
Joint consultation
  Coal-mining Industry, 31-4
  Electricity Supply Industry, 27-31
  Ford Motor Company, 34-8
  machinery for, 161
  Marconi-Elliott Avionic Systems Company, 38-9, 164
  meaning of, 26
  Van den Berghs and Jurgens, 39-40
Joint negotiation
  Electricity Supply Industry, 30-1
  Ford Motor Company, 35

Lecturettes, 57, 200
Lecturing, 198-9
Letter writing, 101-14
Listening, 60-1

Management
  by objectives, 18-22
  evolution of, 4-5
  functional, 22
  line, 17-18
  meaning of, 5
Maps, 12
Marconi-Elliott Avionic Systems Company, 38-9, 164
Meetings
  adjournment of, 178-9
  Chairman of, 170-2
  methods of voting at, 176-7
  minutes of, 179-81
  motions at, 174-6
  notices of, 169-70
  procedure at, 172-9
  valid, 169
Memoranda, 115, 140
Minutes, 179-81
Motions, 174-6

Notemaking, 61
Notices, 169-70
Nottingham and District Productivity Association, 44-8, 166

Open days, 189-91
Oral examinations, 61
Orders, 57-8
Organisation charts, 23-4
Overhead projector, 203

Paragraphing, 107-8
Parenthesis, 94-5
Possessive, 97-8
Posters, 13-16
Précis writing, 118-24
Press releases, 193
Promotion prospects, 7
Public relations, 187-95
Public speaking, 54-7
Punctuation, 89-99

Question mark, 95
Quicker reading, 154-6
Quotation marks, 96

Reference, 107
Reported speech, 120-1
Report writing, 140-56
Roget's *Thesaurus*, 54

Salutation, 104-5
Semi-colon, 91-2
Shop stewards, 34-7
Signature, 109
Span of control, 22
Speeches, 54-7, 198, 200
Staff
  advertisements, 191-3
  appointments, 22
Suggestion schemes, 42-8
Summarising, 118-24
Supervisor's discussion groups, 37
Syndicate work, 199

Talks, 54-7, 198-200
Teaching aids, 201-4
Telephone, 110, 183-7
Trade unions, 49
Training, 2, 160, 161, 186, 197

Urwick Report, 150

Van den Berghs and Jurgens, 39-40
Video cassette recorders, 204
Vocabulary, 53-4
Voting, 176-7

Word arrangements, 89
Word processing, 112
Works
  councils. 41-2
  magazines, 193-4